WITHDRAWN

DILEMMAS OF GOVERNMENT

Britain and the European Community

F E C GREGORY

Martin Robertson · Oxford

First published in 1983 by Martin Robertson
& Company Ltd., 108 Cowley Road, Oxford OX4 1JF.

British Library Cataloguing in Publication Data

Gregory, F.E.C.
Dilemmas of government: Britain and the European
Community.
1.   European Economic Community—Great Britain
I.   Title
337.1'42   HC241.25.G7

ISBN 0-85520-588-1
ISBN 0-85520-589-X

Typeset by Pen to Print, Oxford
Printed and bound in Great Britain by
Billing and Sons Ltd., Worcester

To
D H Gregory
A token of affection

Contents

List of Tables and Figures

Acknowledgements

During ten years of teaching undergraduate courses on British Government and the European Community frequent complaints were heard about the lack of a basic, comprehensive text. Repeating these complaints to the Professor of British Government, Peter G. Richards, the answer, with encouragement, was write a book yourself. This task was approached with some trepidation since I am by training a lecturer in International Relations; however, with the invaluable help and knowledge of the Civil Service of my colleague and contributor Freida Stack, Teaching Fellow in British Government, the attempt has been made.

This book could not have been written without drawing upon the many excellent but scattered studies by other authors. We hope that due acknowledgement has always been given where such material has been used. In some places fresh research was necessary and our deepest gratitude for help and patient counsel go particularly to R. W. G. Wilson, Esq, Clerk to the European Legislation Committee of the House of Commons, and to G. Stapleton, Esq, European Secretariat, the Cabinet Office, both of whom opened many doors for us. Listed at the end are the many individuals in the public service and outside who allowed us to interview them and others, in official capacities, provided written answers to our queries. To all these we extend our grateful thanks.

In addition we must express our particular thanks to Sir Charles Davis, CB, Counsel to the Speaker; Dr Juliet Lodge, Hull University; Mr Peter Lloyd, MP; Dr Roger Morgan, Director of European Studies Centre at the Policy Studies Institute; Professor Peter Richards, Southampton University, Mr Nigel Spearing, MP and Dr Helen Wallace, Civil

Acknowledgements

Service College for kindly reading and offering helpful comments on parts of the early drafts. Also to Mr Bruce George, MP who provided data from the Polis Computer. Preparation of the typescripts was undertaken with great care and without complaint at the many changes by Pam Powell and Joanne Fluck.

Material contained in Stationary Office publications has been reproduced with the permission of the Controller of Her Majesty's Stationary Office. We alone are responsible for all opinions, errors and interpretations. Freida Stack drafted chapter 4 and I drafted, with her help, the remaining chapters. Lastly, we must thank our families for their support and patience during the preparation of this book.

Department of Politics
Southampton University
June 1983

F E C Gregory
F M Stack

Glossary

CAP	Common Agricultural Policy
CET	Common External Tariff
CFP	Common Fisheries Policy
COREPER	Committee of Permanent Representatives
COREU	Telex system linking EC states
DHSS	Department of Health and Social Security
DOE	Department of Environment
DTI	Department of Trade and Industry
EAGGF	European Agricultural Guidance and Guarantee Fund
EC	European Community
ECOSOC	Economic and Social Committee
ECSC	European Coal and Steel Community
EEC	European Economic Community
EEZ	Exclusive Economic Zone
EFTA	European Free Trade Association
EIB	European Investment Bank
ELC	European Legislation Committee (Commons)
EMS	European Monetary System
EP	European Parliament
EPC	European Political Cooperation
EUA	European Unit of Account
Euratom	European Atomic Energy Community
EUROSAC	European election Selection Advisory Committee (Conservative Party)
FCO	Foreign and Commonwealth Office
GATT	General Agreement on Tariffs and Trade
HC	House of Commons
HL	House of Lords

MAFF	Ministry of Agriculture and Fisheries
MEP	Member of the European Parliament
OEEC	Organisation for European Economic Cooperation
PLP	Parliamentary Labour Party
PR	Proportional Representation
UKREP	British delegation to the European Community
UNCLOS	UN Conference on the Law of the Sea

Chronology

18 April 1951 – signing of the Treaty establishing the European Coal and Steel Community (ECSC).

21 December 1954 – signing of the Association Agreement between Britain and the ECSC.

25 March 1957 – signing of the Treaties establishing the European Economic Community (EEC) and the European Atomic Energy Community (Euratom) – 'the Six'.

3 May 1960 – establishment of the European Free Trade Area (EFTA or 'Outer Seven') – included Britain.

9 August 1961 – Britain applies to join the European Communities.

26 January 1963 – Negotiations on Britain's application are broken off at the request of the French Government.

10 May 1967 – Britain's second application to join the European Communities.

27 November 1967 – France puts a second veto on Britain's application.

1 July 1967 – Merging of the separate institutions of the European Communities (EC).

30 July 1970 – Reopening of negotiations on Britain's earlier application to join the EC.

22 January 1972 – Signature of the Act of Accession of Britain to the EC.

1 January 1973 – Actual date Britain becomes a member of the EC.★

5 June 1975 – British Labour Government under Harold Wilson holds national referendum on the issue of

★The dates up to this point are those recorded in official EC chronologies.

staying in the EC on the terms as renegotiated by Labour.

31 December 1977 – Britain's period of transition to full membership obligations ends.

7 June 1979 – Holding of the British part of the first Community Direct Elections for members of the European Parliament.

10 October 1980 – British Labour Party commits itself to seeking to withdraw from the EC.

9 June 1983 – After a major defeat in the General Election, Labour Party leaders re-appraise the attitude of the Party to the EC.

Introduction

It is evident at the time of writing this study (1981–83) that the general public and the main political parties, Labour and Conservative are both less than enthusiastic about Britain's membership of the European Community (EC). Shortly after the 1981 Annual Labour Party Conference had voted for Britain to leave the EC, Edward Heath, who as Conservative Prime Minister had taken Britain into the EC, was complaining that even his own party as the Government had adopted an essentially negative attitude towards the EC. Mr. Heath (*The Times*, 10 October 1981) complained both that the media either ignored or trivialized the EC and that members of the Conservative Government '. . . are over-anxious to thump the table about the alleged wrong doings of our friends and partners [and] make no attempt to inform public opinion of the real advantages of our membership.' No wonder that in a recent study of Britain as a member of the EC, William Wallace (1981, p. 1) wrote 'British opinion remains confused about the objectives of membership and deeply divided over its desirability.' This comment is valid today, and will doubtless remain so for some time.

During 1982 it became clear that the Labour party were intending to fight the coming election with the clear aim of swiftly withdrawing Britain from the EC. Their manifesto of 1983 confirmed this. Statements by the Conservative Foreign Minister, Mr Francis Pym in September 1982, were interpreted as signalling a more positive Conservative attitude to the EC. However, in the 1983 General Election the EC was remarkable for not really being an issue in the campaign. The Labour Party did not seek to bring EC membership to the forefront of the campaign arguments and thus the Conservatives could leave their case, upon the issue of membership, to a simple commitment to remain in and a reminder of the possible loss of jobs if Britain left the Community.

This study will argue that successive British governments since 1973 have adopted an approach to EC membership which is both low-key and negative in attitude with regard to both the accepted obligations of membership and subsequent plans for development in the EC. This attitude is a consequence of the long period of pre-membership debate and its continuance, the political party divisions over membership, and the conflict over what may be termed Britain's preferred form of looser relations with Western Europe and the more legally constrained relationship which was actually attained through EC membership.

Apart from the natural political differences which can arise over any major issue in national policy there are some special factors promoting the likelihood of political disputes which clearly relate only to membership of the EC. Firstly, the period of membership to date has been dominated by Britain's dispute with the EC over the question of the size of our budgetary contribution. It has been argued (G. Denton in M. Hodges and W. Wallace, 1981, pp. 81–4) that British policy-makers have always been aware that the import and export and expenditure patterns in the British economy could produce this situation of high budget contributions. However, it was hoped that this would be offset by an increase in overall economic performance because of EC membership. As Denton wrote in 1972: 'the Heath government was prepared to take the gamble . . .' (G. Denton in Hodges and Wallace, 1981, pp. 98–9). Second, since Mr Heath took this gamble, and subsequently lost office over the question of a pay policy, there has been no Prime Minister with a comparable degree of enthusiasm for EC membership. This is an important factor in the shaping of Britain's policy towards the EC, where there is an evident tendency to stress the negative features of membership and the EC itself, because Britain's system of government is open to the exercise of considerable influence by a Prime Minister. Third, the budget dispute and lack of any generally overt ministerial enthusiasm for the EC has led Parliament, aided by party divisions, to try to scrutinize closely and critically the consequences of EC membership. Fourthly, the Civil Service has at times taken into EC policy-making meetings its normal practice in domestic policy-making, of concentrating on the practicalities of the policy rather than on its conceptual merits. This can produce the appearance of an overtly negative attitude if the British response is too often opened by a long list of objections.

The British system of government will be shown to have been able to cope quite well with the more routine aspects of the legislative, executive, administrative and judicial consequences of membership but this has been at the expense of a further weakening of parliamentary control of the executive. However, it has not been able to overcome the politically highly contentious effects of the EC budgetary system and the CAP upon Britain's contribution to the EC compared with what Britain receives from the EC. These effects have been multiplied by the poor performance of Britain's economy and the general world recession. The main focus of this study is upon the actual machinery of government and how it has responded to the consequences of Britain's joining the EC. Britain has been in the EC for ten years and this time can best be characterized by considering it as constituting a learning period.

The learning factor is evident, for example, in the way the Commons European Legislation Select Committee has developed its scrutiny methods, the emerging adaptation of the judiciary to a new legal order, and the new duties which fall upon ministers and government departments. As an example of the latter point, one may note that when the (then) Agriculture Minister Mr Fred Peart appeared before the Commons European Legislation Committee in 1974, he had to bring with him MAFF officials from the Veterinary Department, the Finance Department and the Beef Division, as well as the officials from MAFF's Special Division, and an official of the DHSS, because of the range of EC activities covered by his department.

Since 1973 there have been changes by statute and executive and administrative practice in the constitution of the state, defined by Hood Phillips (1978, p. 5) as being 'the system of laws, customs and conventions which define the composition and powers of organs of the state, and regulate the various state organs to one another and to the private citizens.' The 1972 European Communities Act giving domestic effect to the Accession Treaty had to be drafted so as to allow EC law to be given precedence in the areas of national activity coming within the scope of the EC treaties. Thus by joining the EC Britain has accepted that in some areas of public policy Parliament is no longer the supreme law-maker or legal authority, that policy-making for Britain is no longer in certain areas the prerogative of the Prime Minister and Cabinet but something shared with the Commission and Council of Ministers of the European Community. Even the ordinary citizen's position has changed; the citizen has new rights and obligations and a second franchise in another system of representative democracy by being able to vote in the elections of Members of the European Parliament (MEPs).

Domestic party political difficulties and the actual terms of membership have contributed to what may appear to be a rather long period of adaptation. When Labour took office in 1974 it was united in opposing the terms of membership negotiated by Mr Heath. Thus from 1974, until the referendum on staying in the EC in June 1975, the Labour Government was preoccupied with renegotiating the terms of entry. Therefore the first two years of membership 1973–75 did not see much positive EC activity by Britain. One minor but important fact was that it took nearly a year for the EC draft proposals, written in English, to arrive in Britain. Furthermore, the actual terms of entry allowed Britain a transition period, extending until 1977, during which certain of the obligations of membership would only gradually take effect.

IMPLICATIONS FOR THE STUDY OF BRITISH GOVERNMENT

The student of British government has traditionally focused attention upon domestic political affairs and paid relatively little attention to inter-state relations. This is partly because it has been British constitutional practice to adopt a 'dualist' view of the relationship between domestic or municipal law and international law. Thus Parliament must legislate to give domestic effect where necessary to international obligations entered into by the executive. Therefore if one Parliament is presumed incapable of binding its successors the internal effects of international obligations need not be assumed to be irreversible.

However, at least for as long as Britain remains a member of the EC, the student of British government must be concerned with inter-state relations. EC membership means that, in a manner not paralleled by any of Britain's other treaty commitments, British domestic policy-making has to be carried out in certain areas within a multinational decision-making structure, and the governmental system of Britain is now not confined within the geographical boundaries of the British Isles.

Source material for many areas of study involving the EC are diffuse in origin,[1] therefore it is not surprising to find the sources relating to British government and the EC also widely scattered.[2] In particular the legal framework provided by the EC treaties has produced a number of especially relevant studies in law texts and journals. At present the available literature in British government studies relating to EC membership exists only, in the main, in isolated chapters in books, and in articles, and one of the objectives of this study has been to draw upon these sources within one volume. Amongst the official sources there are government White Papers, the reports of parliamentary committees, advisory and explanatory information from government departments, the EC and interest groups.

The continuing controversy over membership has in part dictated some of the structure of the study. An analysis of the history of Britain's approach to European integration reveals Britain's preferences in terms of possible types of relationships with other European states. It also helps to make clear the expectations concerning the benefits of membership that existed on Britain's entry. Because there is a popular tendency to blame the EC for many national problems, it is also necessary to try to record the actual as opposed to the 'myths' concerning the obligations of membership. In this context it is important to remember that on a number of issues the decision-making process of the EC is quite slow. For example, an EC Draft Directive on the Adjustment of National Taxation Systems for Commercial Vehicles (R1435 /68) (COM (68)567) which first surfaced in the EC in July 1968, was still awaiting a final consideration of outstanding issues in March 1982.[3]

The minefield of constitutional controversies must also be crossed because of the continuing debate over EC member-ship and its effects on different views of the concept of sovereignty. This involves substantive political issues such as the legislative sovereignty of Parliament and the accounta-bility of ministers to Parliament. As one MP put it, keeping track of British ministers' activities in the EC was a question of whether 'we may, if we are lucky, just manage to catch the tail of the minister before he goes to Brussels . . .'[4]

In the first chapter Britain and the EC, considered as poli-tical systems, are compared and contrasted to provide a basic understanding of the decision-making system by which the EC policies are made. The chapter concludes by reviewing the history of Britain's application to join the EC, covering the period from 1961 to 1972. The second chapter examines the constitutional controversies, the areas of national activity necessarily affected by EC entry and the 1972 European Communities Act. The next four chapters look at the impact of Community membership upon the legislative, executive and administrative branches of government.

REFERENCES

1. See particularly the comments of D. Allen, 'Foreign policy at the European level: beyond the nation state?' in W. Wallace and W. E. Patterson (eds), (1978) *Foreign Policy Making in Western Europe*, Farnborough, Saxon House.
2. A useful bibliography article is K. J. Twitchett, (1979) 'Britain and Community Europe', *International Relations*, vi, pp. 698–714.
3. Department of Transport (1982) *Information on Progress of EC Legislation*, London, International Transport Division.

4. 'Minutes of Evidence – MAFF', *Select Committee on European Secondary Legislation*, HC 87–I, Session 1974, p. 19, comment of Mr Bell, MP.

CHAPTER ONE

Britain and Europe of the Community

The first and general post-entry study of British government and the EC was produced for the Open University; post-experience course (P933) European Economic Community. In this study (*The European Economic Community, National and International Impact*, 1974) Helen Wallace succinctly describes the EC as:

> . . . not a government, nor is it simply an international organisation. It has not replaced the governments of the member states in the fields of activities for which it has responsibilities under the Treaties of Paris and Rome, it has rather added another stage, a further range of complications to the already complex process of policy-making (Open University, 1974, p. 13).

In reviewing the theoretical models which could be applied to the relationship between the member states and the EC, Wallace concludes that neither the inter-governmental model (state-dominated policy-making) nor the functionalist model (commission-dominated policy-making) provide accurate descriptions of the relationship. Therefore Wallace suggests that the relationship between member states and the EC is best considered from the perspective of a hybrid model where both inter-governmental and functionalist relationships can be discerned (see diagram 1).

Joseph Frankel in the same Open University text examines national sovereignty and the EC. He points out that 'all theories of "sovereignty" include not only descriptive but also prescriptive elements. Hence one's evaluation greatly depends upon one's basic convictions about the desirability

of either maintaining the supreme rule of the national state or
of establishing other organizational patterns' (Open University, 1974, p. 62). Frankel also points out that the issue of
state sovereignty and EC membership is further complicated
by the fact that the proponents of European unity in the late
1940s and early 1950s were very attached to 'federation' and
'supranationalism' as the ultimate objective of the process of
developing closer relationships between the Western European states. In the context of the British debate over membership Frankel rightly identifies that debate as being pre-
occupied with the legal framework of the EC and with
unnecessary worries over the vague concepts of the Community in the future having federal and supranational charac-
teristics.

Moreover Frankel's overall conclusions have remained
valid, namely that:

> the methods within the Community will consist of a
> slow evolution from occasion to occasion in which, for
> a long time to come, the members will retain full formal
> sovereignty and probably occasionally insist on its
> exercise. It is highly unlikely that the EEC will develop
> into some equivalent of the classical federation with a
> proper central government (Open University, 1974,
> p. 75).

THE INSTITUTIONS OF THE EC AND THEIR FUNCTIONS

There are a variety of ways of describing the EC. In the study
of international relations the EC is classified as a type of inter-
governmental international institution or organization (IGO).
Feld (1979, p. 216) comments that these are entities established by sovereign states (this distinguishes them from non-
governmental international organizations) and in theory all
the member states in an IGO participate on an equal basis in
its activities; the 'most distinguishing feature of an IGO is its
institutional framework' (Feld, 1979, p. 217) which may be
simple or complex as in the case of the EC whose institutions
approximate to 'the legislative, executive and judiciary

branches of a national government' (Feld, 1979, p. 217).
IGOs are set up under a multilateral treaty which provides
the IGOs' 'constitution' and IGOs are considered to have
international personality. This is a term in international law
which means having 'the capacity to be a bearer of rights and
duties under international law. Any entity which possesses
international personality is an international person or a subject of international law, as distinct from a mere object of
international law' (Schwarzenberger, 1967, p. 53). Among
the descriptions of the EC in international law texts Bowett
(1963, pp. 139–82) has the most apt description of the EC as a
regional institution of limited competence. Figure 1.1 gives
an outline representation of the relationship of the EC institutions to the British government system.

FIGURE I.I: The European Community in outline and its
relationship to the British political system

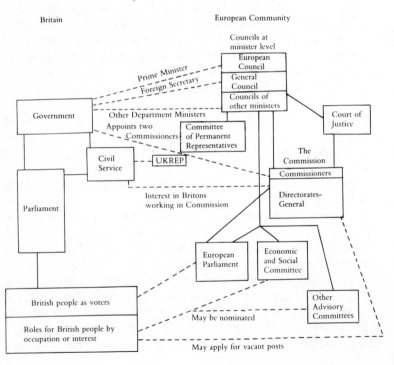

Since 1967 the institutions of the three consituent communities of the EC, the European Economic Community (EEC or Common Market), the European Coal and Steel Community (ECSC) and Euratom (The European Atomic Energy Community) have been merged. The only exception is the Consultative Committee of the ECSC which remains distinct because of its highly specialized functions. Thus one only has to be concerned with one set of institutions covering all three constituent communities.[1]

Very broadly it can be said that the founders of the EC envisaged the gradual development of a federal type of Western European political and economic grouping. Over time, an increasing number of decisions affecting individual states would be taken by the Community as a whole, either by majority voting in the Council of Ministers, or by the Commission exercising delegated powers. However, because of the difficulties of persuading states to cede national powers to supranational institutions, the reality of how the EC works is far removed from the early 1950s' vision of a community of European states.[2] This point has been made explicitly by the current President of the Commission, Mr Gaston Thorn, who recently 'launched a strong attack on nationalist and protectionist tendencies and the insidious return to inter-governmental negotiations and traditional deadlocks'. This could only be avoided, he argued, by stripping governments of the right to veto any Community idea to which they might object.[3] Even the ignoring of Britain's 'veto' in the Council of Ministers (on agricultural matters) in May 1982, does not mean that the national veto has completely vanished. This action was probably more one of annoyance at Britain's tactics over the reform of the CAP and budgetary contributions. Therefore, in studying any topic related to the EC, it is most important that knowledge of the formal structures and processes of the EC should be related to how the system actually works in practice.

A good example of the difference between the Treaty of Rome's institutional arrangements and the institutional arrangements found necessary by the member states was the establishment in 1965 of the Committee of Permanent Representatives (COREPER or CPR). The permanent representatives are national civil servants permanently stationed in Brussels to provide their ministers with a separate, state interest-dominated scrutiny body for Commission proposals and for preparing Council directives to the Commission. Another example is the by-passing of what were supposed to be fixed land-marks in the staged development of the EC. As an instance of this under Article 8 (EEC Treaty) the Common Market was to be established progressively during a twelve-year transitional period. It was proposed that this should take place in three four-year stages. The first stage could be extended to six years when the Council of Ministers should decide on the progress 'acting by a qualified majority on a report from the Commission' (Rudden and Wyatt, 1980, p. 23). This would have been by about 1964, as the EEC Treaty, though signed in March 1957, did not come into force until January 1958. However, in the middle 1960s the Commission 'submitted a rather ambitious proposal to the Council providing for the definitive establishment of the common agricultural policy linked with the introduction of direct revenues for the Communities and increased budgetary powers for the Assembly (Parliament)' (Pryce, 1973, p. 64). This produced strong resistance from France and led to a halt in the EC's development.

This crisis in the EC was not ended until January 1966 when what was known as the 'Luxembourg Agreement' (or Compromise, or Accord) was adopted by the Council of Ministers. This agreement was thought to allow each state a veto over Community developments. As the 'Luxembourg Agreement' is now the subject of much controversy it is worth quoting in full. This agreement took the form of part of a statement from the meeting of the Council of Ministers on 28 and 29 January 1966:

Majority Voting Procedure
(I) Where, in the case of decisions which may be taken by majority vote on a proposal of the Commission, very important interests of one or more partners are at stake, the Members of the Council will endeavour, within a reasonable time, to reach solutions which can be adopted by all the Members of the Council while

respecting their mutual interests and those of the Community.

(II) With regard to the preceding paragraph, the French delegation considers that where very important interests are at stake the discussion must be continued until unanimous agreement is reached.

(III) The six delegations note that there is a divergence of views on what should be done in the event of a failure to reach complete agreement (Rudden and Wyatt, 1982, p. 71)

A careful reading of the above statement shows that the supposed safeguarding of a general national veto actually remained vague, as was in fact acknowledged by a British White Paper (Cmnd 3301, 1967, p. 6) on the legal and constitutional implications of joining the EC. However, certain EC decisions do formally require a unanimous decision by the Council of Ministers, for example, the conclusion of treaties (EEC Article 228) and the admission of new members (EEC Article 237).

The European Community has six principle institutions; the Council of Ministers, the Committee of Permanent Representatives (mentioned earlier) and the Commission, the European Parliament, the Economic and Social Committee and the Court of Justice. In addition since 1974, there have been regular meetings of heads of governments, which act as a sort of superior Council of Ministers. These meetings are now called meetings of the European Council, and are regarded as EC 'summit' meetings, involving the Prime Minister.

However, the Council of Ministers are still as Pryce (1973, p. 4) noted, the 'apex of the Community's regular decision-making process'. Which ministers attend depends upon the nature of the business to be carried out; sometimes the meeting may be the Council of Agricultural Ministers, sometimes the Council of Finance Ministers. Standing with, but slightly above, these meetings is the Council of Foreign Ministers, or General Council. At these meetings the foreign ministers address themselves to the more politically contentious issues; for example in May 1980 the Council of

Foreign Ministers agreed a short-term formula for cutting Britain's budget contribution. The Council of Ministers meetings deal with an agenda divided into A and B sections. The A section items have already been scrutinized and passed as suitable for decision by the national officials in COREPER. The B section contains items such as Commission proposals on which the COREPER officials have not produced a formula for agreement; it is the ministers' task to try and resolve those issues. Given the main preoccupations of the EC in recent years, the Budget, CAP and developing political co-operation, the workload in the Council of Ministers will obviously fall unevenly upon British ministers, with the Foreign Secretary, Treasury ministers and the Agriculture minister bearing a particularly heavy burden. In addition to the filter of national advice, available through COREPER, the Council of Ministers is assisted by a number of committees of senior national civil servants and members of the Commission. These committees make detailed preparation on certain topics for meetings of the Council of Ministers.

Most of the responsibility for the policy initiation, mediation between conflicting national interests and supervision of the implementation of EC law is vested in the Commission as the Community's executive organ. The largest area of the Commission's work concerns routine administration, especially of the CAP. Collectively the Commission is responsible to the European Parliament (EP). The EP can vote the entire Commission out of office on a motion of censure, providing the motion is supported by two-thirds of those voting and a majority of the total membership of the EP.

The Commission has often been criticized as a large and wasteful bureaucracy; the reality is, however, somewhat different. The population of the EC states is over 260 million and in November 1982 it was served by a total Commission staff of 12,197. By contrast, to serve the population of Britain, the Civil Service in 1982 had a staff of 653,500. Michelmann (1978, p. 15) points out that in strict terms 'the word commission . . . refers to the college of political appointees heading the community institution commonly identified by the same name.' These top nationally appointed officials, the commissioners, are responsible for the work of one or more of the Commission's 19 Directorate-Generals. Currently there are 15 commissioners. Britain, like France, Germany and Italy appoints two commissioners. In Britain this is done by the exercise of the patronage power of the Prime Minister, sometimes in consultation with the Leader of the Opposition. It has become customary for a Conservative and a Labour politician to be appointed as the British commissioners. Part of Britain's 'unofficial' quota of 20 per cent of other Commission posts was filled on entry by government nomination, that is, posts above EC grade A3 (British civil service equivalent Assistant Secretary). Now all the posts below Commissioner are filled by a form of competitive entry. The commissioners have been the subject of criticism because although they are community servants, they have a concern about their domestic political careers. This situation leads to a tendency towards conflict rather than co-operation between the commissioners, and to divided loyalties.

The Commission has a natural ally among the institutions of the EC in the European Parliament (EP); both at times seek to make inroads into the directing role of the state interest-dominated Council of Ministers. The EP was originally called the European Assembly and until June 1979 its members were nominated by national parliaments from among their members. The Assembly took to calling itself the European Parliament in 1962 and since June 1979 its membership has been directly elected by the voters in the EC states.

The EP's own information booklet notes that

Absolute precision about the powers of the European Parliament is not possible. The Treaties establishing the European Community lay down some outlines; but particularly in recent years both amendments to the Treaties (notably in the budgetary field) and new relationships between Community institutions (what in Britain would be described as 'conventions of the constitution') have made constant changes in Parliament's role (1978, p. 5).

Thus one has to consider the EP in two ways as an EC institution carrying out the formal advisory and legislative functions conferred on it by the treaties (ECSC, Article 20; EEC, Article 137; Euratom, Article 107). These functions include legislative and budgetary powers, and control of the Commission's activities.

In the passing of EC legislation the powers of the EP are formally limited to being consultative. The Council of Ministers does not have to act upon the opinion of the EP, but the Court of Justice ruled (Palmer, 1981, pp. 116 and 233) in October 1980, that if the Council of Ministers asked for an opinion from the EP it must as least wait for that opinion before taking any further action. This ruling followed an intervention by the Parliament in two isoglucose cases before the court. The EP can also try to influence the way in which the Commission frames proposals by publishing reports. The EP could only actually propose legislation in one area, that of its own system of direct elections. Article 138 (3) of the EEC Treaty states that 'The Assembly shall draw up proposals for elections by direct universal suffrage in accordance with a uniform procedure in all Member States.' However, this article formally lapsed in July 1979 after the Council of Ministers' Decision and Act of 1976, and the holding of the first round of direct elections. Nonetheless, the EP has still been able to propose a uniform electoral system, as the first direct elections were held using separate national systems because the Council of Ministers could not agree in 1979 on a single Community voting system. As before, the EP has now opted in March 1982, for a system of proportional representation (PR), in this case one based on the regional list system.

The EP shares the Community's budget powers with the Council of Ministers, and has the exclusive right to approve or disapprove of the way in which the EC institutions discharge their budgetary obligations. In June 1976 the EP established its own form of Public Accounts Committee, the Control Sub-Committee of the Budget Committee which works with the Community's Audit Board and the independent Court of Auditors established in 1975. The EC budget is divided into two parts: 'compulsory' or 'obligatory' expenditure arising directly out of the treaty provisions such as expenditure on the CAP, and totalling about 70 per cent of the budget, is under the ultimate authority of the Council of Ministers; 'non-compulsory' expenditure, that is, finance for new policies (e.g. Regional Fund) formally set out in the EC Treaty and equalling around 30 per cent of the budget, may be varied by the EP within certain defined limits. Among the constraints upon the EP's powers to vary the patterns of non-obligatory expenditure is the inclusion of the salary costs of the Commission under that budget head. Such costs cannot, in practice, be varied very significantly from year to year. If there are disputes on the budget between the EP and the Council of Ministers, a special 'conciliation' or 'concertation' procedure developed in 1975 is used in an attempt to resolve the differences. Finally, the EP can reject the whole budget, which means that EC expenditure is frozen at the previous year's level until the EP and the Council of Ministers agree a new budget. This power was actually used in December 1979.

Although the EP has, as mentioned earlier, the power to dismiss the Commission on a vote of censure, this is an unlikely move. The EP sees the Commission as an ally against the Council of Ministers, and any moves to press for a vote of censure against the Commission are more in the nature of a lever against the Commission and/or the Council of Ministers. Parliament's most useful power in respect of the Commision is that conferred by Article 140 (EEC) which *obliges* the Commission to reply to Parliament's questions.

The relationship between the Council of Ministers and the EP is rather vague in its definition. Article 140 (EEC) merely says that the Council of Ministers has the right to be heard in the Parliament. In practice, the participation by members of the Council of Ministers in the Parliament's sittings has increased. Every six months the new President of the Council of Ministers makes a statement to the EP on future Council policy and by convention, though not by obligation, the Council answers questions put to it by the Parliament.

In its actual workings the EP is dominated by the 'party groups'. A group of politically like-minded MEPs (varying in size from 10 to more than 21 MEPs) can form a party group and receive secretarial support and a seat on the EP's executive committee, the Bureau of Parliament. The party groups are also represented on the 18 specialist committees of the EP. Britain has 81 directly-elected MEPs; the Conservatives formed the European Democratic Group, the Labour members sit with the Socialist Group and the Scottish Nationalist MEP sits with the group of European Progressive Democrats. David Marquand (1979, p. 75) has argued that there are two major differences between the European Parliament and the British Parliament. First, the EP functions on the continental pattern of consensus and discussions; second, committee work is a much more important way for MEPs to exercise influence than is Question Time.

The EC's Economic and Social Committee is another consultative body which owes its origin to a continental view that a person should be represented not only politically (in the EP) but also in terms of his or her other 'socio-economic' interests. Thus the Economic and Social Committee contains national representatives from various walks of life. In 1978 among the 24 British members were: Mr David Basnett, General Secretary and Treasurer of the National Union of General and Municipal Workers; Mr H. Lobel, the Chairman of Glass Ceramics Ltd; Mrs A. Prys-Davies, former Chairman of the Consumers Association; and Mr A. E. Sloman, Vice Chancellor, Essex University.

What Pryce (1973, p. 75) calls the 'creation of a new dimension of government by the Community' required a legal system as well as institutions for legislative, executive and administrative functions, in order to ensure that the EC laws were upheld and that there was justice in the way in which the treaties were interpreted and applied. All the EC treaties lay down (e.g. Article 164, EEC) that 'The Court of Justice shall ensure that in the interpretation and application of this Treaty the law is observed.' The Court's role is confined to the application and interpretation of Community law, but it may rule in an individual case on the conformity of a member state's law with Community law. Unlike Britain, where Parliament is the highest court in the land, the European Court is the EC's supreme judicial authority and there is no appeal against its rulings. Each country has one national as a judge by informal custom, and the judges are appointed by inter-governmental agreement. The judges are assisted by four advocates general who, again by custom, come from the four largest states (Britain, France, Germany and Italy). At present the members of the Court from Britain are Judge Lord Mackenzie-Stuart (formerly of the Scottish Court of Session), and Advocate-General Sir Gordon Slynn (formerly a judge of the Queen's Bench Division).

It is generally accepted that one of the most difficult tasks for the Court is to ensure respect for EC laws when these are broken by the member states. The British Government formally broke the treaty when it failed to ensure that Council Regulation 1463/70, concerning the tachograph, was implemented by the due date of 1 January 1976. In this case Britain was granted an understanding by the Community that the tachograph would be introduced as soon as possible, and this eventually happened. The British Government was also the subject of an action by the Commission for introducing a pig subsidy contrary to the EEC treaty; the Court ordered the British Government to cease the subsidy and the order was obeyed. In practice, member states do comply with decisions of the Court though they may take a long time to do this. In 1982 the Court ordered Britain to cease restricting the entry of French chickens by imposing health regulations (especially relating to Newcastle disease), and it was reported (*The Times*, 6 October 1982) that this order had not yet been complied with.

In this instance the allegation of a British failure to adhere to EC law brought forth a personal response by the Minister of Agriculture, Mr Peter Walker, in a letter to *The Times* (9 October 1982). Mr Walker pointed out that the Court had confirmed the right of member states to take measures to protect animal health, but had felt that Britain's measures were unduly restrictive of Community trade. Although the Court required Britain to comply with its judgement it was explicitly noted that this would be done within the context and time it took for the Commission to gain member states' agreement to an adequate form of animal health regulations.

The Court has no way of compelling states to comply, any more than a British court can compel a government to comply with its judgement. States comply because, as in the domestic case, failure to do so brings serious consequences; in this case a state would risk breaking up the EC. Moreover, states acknowledge the international law principle of reciprocity, that is, a country may itself comply in order to ensure that in future another state complies.

Periodically the EC system and its institutions are the subject of internal studies concerned with structural reform and the development of future policies. For example, in January 1976 the EC published a report on 'European Union' prepared for the European Council by M. Leo Tindeman, the Belgian Prime Minister. In this report M. Tindeman suggested that the goal of European political and economic union had to be accompanied by the development of common foreign policies.[4]

The most recent studies of the EC are the Spierenburg Report on the Commission[5] and the Report of the Committee of Three on 'The European Institutions – Present and Future'.[6] In general, the Committee of Three reported that there was little movement towards common policies, that a very large amount of EC effort was required to produce only modest developments, and that members tended to remain content with narrow and static interpretations of the treaties. Whilst welcoming the establishment of the European Council, the Report noted that it could be weighted against the interests of the smaller countries, and that any decision taken by it still had to be processed through the normal or treaty-based EC procedures. The Report reserved most of its criticism for the Council of Ministers which it felt had become too intergovernmental in character and too little *communautaire*. Moreover, the increasing use of specialized Councils of Ministers had lessened the overall directing role of the foreign ministers acting as the General Council. The Report recommended an increase in the authority of the President of the Council; more use to be made of majority voting; an increased willingness to delegate, perhaps to COREPER; and a reassertion of the role of the foreign ministers in the General Council.

The Committee accepted and endorsed the recommendations of the Spierenburg Report on the Commission.

These were for a smaller number of commissioners (only one from each country); a reduction and reorganization of the commissioners' functional departments, and a stronger Commission presidency. The general aim was to restore 'collegiality' to the Commission. On the European Parliament the report recommended that the EP should have a formal link with the European Council and, should it wish, to give written views on major issues to the European Council.

Overall, the Report urged a modest measure of institutional reform, in order that the EC could more easily adjust as a working community were the EC enlarged to 12 member states. The Committee does not believe that there is any merit in proposing that European union should be an immediate political goal because an inconclusive 'excess of ambition' only produces 'confusion, frustration and finally indifference'. However, these modest reform proposals have yet to be even partially implemented. The EC remains preoccupied with budgetary and CAP issues. Even the admission of new members is not proceeding as smoothly as was hoped, as the French have indicated that they might veto Spain's application because of the continuing internal EC difficulties.

DECISION-MAKING IN THE EC AND ITS RELATIONSHIP TO THE BRITISH POLITICAL SYSTEM

The EC has two types of decision-making machinery; one is known as the 'Community method' and covers economic policy issues within a fairly strict interpretation of the provisions of the EC treaties. The other is known as the 'Davignon' or European political co-operation procedure (EPC). The EPC procedure covers the more political activities especially the co-ordination of external relations which have been undertaken by the member states outside the formal areas covered by the EEC treaty. This distinction between the two sets of decision-making machinery is somewhat artificial as it is sometimes very difficult to deal separately with the economic and political aspects of a policy

issue facing the EC states. However, on occasion it has been
necessary to hold 'Community' ministerial council meetings
in a different city to EPC council meetings, in order to meet
the wishes of states to keep the decision systems apart.

Two examples will illustrate how these different EC
decision-making structures operate. The tariff and trade
negotiations conducted under the auspices of the General
Agreement on Tariffs and Trade (GATT) are conducted for
the EC under the Community methods, because the subject
matter falls clearly under the provision of the Rome Treaty.
Thus the Council of Ministers lays down the general negotiating guide lines for a GATT meeting and these guidelines
are then used by the Commission in the actual day-to-day
talks. The member states are kept in close touch with the
talks via the Commission meeting the COREPER officials in
the Article 113 Committee, Article 113 being the article of
the EEC treaty referring to the concluding of tariff and trade
agreements based upon uniform EC principles. The conclusion of an agreement with, for example, GATT, is the
responsibility of the Council of Ministers acting unanimously
on behalf of the Community (Article 114 EEC).

The EC's response to the Falklands crisis reveals both sets
of decision-making machinery in operation.[7] The EC's diplomatic response to the crisis was worked out by national
officials and ministers using the EPC machinery, with
COREPER as the intermediary between decisions within
states and decisions in the Council of Ministers. The trade
sanctions details were however formalized through the
'Community method' machinery by the Commission with
national consultations, and then sent for approval, again via
COREPER, to the Council of Ministers. Domestically this
has an impact on the House of Commons because its EC
Scrutiny Committee, the European Legislation Committee
(ELC) has a remit which only covers 'Community method'
proposals as diplomatic responses are not normally closely
monitored by the Commons. Therefore the ELC only
became formally aware of the EC's response to the Falklands
crisis when the Commission produced a document on the
implications of the sanctions policy for the trading practice of
member states. Because the EC response involved the

adoption of a Community position regarding external political relations, not a formal EEC function, the crisis itself was handled by the EPC machinery. At the lowest EPC level, a Correspondent from each state's foreign ministry, a junior official (in Britain a First Secretary in the EC department's external affairs section) who co-operates with the other states' Correspondents on a day-to-day basis. They are linked by a telex called COREU. The Correspondent reports to the Political Director in the national foreign ministry (in Britain he is a Deputy Under Secretary in the FCO responsible for EC political affairs). The Political Director reports to the Foreign Secretary and then advises the ambassador attending the COREPER meetings. Ultimately the EC's decisions on the Falklands crisis were taken by the Council of Foreign Ministers.

In order to illustrate how the treaty based decision-making system works, a hypothetical major item of Council legislation will be traced through the EC and the British system. In outline form the sequence has been set out in Figure 1.2. No particular legislative proposal has been selected because of the difficulty of giving an example which is sufficiently 'typical', given the broad range of topics that can be the subject of an EC legislative proposal. For example, some instruments such as those dealt with by the Management Committee for agriculture may move so fast that little time for wide consultation is available, whilst others like the Common Fisheries Policy may be very slow-moving and go round the system more than once. Moreover it is important to remember that EC decision-making is unlike decision-making at the national level where sometimes, for example, a Prime Minister will not seek a compromise position amongst Cabinet views but rather will seek to impose a prime ministerial view by virtue of that office. By contrast, a former Agriculture Minister, Mr John Silkin, has stated 'the basis of the [agriculture] price review, indeed of many of the decisions in the Community, are those of the consensus package at the end of the day' (HC 43–II, 1977, p. 33).

An idea for EC legislation usually arises on the initiative, under the treaty authority, of the Commission, although the initiative could come from the member states, the EP or

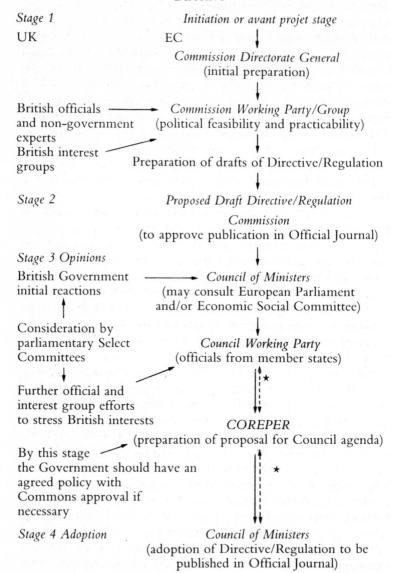

FIGURE 1.2: The Preparation of an EC Council Regulation or Directive

Stage 1
UK

Initiation or avant projet stage
EC

Commission Directorate General
(initial preparation)

British officials ⟶ *Commission Working Party/Group*
and non-government   (political feasibility and practicability)
experts
British interest
groups   Preparation of drafts of Directive/Regulation

Stage 2   *Proposed Draft Directive/Regulation*

Commission
(to approve publication in Official Journal)

Stage 3 Opinions
British Government ⟶ *Council of Ministers*
initial reactions   (may consult European Parliament
                  and/or Economic Social Committee)

Consideration by
parliamentary Select   *Council Working Party*
Committees   (officials from member states)

Further official and
interest group efforts
to stress British interests   *COREPER*
                  (preparation of proposal for Council agenda)
By this stage
the Government should have an   ★
agreed policy with
Commons approval if
necessary

Stage 4 Adoption   *Council of Ministers*
                  (adoption of Directive/Regulation to be
                  published in Official Journal)

★If a proposal is complex and/or contentious it may remain between these stages for
some years before final adoption.

from an amalgam of pressures and interests.[8] The initial preparatory work is carried out by the relevant Commission directorate-general. A Commission document is then sent to a Commission working party or group. This is the stage for wide-ranging discussions about the political feasibility and practicality of the proposal. These discussions are attended by officials from the relevant British government department, or departments, and any appropriate non-government 'experts'. The discussions are aimed at producing a draft regulation / directive (these terms are defined in chapter 2) and interest groups in Britain will make their first inputs at this stage through a government department and possibly through a European interest group association.

The draft regulation / directive must then receive the sanction of the full Commission. If this is received the draft is published in the Official Journal and sent to the Council of Ministers. The British Government should, at this stage, begin to formulate some views on the proposal. The Council may, and sometimes must, consult the EP and / or the Economic and Social Committee. At this stage the proposal will come on the agenda of the British parliamentary EC Scrutiny Committees and government departments will provide an explanatory memorandum to accompany the proposal. The proposal may also be considered by one of the departmental Select Committees in the Commons.

The Council will send the draft regulation / directive to a council working party or group which may be standing or *ad hoc* in character. Council working parties or groups consist solely of officials from member states, and this is where British officials will conduct formal negotiations with the officials from other states. These meetings are usually chaired by an official from the state holding the Council presidency. This inter-nation discussion stage may take some time; for example, a Council working group was examining the draft Seventh directive (Group Accounts) in the Company and related law harmonization programme, from September 1978 to December 1981. In the British Government system, this stage allows ministers, officials and interest groups some time to attempt to exert national or sectoral interests. However, the pressures upon the Commons' timetable and its EC scrutiny system means that MPs are only likely to have a limited opportunity to try to influence ministers, unless a proposal is slow-moving. By contrast, the Lords EC Scrutiny Committee has the remit and time to produce a detailed examination of an important draft regulation / directive.

The draft regulation / directive is sent by the Council working party to COREPER which prepares the proposal for the Council of Ministers to adopt, either without discussion or as an uncontentious 'A' item or for discussion before decisions as a 'B' item. Some 'B' items may not reach the Council of Ministers until after a further stage at Council working party level. At this stage a British government should have its policy on the proposal quite clearly set out and, if the proposal is contentious, the Commons should have been able to debate the issue so that the minister responsible is aware of the feeling of the House.

If the draft regulation / directive is adopted it will be published in the Official Journal. A regulation takes effect 20 days after publication, unless otherwise specified. A directive takes effect upon notification, and states usually are given a specified time limit within which to implement the provisions. If the regulation requires any new or changed supplementary domestic legislation this will have to be prepared and passed by Parliament. Once a directive is adopted it is most likely to be given effect in Britain by an order, subject to the affirmative resolution procedure in Parliament, as specified in Section 2 (2) of the 1972 Act. However, this does not involve a parliamentary procedure which gives members great scope for influence. If an Act of Parliament is required then, of course, Parliament has more opportunities for influence.

In general, the processing of an EC legislative proposal seems to increase the opportunities for the exercise of ministerial and official power and influence, and the opportunities for non-parliamentary pressure-group influence. (These points shall be discussed further, in later chapters.) It does not appear to be a system which offers Parliament, especially the Commons or non-parliamentary political party organizations, much scope for influence, except upon the more highly controversial issues, or those that are slow-moving. However, slow-moving issues may also be either very technical in character, or only affect a restricted range of activities. Such issues will be unlikely to arouse the interest of more than a few MPs.

The fact that Britain would have to accept decisions not tailored exactly to her own preferences, but which were rather the results of a 'consensus package' was one of the reasons for the controversies surrounding Britain's approach to the issue of whether or not to join the EC. As Mr George Younger, Secretary of State for Scotland said: 'Taking Britain into the European Community was a fundamental aim of successive governments from 1961, yet membership remains a political football.'[9]

THE HISTORY OF BRITAIN'S APPLICATION TO JOIN THE EC

The European Communities were established in two stages; the European Coal and Steel Community (ECSC) was the first community to be set up in 1951. In 1957, following two years of negotiation, the ECSC members agreed by the Rome Treaty, to set up two further communities, the European Economic Community (EEC or Common Market) and the European Atomic Energy Community (Euratom).

King (1977, chapter 1) points out that until 1960 no British government seriously considered joining any of the Western European supranational initiatives. Attlee refused to place Britain's iron and steel industry into the ECSC, and in 1955 Eden withdrew the British representative from the EEC and Euratom talks. In general, British politicians before 1960 saw Western European unity as irrelevant to Britain's post-war recovery, perceived Britain's status to be that of a world power, and recognized the deep historical gulf between Britain and Europe.

However, in 1954 Britain did negotiate an association agreement with the ECSC.[10] This agreement with the ECSC marks a shift in British Government attitudes towards non-military co-operation with other Western European states. The treaty provided for a standing Council of Association

between the British Government and the ECSC high authority. The aims of the association were to provide a continuous
exchange of information and consultation on matters of
common interest, such as pricing arrangements, and to
examine the impact of any trade restrictions imposed either
by Britain or the ECSC. Commenting on the treaty, Duncan
Sandys as the Conservative Minister leading the debate told
the House of Commons, in February 1955, of the long-term
significance of the agreement: 'It provides the machinery to
facilitate consultation and co-operation. It creates a framework within which we sincerely hope a closer association
between Britain and the Community will progressively
develop' (537 HC Deb. Col. 886). This association of Britain
and the ECSC was maintained right up to our entry to the
EC in 1973, and its progress was reported to Parliament each
year. As an example of the value of the ECSC association in
1967, the UK and ECSC set up a study group of senior
officials to examine the problems arising from the continued
excess of steel-making capacity in relation to demand.

However, as Kitzinger (1968, pp. 29–33) has pointed out,
there were considerable problems attendant on any EEC
association; not least, the reconciliation of the conflicting
interests of Britain and France, and the institutional arrangements for policy-making.

In the mid 1950s the Eden Government could see advantages in economic links with other Western European states,
but no advantage from a political union. Once it became clear
that a European economic group was to be formed by the six
ECSC states, Britain began to produce proposals through the
medium of the OEEC for a free-trade area as opposed to a
customs union. These proposals were worked out under
Prime Minister Eden and were technically known as 'Plan
G'. Miriam Camps (1965, chapter 7) suggests that what was
represented by this divergence between countries such as
Britain, Norway, Denmark and Sweden (pro-free trade
area), and the Benelux states, France and Italy (pro-customs
union) was a distinction between 'functionalists' and 'federa-
lists'. Camps also gives a good analysis of Britain's mixed
motives regarding the establishment of the free-trade area
alternative to the EC – the European Free Trade Area (EFTA

or the 'Outer Seven'). At the most optimistic end of the policy scale, Britain might have been able to persuade the EC to be involved in a looser European free-trade area and to produce the form of association with the EC which Britain favoured. However, de Gaulle vetoed this idea in 1958. At the pessimistic end of the policy scale at the very least, an EFTA would keep other countries from joining the Six and so minimize the economic consequences for British trade and industry of widespread European trade barriers.

The Stockholm Convention, of November 1959, which brought EFTA into being in 1960 (the members were Austria, Britain, Denmark, Norway, Portugal, Sweden and Switzerland) contained the following main provisions: a schedule of tariff reductions to enable its members to trade with the same freedom between themselves as the Six could in the Common Market; the right of the EFTA Council to modify the Convention if members so required (making it potentially a more flexible arrangement than the Rome Treaty). Also, unlike the Rome Treaty, the Stockholm Convention contained a formal provision under which a member could leave on 12 months' notice.

Britain's reasons for not seeking an association with Euratom similar to the association with the ECSC, were different to those pertaining to the issue of her relations with the EEC. Britain, like the United States, had wanted to promote a Western European nuclear development, favourable to its own commercial interests, and without any military nuclear programme. Britain's preference in 1957 was not for a Euratom but a looser agency under the framework of the Organization for European Economic Co-operation (OEEC) – the ENEA (European Nuclear Energy Agency) which was to sponsor several loosely organized nuclear programmes. Britain became involved with Euratom in 1959 when, under ENEA auspices, Britain became the dominant partner with Euratom (and some minor partners – Norway, Sweden, Denmark, Austria and Switzerland) in the 'Dragon' project in the field of high temperature gas reactor research. The project was carried out at Winfrith with Britain providing 90 per cent of the administrative staff, 70 per cent of the employees, and having a 60 per cent share of the contracts.

Britain thus obtained the relationship with Euratom best suited to her technological and commercial interests, like the ECSC relationship 'with, but not of', (Nau, 1974).

Thus it becomes clear that in the late 1950s Britain's preferred form of relationship with continental Western European countries comprised loose, general or *ad hoc* arrangements for functional co-operation. These were typified by the association with the ECSC, the establishment of EFTA, and the arrangements with Euratom. However, these arrangements still left unresolved the issue of Western European trading relations as a whole, and the question of whether, as Britain had originally hoped, some compromise economic association could be worked out between the Six and the other Western European states. In addition, Britain began to speculate on the consequences for her political position and European / American links if the Six started to develop an ability to put forward common policies on external political issues. It was political questions such as these which formed part of Prime Minister Macmillan's move towards seeking membership of the EC.

Britain's application to join the EC, and considerations of the terms of membership, can best be understood as a lengthy process spanning the years 1960–75. The initial decision to seek entry was taken in 1960: the first application was made during 1961–63; the second application during 1967–71. Moreover it was a process that never attracted whole-hearted support from the Labour and Conservative parties, although the Conservative party has of recent years appeared less anti-EC than the Labour party. The Liberal party (now allied with the SDP) has long been viewed as the pre-eminent pro-EC British political party. However, before 1960 the Liberals were more in favour of free-trade areas rather than EC-type customs unions. It was not until the 1962 Liberal Party Assembly at Llandudno that the party passed a resolution in favour of joining the EC. Douglas (1971, p. 274) has also pointed out that opinion polls in both 1962 and 1970 showed that there were anti-marketeers in the Liberal party ranks as well as in the two main parties.

Although King (1977, p. 10) may be correct in his assumption that, from 1960–61, for Britain 'It was Europe or nothing', the lack of choice did not produce consensus. The length of time it took to enter the EC, and the variable nature of the arguments advanced to support membership, contributed to the controversy over membership. Waltz (1967, p. 265) talks of Macmillan attempting to 'sidle into Europe'. Barbara Castle (1980, p. 80) recalls feelings of being 'inched into the Market by a succession of small *faits accomplis*'. Crossman (1977, p. 586) notes that Prime Minister Wilson, in July 1969, felt that for domestic political reasons and as a negotiating strategy 'we oughtn't to be over eager'.

There are two basic reasons why the decision that Britain should enter the EC produced controversy. These are the near impossibility of producing any form of generally acceptable cost-benefit analysis of EC membership, and the relationship of this fact to deep-rooted political differences concerning EC entry. Both Macmillan in 1960 and Wilson in 1964 asked the Civil Service to undertake an examination of the political and economic aspects of EC entry, and there is considerable similarity between the outcomes of these two examinations.

The report prepared for Macmillan argued that association with the EEC, as Britain already had with the ECSC, would provide less advantages than membership and was not likely to be negotiable with the rest of the Community. The consensus seems to have been that the economic arguments for and against membership were finely balanced, and that in the end 'the economic case for joining was secondary!' (Camps, 1965, p. 261). However, it was considered that British industry might be able to benefit from the advantages of larger-scale production for an expanded market, and that somehow the British economy would grow more healthy because of 'the forced draught of competition' (Camps, 1965, p. 621). This last point of a sort of necessary shock to the then poorly performing British economy was stressed by Heath in the context of ultimately producing an economically stronger Britain, which could then provide the basis for Britain to give a new political leadership to the European Community.[11]

Thus the political arguments for entry are now believed to have been the decisive ones. Essentially these can be reduced to an admission that Britain's relative status in the world had declined, certainly in regard to the relationship with America; a realization that the Community of the Six was gaining in relative economic strength and hence political influence; and that the changing Commonwealth would not provide an alternative form of political and economic group or accept any form of British domination as in the days of Empire. Nonetheless it was believed in the early 1960s that Britain's entry into the Community need not affect, and could indeed strengthen Commonwealth ties (expanded markets) and produce a more equal Atlantic partnership with America. Thus, it was thought, Britain might get the best of both worlds: she would be politically and economically stronger from EC entry, and her Commonwealth and American links would also be strengthened.

Michael Charlton (1982) believes that the years 1958–60 were the crucial years for what Mr Heath called 'a gradual making-up of minds' on Britain's relationship with Europe of the Six. First, Suez had shown to the then Prime Minister, Macmillan, how weak Western Europe was in the face of the pressure Russia and America could exert. Second, the Cabinet was considering changing Britain's agricultural support system from one based on the taxpayer to one based on the consumer. Because of this, Britain's agricultural support policy might have ended up looking very like the EEC's Common Agricultural Policy (CAP) and consequently the CAP did not need to be an obstacle to entry. Finally, by 1962 both American and Commonwealth contacts had accepted and even advocated, in the case of American Under Secretary of State George Ball, that Britain should join the EC. Thus, Charlton (1982) concludes 'The British decision was, in essence, a political one. The recovery and the exercise of sufficient sovereign power and influence in the second half of the twentieth century had ben judged, after 'quite calm deliberation' (Macmillan's words), 'to lie in membership of the EEC'.

Charlton's comments on Macmillan's decision could also, in part, be applied to Wilson's decision to make the second application. In this instance Wilson ordered the Civil Service to produce very detailed studies for the Cabinet of the economic and political arguments for entry, in order to sway the anti-marketeers. Wallace (1977, p. 86) argues that, as with the brief for Macmillan, 'the economic arguments were finely balanced; it was the political arguments which might be seen as compelling, if the Cabinet accepted them.' Indeed, Crossman (1977, p. 612) suggests that Wilson, Brown, Stewart, the Foreign Office and Whitehall in general believed that 'there is no greatness outside.'

Not only were the general economic arguments for entry finely balanced, some of the additional future economic advantages rested upon a belief in government in the continuation of a period of general economic prosperity such as had produced the early high rates of economic growth in the EEC of the Six. In Macmillan's period the relatively poorly performing British economy was portrayed as likely to be helped to greater economic growth within the prosperous EEC.

During Wilson's 1964–69 premiership the British economy showed some signs of improvement and this, plus Wilson's stress on 'new technology' permitted a variation on the economic arguments for entry. 'New technology' was advanced as a solution to Britain's economic problems, and as her special contribution to the EC, to produce a greater capacity to compete with the industrial strength of the United States. The improvements in the economy also allowed Wilson to try to differentiate between Labour's approach to EC entry and that of the Conservatives. Heath and the Conservatives, the Labour party argued, were for EC entry at any price, whereas Labour was only in favour of entry at the 'right' price. If the economic arguments were inherently controversial it is harly surprising that the political controversy should have been so long-lasting.

The relationship between the Conservative and Labour parties in the 1960s has been analysed by R. J. Leiber (1970) and the following paragraphs are based on his study. Leiber argues that the two main parties had drifted to the political centre. The Conservative party thus saw great electoral advantages in appearing as the main pro-Europe party (initially taking away some Liberal party appeal) and being seen to contrast, in electoral terms, with a rather insular-looking Labour party beset by internal wrangles. This desire for electoral appeal by the Conservatives was also to override the general notion of a bipartisanship in foreign policy. The bipartisanship had in any event been damaged by the Labour party's attitude over Suez. Therefore in order to have electoral appeal and because of any poor relations between th two main parties, Leiber concludes that 'the Conservatives consciously chose not to make the issue bipartisan.'

Whether the issue of EC entry could actually have been made truly 'bipartisan' in 1960 is another matter, but it does seem at least as if some of the continuing arguments over membership can be related to this absence of a consensus between the main parties on the original question of entry. When the Labour party came round to support the general idea of entry in 1961, they had to show a distinction between their EC entry policy and the Conservative policy. This initially took the form of saying that entry was acceptable, but only with strict reservations. George Brown reports in his Memoirs (1971, p. 216) that at the 1961 Labour Party Conference the NEC accepted a resolution that conference would not approve EC entry unless:

(1) British agriculture and horticulture were protected;
(2) EFTA was protected;
(3) the Commonwealth was protected;
(4) Britain '. . . retains power of using public ownership and economic planning as measures to ensure social progress within the United Kingdom'.

Brown also notes that Gaitskell was not very enthusiastic over EC entry and that only with great difficulty was the Labour Party able to agree to even try and get in.

It is important to realize, however, that Labour party attitudes to EC entry became less 'anti' by the mid-1960s. When Labour won the 1964 general election, after Britain's first application had been vetoed, the circumstances facing the party and its internal composition had changed. R. L. Pfaltzgraff Jr (1969, p. 172–3) lists five significant reasons for changes in party attitudes:

(1) Britain's economic crisis now suggested to many in the Labour party that Britain would benefit economically from EC membership;

(2)   in the 1964 and 1966 general elections a large number of younger pro-Europeans became Labour MPs;

(3)   the party realized that the Commonwealth countries were seeking their own trading agreements with the EC;

(4)   the EC certainly did not seem to be developing into any form of federal political entity;

(5)   the EC did not really appear to be so much of a capitalist club as was once thought.

Nevertheless, as George Brown (1971, p. 219) records, when Prime Minister Wilson decided to apply for entry in 1967 'voluminous records of all our talks had to be taken to satisfy suspicious colleagues in the Cabinet.' The Labour party was still not whole-heartedly behind EC entry.

Nevertheless, it seemed that a Labour Prime Minister might be able to persuade the party to accept EC entry, if not on terms negotiated by a Conservative government. Therefore, as the Conservatives under Heath took Britain into the EC but lost the next general election, the incoming Labour government was committed to renegotiating the terms of entry. The new Foreign Secretary, James Callaghan, told the Council of Ministers in January 1974 that the Labour party's election manifesto had stated that the Conservative Prime Minister Edward Heath's terms of entry involved 'the imposition of food taxes on top of rising world prices, crippling fresh burdens on our balance of payments, and a draconian curtailment of the power of the British Parliament to settle questions affecting vital British interests' (Cmnd 5593, 1974, p. 13). On agriculture the Foreign Secretary said that the Labour party wanted changes in the CAP, because it was too costly and harmed world food trade, and changes in the financing of the EC budget especially relating to expenditure in the CAP.

The 1975 White Paper on the results of the renegotiation actually appeared to find few practical difficulties. Moreover, the Government acknowledged as a general point that the era of cheap world food prices was over. The renegotiation produced a response from the EC in terms of a greater flexibility in the agricultural price structure to meet the varying needs of member states, agreement to discourage surplus stocks and production (e.g. 'butter mountains') and an acceptance that 'a fullscale reappraisal of the CAP was required' (Cmnd 6003, 1975, p. 12). However, the reform of the CAP has proved to be a major difficulty and the current Conservative government is still having to press hard for reforms. On the related issue of budgetary contributions, the EC produced a corrective mechanism to give Britain refunds and promised to develop expenditure policies which would bring more benefits to Britain, for example, the Regional Fund and sugar import subsidies.

In the renegotiation of the terms of entry the Labour Government also expressed concern about the prospects of a transition from the simple customs union stage to full economic and monetary union, VAT policy harmonization, and possible loss of the powers of Parliament to make nationally applicable regional, industrial and fiscal policies. However, the Government found that actual economic and monetary union was still somewhat remote, and it was to find in 1979 that it could even stay outside the European monetary system when that was established. Regarding planned policies the Government reported that there was no problem for Britain in 'pursuing effective regional policies adjusted to the particular needs of individual areas on the country' (Cmnd 6003, 1975, pp. 18–19). About industry, it was found that the Government's nationalization proposals, and the establishment of the National Enterprise Board and of planning agreements, would not be hampered by treaty obligations. On fiscal policies the Government found that it could resist any VAT harmonization policy that it did not like and more generally that 'membership of the Community does not limit their (government's) powers to pursue effective fiscal policies' (Cmnd 6003, 1975, pp. 18–19).

The referendum in June 1975 produced a 67.2 per cent vote in favour of remaining in the EC on the terms that the Labour Government had renegotiated. The referendum may be dismissed as a political device designed to placate Labour anti-marketeers. However, the renegotiations did produce an important belief that vital national interests could really be safeguarded within the framework of EC membership because of changing attitudes by other member states and a greater awareness of how the EC functioned.

After the completion of the Labour Government's renegotiation, the Labour party leadership publicly accepted that the powers of the Community treaties were limited and that member states retained both considerable freedom of manœuvre and ultimate control. Prime Minister Wilson told the Commons:

> Many of us, including myself, have at various times been half terrified by reading legal jargon, the apparently fussy legalism and theology, not to mention interference in things, such as beer, milk, hops and uneviscerated chickens. Much of this nonsense has now stopped – certainly those fussy Commission initiatives to which I have referred on these items. The Foreign Secretary and I have found the Market much more flexible than I think either of us expected, both in individual questions and in what we have noted as a substantial shift of power over these past 12 months. It is remarkable how flexible it can be when there is a British Government who are prepared to stand up for British interests. . . . A fundamental change not in the Treaty but in the practice has been brought about by the new system of Heads of Government summits of a regular, routine character. . . . This system has, already, *de facto* reasserted a degree of political power at top level, not only over the month-by-month decisions but over the general method of operations of the Market (Cmnd 5999, 1975, p. 10).

One might argue that the record of Britain's membership since 1975 has been one of a continual stress upon Britain's 'vital interests', with Prime Ministers Callaghan and Thatcher constantly seeking adjustments to Britain's financial contribution to the EC. It is necessary to remember the arguments for membership in which, although political considerations predominated over economic considerations, certain economic arguments had some significance, namely the advantages of a larger market and the supposed benefits of the 'shock' of competition to British industry. The economic arguments have to be related to circumstances which did not exist in the 1960s or were not fully appreciated. Firstly, it is generally understood that in a customs union the maximum gains from tariff reductions occur in the earlier years, and that the greatest gains go to the most economically strong members. Britain, as a later entrant and (relatively speaking) an economically weak one at that, was unable to gain as much from tariff reductions as the original members. Secondly, in the 1960s no one could have foreseen such a profound world recession in the 1970s and 1980s, and Britain actually entered the EC, not in a continuing period of general economic expansion, but at the start of a recession period.

Consequently, although political considerations were the major reasons for entry, since entry, successive governments have actually had to be concerned mainly with the economic considerations, not just for party political reasons but also because of severe domestic economic problems and the world recession. Moreover, the economic problems produced new attitudes towards the original political considerations. For example, the EC, speaking with one voice at a world energy conference, might once have been seen by British politicians as enhancing Britain's position in such a meeting. However, when just such an arrangement was proposed for an actual world energy conference in 1974, Britain objected to a single EC policy line. By then Britain was arguing that as an oil-producing country her interests were not identical with the other EC members who were not oil-producers. Britain also had no intention of allowing British North Sea oil to be considered as an asset to the whole Community.

The interesting aspect of Britain's current relations with the EC is that a relationship seems to be forming with the Community which requires that British EC policy is operated in two parts: a 'communitaire' policy on political co-operation, which balances the negative effects of confrontation policy on budgetary and CAP issues.

Lord Carrington tried to develop EC co-operation in the foreign policy sphere with peace initiatives over Afghanistan and the Middle East. In this context the British proposed the

creation of a small new EC secretariat to help manage a
common foreign policy. Not all EC partners shared British
enthusiasm for this effort; though it clearly reflects the
original British aims of gaining enhanced political influence
in the world, a grouping of European states. As the EC
countries are actually contributing to Western peacekeeping
forces in Sinai and Lebanon, this certainly gives the EC a
visible presence in international affairs.

This *communautaire* policy is, however, in contrast to
Britain's stress on its national interest in economic relations
with the EC. Mrs Thatcher has stressed very bluntly that she
wishes to see major changes in the EC's budgetary system
and in the CAP. Once again, it seems, Britain is heading for
confrontation.

NOTES AND REFERENCES

1. See particularly H. Arbuthnott, and G. Edwards (eds) (1979),
    A Common Man's Guide to the Common Market, London,
    Macmillan; A. J. C. Kerr (1977) *The Common Market and How
    it Works*, Oxford, Pergamon Press; S. Henig (1980) *Power and
    Decision in Europe*: London, Europotentials Press; R. Pryce
    (1973) *The Politics of the European Community*, London,
    Butterworth.
2. Among the considerable literature on the 'vision and reality'
    of European regional integration see particularly E. B. Haas
    (1958) *The Uniting of Europe*, London, Stevens and Sons; and
    L. N. Lindberg and S. A. Scheingold (eds), (1971) *Regional
    Integration: Theory and Research*, Cambridge, Mass., Harvard
    University Press.
3. *Europe 82*, July 1982, p. 15.
4. The details of this report were published in *The Bulletin of the
    European Communities*, Supplement, 1/76, pp. 16–18 and com-
    mented on in the British parliamentary EC scrutiny process
    by the **44th Report, House of Lords European Community Com-
    mittee**, 'Tindemans', HL 277, Parliamentary Papers (Lords),
    Session 1975–76, Vol. VIII.
5. For details see European Communities Commission (1979),
    Reforming the Commission, Background Report No. ISEC/
    B42/79.
6. European Communities Commission (1980), *The European*

Institutions – Present and Future, Background Report No. ISEC/B13/80.

7. The following comments are based upon C. Twitchett, 'The Falklands – Community diplomacy at work', *Europe 82*, July 82, pp. 10–11; and C. and K. Twitchett (1981) *Building Europe: Britain's Partners in Europe*, London, Europa Press, pp. 1–16.

8. The discussion of the progress of an EC legislative proposal in relation to Britain's machinery of government has been derived in part from A. J. C. Kerr (1977), *op. cit.*, ch. 4; *EEC Checklist*, (1982) London, British Bankers' Association, p. iii; and *Harmonisation of Company and Related Law in Europe – Timetable and Progress of Draft Directives and other Proposals*, July, 1981, Companies Division, Department of Trade.

9. Mr Younger's comments in *The Scotsman* were cited in *Europe 81*, June 1981, p. 8.

10. UK Series. Misc., No. 35 (1954), 'Agreement concerning relations between the UK and the ECSC', Cmnd 9346, Dec. 1954, *Parliamentary Papers*, Vol. XVIII, Session 1952–55.

11. See the comments on Mr Heath in M. Laing (1972) *Edward Heath – Prime Minister*, London, Sidgwick & Jackson, pp. 231 and 248; and D. Hurd (1979) *An End to Promises – Sketch of a Government 1970–74*, London, Collins, p. 12.

CHAPTER TWO

Membership Obligations and Constitutional Controversies

In order to understand how the government of Britain has been affected by EC membership it is necessary to describe briefly the provisions of the EC treaties and the consequent obligations accepted by a member state. This forms the background to the constitutional controversies over membership, how membership was to be given effect in Britain under the 1972 European Communities Act, and the acceptance of re-negotiated terms by the 1975 referendum.

The obligations of membership can be categorized in a number of ways. They can be considered with reference to the activities of the state and its people which may come within the scope of Community policy-making powers, for example, trade and agriculture. The obligations, for a post-foundation member like Britain, may also be divided into those covered by the pre-accession legal provisions and those still in the process of being negotiated. Obligations in the former category have to be accepted as they stand, unless the other members agree to modifications. The obligations being developed at or after entry involve the new member in the EC's bargaining process, and require a government to attempt both to rank its policy goals and take a broad view of the national interest to reconcile possible conflicting policy aims. In fact, British governments have found it very difficult to view EC membership as involving a balancing out of advantages and disadvantages between the member states because of the consequences of the Community's budgetary policy and agricultural expenditure upon the size of Britain's financial contribution to the EC. Lastly, obligations can be categorized according to whether they involve immediate direct internal effects, as with EC regulations, or whether they allow the member-state flexibility in the timing and manner of implementation, as is the case with EC directives.[1]

Because any assessment of the obligations of membership involves a degree of subjective analysis, there is no generally accepted statement of how Britain has fared as a Community member. However, there is a wide range of sources that may be consulted, of which the following are examples. Between May 1967 and March 1975 nine White Papers were published covering the various implications of membership and the re-negotiated terms of membership. These provide various governments' views on membership. A comprehensive and somewhat different set of perspectives is provided by the European Parliament's 1975 Report (Doc. PE 37.460–464) entitled 'The effects on the United Kingdom of membership of the European Communities'. Since entry, successive governments have produced two White Papers in each parliamentary year, entitled 'Developments in the European Community'. The most comprehensive series of reports on the effects of membership are provided by the EC Scrutiny Committees of the Lords and Commons. Among other useful sources there is a detailed assessment of 'gains' and 'losses' from membership in W. Wallace (ed.), *Britain in Europe* (1980).

THE OBLIGATIONS OF MEMBERSHIP

In the formal legal sense the obligations of membership derive from the three foundation treaties (see Appendix I) for the Coal and Steel Community (ECSC), the Economic Community (EC), the Atomic Energy Community (Euratom), their Annexes and Protocols, the Rome Convention, the Brussels Treaty of Merger, the Brussels Treaty of Accession with Annexes, and the 1972 Luxembourg Treaty on Budgetary Matters. These primary sources of EC law can be supplemented by the law-making powers of the Council of Ministers within the general provisions of the treaties. However, such changes in the obligations of EC membership are subject to the unanimous agreement of all member states.

The secondary sources of EC obligations come from the exercising of their treaty functions by the Council of Ministers or Commission to make administrative acts and the European Court's judicial acts. In essence, one can regard the European Court's function as to give precise expression to the obligations of membership, when doubt may exist, through the medium of case law or the jurisprudence of the Court.

The administrative acts can be of four types: regulation, directive, decision and recommendation, and each has different consequences in terms of obligations. The regulation applies to all EC members and is binding in its entirety. It has direct application in member states, although some national legislative or administrative act may be necessary to give precise effect to it. The regulation has been described as 'by far the most important source of secondary legislation of the European Communities' (Mathijsen, 1972, p. 183). The directive has direct effect but is only binding as to the desired results, and member states may select their own method of implementation. A decision, usually in implementing an EC obligation, only applies to the state, company or even individual to whom it is addressed. Recommendations (or opinions) have their literal meaning; they have no binding force. It is important to remember that governments can delay the implementation of all EC administrative acts to suit national circumstances or to seek changes in the acts. For example, it took Britain until the end of 1981 actually to implement the EC regulation on the introduction of the tachograph.

Some confusion over the relative status of the regulation and the directive was caused when the Court of Justice in 1970 gave a number of judgements which implied that although under Article 189 (EEC) only regulations have direct application, this did not mean that other EC Acts were precluded from having a similar binding effect. However, the Court of Justice never said that the directives were directly applicable as that term is applied to regulations. Usher (1981, p. 24–27) therfore argues:

> any provisions of Community law which are clear, unconditional and leave no discretion may, within the

limits of their legal nature give rise to rights and obligations enforceable by individuals before their national courts. To describe this concept, which is not automatic and in practice has largely been relevant where there has been a failure to perform a Community obligation, it is preferable to use a separate term, 'direct effects'.

In this book, the term 'Britain' has been used as a brief name for the country's full title of the United Kingdom of Great Britain and Northern Ireland. However, it must be noted, for the subject matter of this chapter, that the different legal systems in the United Kingdom do cause special problems for Britain as an EC member. The EC obligations, those accepted on entry and the subsequent obligations, may have to be enacted in Britain in three different legal forms; one form for England and Wales, another for Scotland and another for Northern Ireland. The existence of three different legal regimes in Britain causes continual difficulties when any proposals for legislative harmonization arise in the EC, because Britain may not exist as a single legal entity in respect of, for example, company law.

In political terms the sources of obligations are not as important as the areas of national activity affected by the obligations. Some measure of the areas of incompatibility between Britain's pre-entry laws and EC obligations can be shown (Wall, 1973, pp. 81–6) by the fact that only 31 Acts of Parliament needed to be changed, and only one of those, the 1969 Customs Duties (Dumping and Subsidies) Act, needed to be repealed. Of the remaining 30 Acts, six related to customs tariff, ten to sugar, three to seeds, and among 12 miscellaneous acts, the most noteworthy were the 1967 Agricultural Act, and the 1953 Iron and Steel Act. As one might expect therefore, from even a general knowledge of the EC, the initial changes mostly had to be made in relation to agriculture, the iron and steel industry and trade.

The Lord Chancellor in the 1967 White Paper 'Legal and Constitutional Implications of Membership of the European Communities' (Cmnd 3301, 1967, p. 9) defined the extent and nature of the obligations of membership. Firstly he pointed out that the powers granted to EC institutions 'are limited to the purposes laid down in Articles 2 and 3 of the EEC Treaty, Articles 2 and 3 of the ECSC Treaty and Articles 1 and 2 of the Euratom Treaty, which are mainly economic purposes'. These can be broadly understood as relating to customs duties, agriculture, the movement of labour, services and capital, transport, monopolies, monopolies and restrictive practices, state aid for industry and the regulation of the coal and steel and nuclear energy industries.

Secondly the Lord Chancellor explained (Cmnd 3301, 1967, p. 9) that Britain could control developments in the EC once she was a member: 'By the terms of the treaties themselves neither the objects nor the particular purposes can be extended except by unanimous agreement.' Moreover, even the permissive Articles 99 and 100 of the EEC Treaty dealing with harmonization and approximation of national policies and practices are not only limited to economic and financial activities, they are also subject to the unanimous approval of the Council of Ministers.

However, the harmonization proposals proposed by the European Commission can cover many matters and involve a considerable amount of preparatory work by government departments and interest groups, and necessitate sometimes lengthy parliamentary inquiries. This work may take many years and in the end only achieve a form of compromise among the interests of member states which some may regard as far from desirable. Plaskitt (1981), who has examined the reports of the House of Lords EC Committee relating to harmonization proposals, notes that these reports have sometimes been critical of harmonization proposals for going beyond the provisions of the EEC Treaty, producing legal provisions which are either less strict than the superseded national provisions or which undermine the basic aims of those provisions.

The official government discussions of the obligations of membership consider these obligations under the following headings: the Common Agricultural Policy (CAP), Trade and Industry, Capital Movements, Value Added Tax (VAT), Regional Policies, Coal and Steel and Atomic Energy.

The chief objectives of the CAP were listed as being to raise agricultural production, to ensure a fair standard of living for the agricultural community, to stabilize markets, to guarantee supplies and to ensure the delivery of supplies to consumers at reasonable prices. In 1967 the White Paper on the CAP (Cmnd 3274, pp. 4–5) listed the differences between the EC and British agricultural support systems as being first, that in the EC farm incomes were supported by import levies and tariffs, support buying and export subsidies. However, it was suggested that these methods did not 'in general provide the same degree of certainty of return to producers as our own system of guaranteed prices and deficiency payments'. Second, in the EC the cost of agricultural support was borne by the consumers in prices paid for agricultural produce, whereas in Britain the taxpayer paid for the support. Third, the EC import policy was essentially designed to safeguard domestic producers, whereas the British policy was to encourage cheap food imports and at the same time assure minimum returns for home producers. In general the concern in 1967 was focused on the fact that there would be a structural impact on British agriculture and that there would be a 'cost' in terms of Britain's financial contribution to the CAP. Britain therefore felt that a transitional period was necessary for her to adjust to the CAP.

The White Papers show that there are really two principal issues for Britain in the CAP: the overall cost of the CAP and Britain's contribution to it, and the effects of the CAP on Britain's agricultural system. The 1970 White Paper 'Britain and the European Community: An Economic Assessment' (Cmnd 4289, p. 5) noted that the move towards the 'own resources' (revenue raised directly for the EC) system of financing the CAP meant a rise in the EC's budgetary powers. Moreover, the gradual completion of the single market stage for a wide range of agricultural products was leading to agricultural surpluses and a rise in the 'guarantee' expenditure of the CAP (from £154 million in 1966–67 to £831 million in 1968–69) of which the major beneficiary was France. In contrast, the 'guidance' expenditure of the CAP (for such things as agricultural modernization) which might benefit Britain more, had risen much less (£51 million in 1966–67 to £119 million in 1968–69). The British Government thus foresaw a balance of payments problem arising because of the increased cost of food imports (Britain is a major food importer) as well as a problem over the cost of our contribution to the CAP.

The 1971 White Paper on the UK and the EC (Cmnd 4715, p. 22) commented on the progress in negotiations on agricultural issues that 'the transitional arrangements provide a sound basis for a smooth and orderly transition for our farmers and growers under conditions of fair competition and stability.' The only special agricultural issue that was noted related to Britain's hill farmers, and there it was stated that Britain would be able to continue giving special assistance to that group of farmers.

The European Parliament's 1975 report on the effects of membership on Britain noted that the objectives of Article 39 of the Treaty of Rome were similar to Section 1 of the 1947 Agricultural Act, and that the CAP is only outlined by the Treaty of Rome. The CAP is developed by directives and regulations. 'It is, therefore, in constant evolution. Britain in the Common Market is able to add its voice powerfully to direct the CAP in a direction suited to its own interests' (EP, 1975, p. 28). Moreover, in the area of support to beef producers the EC moved towards direct payments to farmers as opposed to intervention payments, a move 'favoured by Britain' (EP, 1975, p. 38).

Clearly, in respect of agriculture, British governments are constrained in policy-making by adherence to the CAP, yet they can help to shape its development along lines more favoured by Britain and, hopefully, press for the acceptance of schemes to reform the CAP. The effects of membership in this area, and the related Community budget problems, have obviously had a significant impact upon the workload of the executive and the legislature. Freida Stack's Table 4.2, which gives the frequency of ministers' attendance at the Council of Ministers in 1978–79, shows the most frequent attenders were ministers from the Foreign Office, the Treasury and the Ministry of Agriculture.

No other single area of national policy has been affected in quite such a wide-ranging manner as agriculture. The next policy area where the EC made a significant Community development was in trade policy, with the completion in July

Table 2.1 Transfers of powers from national authorities to the Community institutions

Instruments	Powers of national authorities	Role of Community institutions	
		Influence on national decisions	Own decisions
Public finances			
Current expenditure	Unchanged (but not non-discrimination between suppliers)	Directives (adopted or proposed) on procedures for award of public contracts	
Public investment	Modified (discussions)	Moves toward consultation, particularly in transport and energy	
Transfers to individuals	Unchanged (provided no discrimination between nationals of different Member States)		Social Fund
Operating subsidies to undertakings	Limited (monitoring by the Commission)	Verifying compatability with the common market (Arts 92 and 93)	EAGGF
Capital subsidies	Limited (monitoring by the Commission)	Verifying compatability with the common market (Arts 92 and 93)	The Commission has proposed principle of development to industry
Transfers to the rest of the world	Unchanged		European Development Fund
Indirect taxes	Limited: prohibition of discriminatory taxes (Arts 95 to 98)	Monitoring of non-discrimination and tax reductions	ECSC levy
	monitoring of tax reductions (Arts 92 and 93)	Proposals for harmonization (based on Art. 99) (moves towards alignment of VAT rates)	Own resources (Treaty of 22.4.1970)
	general introduction of the VAT system (decision based on Art. 99)		

Direct taxes on personal incomes	Unchanged	
Corporation tax	Unchanged	Proposals for harmonization (based on Art. 99)
Customs duties:		
intra-Community	Abolished (1.7.1967)	
third countries	Abolished: inroduction of the CET (1.7.1967) (special cases of the associated States in Africa and Madagascar, and Greece; generalized preferences for developing countries from 1.7.1971)	Fixing of CET and rates for agricultural levies
Social security contributions	Unchanged	Social security scheme for migrant workers
Property tax and estate duty	Unchanged	
Transfers from the rest of the world	Unchanged	
Loans to undertakings	Limited (insofar as loans are construed as State aid — Arts 92 and 93)	Verifying compatability with the common market
Loans to the rest of the world	Unchanged	
Borrowings from the home market	Unchanged	ECSC loans EIB loans
Borrowings from rest of the world		
intra-Community	Unchanged	
third countries	Unchanged	The ECSC and EIB can borrow on the markets of member states or third countries
Balance on current transactions	Modified	Council opinion on short-term economic policy
Balance on revenue and expenditure	Modified	Council opinion on short-term economic policy

Instruments	Powers of national authorities	Role of Community institutions	
		Influence on national decisions	Own decisions
Regulations directly affecting certain economic parameters			
A – *Money and credit*			
Direct monetary instruments (re discount rate, open-market transactions, etc.)	Modified	Moves towards consultation (Monetary Committee, Short-term Economic Policy Committee, Committee of Governors of Central Banks)	
Regulation of bank lending	Modified	Moves towards consultation (Monetary Committee, Short-term Economic Policy Committee, Committee of Governors of Central Banks)	
Regulation of capital transactions	Unchanged		
Exchange controls: *vis-à-vis* member states	Abolished	Possibility of authorization by the Commission	
vis-à-vis third countries	Unchanged		
B – *Other regulations directly affecting certain economic parameters*			
Regulation of prices	Limited Abolished in the case of coal, steel and agricultural products		Fixing of agricultural prices, monitoring of coal and steel price lists
Regulation of salaries and wages	Limited: prohibition of discrimination based on nationality (Art. 48) equal pay for equal work for men and women (Art. 119)		

Exchange rate adjustments	Limited (prior consultation)		
Regulation of imports and exports trade agreements:			
intra-Community	Abolished (free movement)		
with third countries	Abolished (common commercial policy)		Formulation of a common commercial policy; negotiation with third countries
Institutional framework and rules and regulations			
System of property ownership	Unchanged		
Commercial legislation	Modified (moves towards approximation)	Directives for the approximation of provisions directly affecting the functioning of the common market (Art. 100)	
Rules on competition	Modified by the precedence taken by the Community rules		Monitoring application of Arts 85 and 86
Regulation of working conditions	Limited: prohibition of discrimination based on nationality (Art.48) maintenance of equivalence between paid holiday schemes Art. 120)	Studies and opinions to promote close co-operation	
Technical regulations	Limited	Directives for the removal of technical barriers to trade (Art. 100)	
Immigration controls member states	Abolished (free movement of workers, freedom of establishment)		
third countries	Unchanged		
Economic information	Unchanged	Medium-term programme	Statistical Office of the European Communities

Source: *The Economy of the European Community*, Periodical 1–2/1982, Office for Official Publications of the European Communities, 1982, pp. 10–13.

1968 of the Customs Union. This 'involved the complete abolition (other than in exceptional circumstances) of tariff and quota restrictions *between* member states, and the replacement of the national external tariffs of the member states by a *Common External Tariff* (CET) which is applied against imports from all third countries except those having preferential arrangements.' (Cmnd 4715, 1971, p. 22). The EC was also seeking to develop a common approach to trade policy in forums such as GATT. Table 2.1 gives some indication of the extent of the obligations.

Apart from the completion of the CET, the Government in 1970 noted that 'Progress in implementing other provisions of the Treaty affecting industry and trade has been less rapid' (Cmnd 4289, p. 25). The EC had established a common system of VAT but not a common rate; there was free movement of labour with attendant health and social security rights; limited progress had been made on simplifying the operations of companies across frontiers; the objectives of regional policies were comparable to Britain's policies, and on the formulation of common road, rail and inland waterway transport policies it was noted that this 'had proceeded slowly' (Cmnd 4289, 1970, p. 25).

The ECSC Treaty is 'designed to ensure an orderly supply of coal and steel to the Community, whilst at the same time taking account of the needs of third countries; to promote the orderly expansion and modernization of production; and to provide better conditions of living and employment for the workers in the industries' (Cmnd 4715, 1971, pp. 37–8). Moreover, EC levies on coal and steel produced by the member states are used to help develop the industries and retrain redundant workers in those industries. Thus for the coal and steel industries:

In general, the present relationship between the Government and the coal and steel industries will continue, although the Secretary of State for Trade and Industry's powers to give directions of a general character will need to be modified. The industries will be free to develop on fully commercial lines. There is no question of their having to cut back production. The powers in the Treaty relating to the establishment of production quotas can only be used in times of 'manifest crisis' and with the agreement of the Council of Ministers, of which we shall be a member (Cmnd 4715, 1971, p. 38).

The Government would also participate in future EC coal and steel pricing policy. Finally, the ECSC provisions are flexible in that although policy was aimed at reducing coal production capacity at the least social cost, because in the past there were cheaper alternative forms of energy, this policy 'is being increasingly reconsidered in the face of the threatening energy shortage' (EP, 1975, p. 79).

The aims of Euratom, expressed in its foundation treaty, are concerned with the peaceful uses of atomic energy, the promotion of nuclear research and the dissemination of technical information. Joining Euratom had no affect on Britain's military nuclear activities, nor were Euratom safeguard regulations seen as placing any additional restraints on Britain's civil nuclear industry. In fact Euratom's scale of activities is very small, probably no more than 6 per cent of the member state's total activities in this field. Moreover, Britain, having a nuclear research activity that in 1975 roughly equalled the total research expenditure of the Six, could be expected to benefit from participation in Euratom research programmes as a major contributor, as happened with the 'Dragon' project on high temperature gas reactor research and the JET (Joint European Torus) project for developing a fusion reactor.

So far, the examination of the impact of the obligations of membership has covered agriculture, trade, industry, tariffs, coal and steel, and nuclear power. The only remaining area of domestic affairs that was affected by pre-entry developments was social policy. Britain, like other member states, is committed to obligations in three particular areas under the EC social policy. First, she is committed to allow the free movement of citizens between member states, and to give reciprocal social security benefits to the citizens of other EC states. This obligation has apparently produced few problems for the British Government. There has been no massive inrush of continental workers into the UK; in 1972, 12,600 entered, and in 1973, 6,402 entered. Nor has there been a major outflow of British workers to the Continent. Social security benefits arrangements seem also to have been relatively trouble-free. In the first year of membership there was only one legal dispute over a Dutch citizen, Ms Van Duyn, and her case was complicated by her membership of the Church of Scientology.[2] Second, under the European Social Fund, grants are available for purposes such as developing facilities in depressed areas. Britain has been a major beneficiary of such grants, receiving in 1979 26.62 per cent of the fund allocation (Italy was first with 36.35 per cent). Third, under the Social Action Programme, Britain may have to adjust some national laws if harmonization proposals in areas such as working hours are accepted by the Council of Ministers.

The major problem in any assessment of the obligations arises from the development of EC policy in many areas. Britain, as a member, participates in decision-making, but whilst a national veto may be acceptable to other states for the protection of vital national interests, at other times Britain has to accept that in some areas EC policy may be similar to a nationally produced policy, in other areas it may be dissimilar.

Another difficulty, as the Commons Scrutiny Committee has found, is to know at any given time precisely what instruments and in what final forms they are actually applicable in Britain.[3] Some idea of these difficulties is provided by a Department of Transport 1982 paper on 'Information on Progress of EC Legislation'. This covers the areas under the responsibility of the Department of Transport, such as motor vehicle regulations, drivers' hours, and international road haulage. Of the 44 proposals listed for EC regulations / directives / decisions, only about eight had actually reached the stage of being in force, or nearly in force, in Britain in 1982, and 27 of the proposals had first appeared in the EC in the late 1960s or 1970s.

It is evident from the preceding pages that the scope of EC obligations, quite wide in its coverage, is nevertheless still concentrated in particular areas. These are the areas which remain central to the proper operation of the Treaty of Rome, namely the CAP, Common External Trade policy, and free intra-Community trade, broadly defined to cover not just the free movement of goods but also the free movement of labour and services. Intra-Community trade also requires the elimination of the non-tariff or technical barriers to trade, and so must include elements of a common transport policy. What is not covered by the Community instruments are national activities such as defence, the maintenance of law and order, many areas of industrial policy, and the content of national fiscal and monetary policies.

Finally it must be recognized that various governments' pre-entry portrayal of the EC as an organization primarily concerned with politically less controversial economic policies is not really correct. Since Britain joined the EC, politicians of all parties have become more aware of the domestic political significance of sharing sovereign powers with other states within the very rule-orientated organizational framework of the European Community.

THE CONSTITUTIONAL CONTROVERSIES

The Conservative Minister for Trade and former Solicitor-General Sir Geoffrey Howe (1973, p. 13), writing on the 1972 EC Act, admitted that: 'entry into the Community does involve a challenge to our legislative and constitutional procedures.' The question is what sort of challenge and whether entry into the EC contributes an irrevocable step. Fundamentally EC entry has posed a challenge to the concept of sovereignty as it had been traditionally understood in Britain.

The concept of sovereignty may be simply defined as the power to give orders to all and receive orders from none. In Britain the controversies about the concept of sovereignty centred on what interested parties – politicians, lawyers and other commentators – understood by the concept of 'sovereignty' as applied in two contexts. These were Britain's sovereignty as a state and, domestically, the sovereignty of the British Parliament. In both these contexts questions were raised about the impact of EC membership upon the two applications of the concept of sovereignty. Moreover, it must also be understood that sovereignty has a separate meaning in each application.

SOVEREIGNTY IN INTERNATIONAL LAW

In the realms of international law Britain is a sovereign state and thus a subject, a bearer of rights and duties, of international law. Subjects of international law are presumed to be entities exercising exclusive control over a portion of the earth's land surface and some adjacent waters.[4] There is no form of authority superior to the sovereign state, except where a state in the exercise of its sovereignty allows some other entity to exercise some of its powers or accepts some other form of limitation on its competence.

It is obvious from even a cursory knowledge of international relations that the sovereignty of a state is not an absolute but an attribute of a state which may vary, in degree, according to the state's political and economic circumstances. For example, the sovereignty of Poland is limited by its links with Russia, and the sovereignty of the Lebanon has been limited by foreign invasion, domestic factions, and the presence of the PLO. Even if a state can resist inroads into its political sovereignty it may still be economically dependent on trade, aid or investment from other states. Economic dependence can in turn lead to political dependence. Because few states are either so remote, self-sufficient or powerful that they can be completely sovereign, it is more usual to acknowledge that states are, in varying degrees, interdependent with other states. In the case of Britain, various forms of interdependence existed long before the country entered the EC. Our defence policy was conducted within the framework of NATO; there was the 'special relationship' with America, most evident in the supply of nuclear weapons technology; and Britain needed to trade with other countries, especially for foodstuffs and raw materials.

In international relations the usual way in which a state modifies its exclusive powers is by means of a treaty (any form of document which sets out mutually acceptable obligations) with another state or states, or international body such as the United Nations. The signing of a treaty presupposes that the parties to the treaty have reached a *consensus ad idem* or complete agreement on the objectives which are to be the subject of the treaty. Therefore Britain's negotiation and signature of the Treaty of Accession,[5] to the European Community was not a derogation of national sovereignty in terms of international law, but an actual exercise of sovereignty.[6]

Under Britain's constitution the conduct of relations with other states or international organizations is a crown prerogative exercised by the government in power. Therefore, in the making of a treaty, Britain's sovereign power is exercised not through Parliament but through the executive. As Dicey (1965, p. 465) commented, 'a Treaty made by the Crown, or in fact by the Cabinet, is valid without the authority or sanction of Parliament.' Thus there is no question of parliamentary sovereignty being in any way infringed because here Parliament has no role. However, it may be asked if there is anything unconstitutional in the executive agreeing to a treaty which imposes limitations on the exercise of Britain's sovereign powers. The answer is no – British governments have acceded to many treaties which impose some limitations on Britain's sovereignty; for example, membership of the United Nations and the General Agreement on Tariffs and Trade.

However, treaty-making is only one element for Britain in entering into new international obligations, if these entail new internal obligations. This is because it is a principle of law in Britain that a treaty entered into by Britain does not in itself affect British law. The reason for this stems from the British view of international law and domestic law as two separate legal orders. Therefore if it is necessary to give effect in Britain to treaty obligations, Parliament must pass the appropriate act or other legislative measure such as an affirmative resolution. But as Yardley notes (1974, p. 34): 'successive Lord Chancellors have stated it would remain within the power of Parliament to repeal by a subsequent Act any former Act applying a treaty which had been made.'

The preceding points about national sovereignty can be related to the existence of different political perceptions of the degree to which Britain is necessarily dependent upon other countries for trade, defence, and general political and economic support. Arguments about Britain's external dependency on other states also involve considerations of how such external links can most advantageously be arranged. For example, should Britain seek to develop a more independent economy, defence policy and global political role? Or, if it is believed that Britain is necessarily dependent on other states for trade, etc., how can those relationships be best arranged? Among a range of possibilities there could be a world-wide free-trade area, Commonwealth preference, or a more restricted form of links with selected countries such as the members of the EC.

Moreover, questions can be asked about the nature of the links with other states; should they be confined to meeting specific and limited mutual needs (as was the case with EFTA) or is the meeting of specific mutual needs best accomplished by developing more general inter-state links as in the EC treaties? Thus either one can argue that British national sovereignty is enhanced by accepting the obligations of EC membership because it is the only way to fulfil Britain's needs and aspirations, or, in contrast, it can be argued that alternative ways of meeting Britain's needs and aspirations would involve relatively smaller losses of national sovereign powers. Each view is an exercise of political judgement.

However, in international law political judgement can be supported either way on the issue of national sovereignty. Although it is always assumed that when states enter into treaties they accept that the obligations should be kept (*pacta sunt servanda*) states can claim that a fundamental change in the original circumstances and assumptions regarding membership (*rebus sic stantibus*) makes the adherence to treaty obligations damaging to vital national interests.[7] Although the Treaty of Rome does not specifically refer to states' rights to leave the Community, it is acknowledged that states can leave the EC because membership does not deprive them of their sovereign powers.

Recently there has been a development in the EC which has re-awakened debate in Britain as to the impact of EC membership upon Britain's position as a sovereign state. It was clear from the previous discussion of the obligations of membership that the main political parties felt that neither the content of the EC treaties nor the way the EC conducted its affairs imposed any serious limits upon Britain's national sovereignty, because the scope of the EC treaties was limited and could not be extended except with the unanimous agreement of all member states and, in normal business, states' interests were protected by the Luxembourg Agreement.

Currently, however, this last point is an open issue because the political device expressing a requirement for unanimous agreement, found in the Luxembourg Agreement or Compromise of 1966, has not been made a formal legal right, and obligation by an amendment to the Rome Treaty and the device has been challenged. On 18 May 1982 the Council of Agriculture Ministers adopted the 1982 price package by qualified majority, ignoring the British 'veto'.[8] Britain has argued that this move is unacceptable because, as Foreign Secretary Francis Pym told the Commons, 'The procedure was regarded as an inherent and essential safeguard.' The Agriculture Minister, Peter Walker, had previously suggested (*The Times*, 19 May 1982) that the acceptance of a decision by majority vote violated one of the basic principles on which Britain had joined the EC.

It has already been pointed out in chapter 1, that the 1966 Luxembourg Compromise was really just a formal expression of different viewpoints on EC decision-making at the Council of Ministers level. Moreover, its status had been explicitly recognized in the 1967 White Paper on the 'Legal and Constitutional Implications of United Kingdom Membership of the European Communities'. The White Paper (Cmnd 3301, p. 6, para. 14) simply notes that in 1966 'The French delegation considered that when very important interests were in issue discussion should continue until unanimous agreement was reached; but this was not accepted by the other countries and it was simply noted that there was a difference of opinion.' This form of expression, a noting of different opinions, was all that Mr Pym was able to report to the Commons (Weekly Hansard, 22 June 1982, Col. 155) after further EC discussions on the voting on the 1982 agricultural price package. However, he did add that five members of the EC supported the British view concerning the importance of the 'veto' as a safeguard for vital national interests.

This is clearly an issue which Britain and other states alike, opposed to decision by majority voting, will not allow to be forgotten, because of the implications that the EC is becoming federal in political character. At present if the EC were to move towards a federal political grouping it would attract a signifant and hostile reaction from both the Labour and Conservative parties. However, politically, states can nullify EC legislation, ignore the supremacy of EC legislation, and ignore EC enforcement efforts. As Lasok and Bridge (1982, p. 303) have pointed out 'a recalcitrant state cannot really be forced to abide by the judgement of the Court.'

There are a number of recent examples of state practice to support these contentions: in 1979–80 France refused to permit the import of British lamb and mutton, despite decisions by the Court of Justice that France was in breach of EC rules.[9] More recently the Commission has been complaining that member states have been nullifying the EC's internal free-trade policy by implementing non-tariff barriers to restrict internal trade. Therefore Taylor can clearly support his argument (1981, p. 253) that 'in the legal area, as in other "policy" areas, the practice of the European Communities differs sharply from the federal model.'

Considering sovereignty in the sense of Britain's status as a sovereign state, one can therefore argue that Britain has delegated no more sovereignty than necessary in the exercise of her sovereign rights to enter, voluntarily, into a particular international agreement and Britain has the right to leave the EC. Moreover, if the EC conducts its affairs with more members supporting the French statement in the Luxembourg Compromise or Agreement, Britain will have gained more secure protection against decisions being implemented which she regards as against her vital national interests.

THE SOVEREIGNTY OF PARLIAMENT

The main issues dealt with in this section are the impact of EC membership upon the sovereignty of Parliament, the status and significance of the 1972 EC Act, and the relationship between Parliament and judiciary. The impact of EC membership upon parliamentary relations with the executive and upon the machinery of government are discussed in the following chapters.

In domestic politics as in international politics it is usual for the word sovereignty to be qualified by an adjective describing the source of power. In Britain we normally speak of parliamentary sovereignty because Parliament is the supreme law-making authority. Thus the successful passage of the 1972 European Communities Act through Parliament was itself a demonstration of the exercise of parliamentary sovereignty. However, such was the general controversy over EC membership that its impact on domestic understanding of sovereignty has been widely commented upon by lawyers, constitutional experts and politicians. Moreover, it has to be accepted that if the political fact of membership is still open to question, the constitutional issues must also be considered as remaining unresolved.

Legal and constitutional commentators face two main difficulties in assessing the consequences of EC entry. First, is the problem of traditional understandings of the sovereignty of Parliament, and second, the problem of how those understandings are to be reconciled with the fact of Community membership. Mitchell (1979, pp. 40–1) has pointed out that the sovereignty of Parliament has two meanings: the positive meaning, i.e. that Parliament's legislative authority is unlimited, and the negative meaning, i.e. that no body or court can question the validity of a statute and must apply the latest one.

The concept of the sovereignty of Parliament is open to a number of interpretations which have been the subject of wide discussion by legal and political analysts, in the context of Britain's entry to the EC.[10] In origin the concept dates from the eighteenth century and means that in Britain the

supreme law-making power resides in the Queen in Parliament (Lords and Commons). The law or rules relating to
the powers of Parliament are derived from legal writings and
judgements. The two questions that arise from these rules
are: Can one Parliament bind its successors?; and If one
Parliament can bind its successors, would it follow that the
courts could pronounce on the validity of subsequent legislation? The followers of Dicey argue for the continuing
supremacy of Parliament. However, they recognize an
inconsistency in respect of transfers of power as in the 1931
Statute of Westminster. More modern constitutional lawyers
have observed that just because a legislature is sovereign it
does not have to retain a totally immutable procedure,
manner, and form of legislating. However, they would still
argue that no single Act of Parliament can be guaranteed in a
legal sense to bind future Parliaments. Thus the binding force
of the Statute of Westminster is derived from the external
factors of the realities of Britain's changed relations with the
Dominions and, internally, from political self-restraint by
British politicians. The key question is whether British
politicians are prepared, in effect, to regard the 1972 EC Act
as having a similar status and consequent effect on their
actions as the 1931 Statute of Westminster.

An official and rather bland view (Cmnd 3301, pp. 8–10)
of the legal and constitutional implications was provided in a
1967 White Paper presented by the (then) Lord Chancellor.
On the precedence over domestic law to be given to Community law, the White Paper noted that although in future
cases Parliament might have to refrain from passing inconsistent legislation, 'This would not involve any constitutional
innovation. Many of our treaty obligations already impose
such restraints.' The White Paper also pointed to an increased
role for the judiciary because Community 'provisions are
framed in more general terms and more is left to judicial
interpretation.' Basically the White Paper suggested that the
major issue was 'the constitutional innovation . . . in the
acceptance in advance of part of the law of the United
Kingdom of provisions to be made in the future by instruments issued by the Community institutions – a situation for
which there is no precedent in this country.' The White Paper

also added the comment that 'these instruments, like ordinary delegated legislation, would derive their force under the law of the United Kingdom from the original enactment passed by Parliament.'

Despite the 1967 White Paper's assumption that all would be well, there is no generally accepted legal solution to the conflict between parliamentary sovereignty and the obligations of EC membership. This was succinctly stated in the case of *Blackburn v the Attorney-General* in 1971. A Mr Blackburn had attempted unsuccessfully to get the Appeal Court to declare the British application to join the EC illegal because it involved an apparently unchangeable surrender of part of the sovereignty of the Crown in Parliament. Lord Denning, Master of the Rolls, stated (Yardley, 1974, pp. 30–1) 'We have all been brought up to believe that, in legal theory, one Parliament cannot bind another and that no Act is irreversible. But legal theory does not always march alongside political reality.' Lord Denning went on to refer to the granting of independence to dependent territories, and argued 'Freedom once given cannot be taken away. Legal theory must give way to practical politics.'

But freedom given to territories overseas is different to restraints accepted upon one's own domestic circumstances by treaty. As has already been noted, in international law, restraints imposed by treaty need not be accepted for all times. The resolution must lie in the meaning politicians wish to give to Lord Denning's terms 'political reality' and 'practical politics'. This much is also admitted by Mitchell (1979, p. 46) who, after arguing that parliamentary sovereignty is not really a stumbling block to EC membership, admits that 'there is a political content to the concept of sovereignty of Parliament which differs in ways from the legal content' and that therefore the political debate need not come to an end. This political element in the debate over parliamentary sovereignty is also examined by Hartley and Griffith (1975, pp. 382–5) who conclude that although

> the provisions of the European Communities Act are ineffective in so far as they seek to limit the power of Parliament to legislate in the future – the doctrine of

parliamentary sovereignty is not something which has existed from the beginning of time, nor is it self-evident in logic. It was developed by writers and courts to meet the needs of the times. It is not immutable: it can be changed by the courts if they decide to follow another doctrine.

Moreover they argue that if Britain's EC entry becomes truly established as an accepted political fact then 'the doctrine of parliamentary supremacy will cease to be the bedrock of the constitution and the primacy of Community law will be accepted.'

THE EUROPEAN COMMUNITIES ACT 1972

In simple terms this Act (1972, C. 68; see Appendix 2) was introduced to give domestic effect to Britain's membership of the EC, both in terms of the obligations of membership as they existed in 1972, and as those obligations might be developed through the due Community processes. However, the constitutional and political aspects of the Act are far from simple and non-controversial. An important feature of the Act is that it increases the scope of executive policy-making by delegating power to a minister or department to implement an obligation by 'means of orders, rules, regulations or other subordinate instrument' (1972 EC Act 2 (2)). This power means a corresponding loss of control over the executive by Parliament, as long as the Act exists in its present form, because under Section 2 and Section 1 (relating to EC treaty-making) obligations usually take effect after Parliament has only had a limited opportunity to discuss the measures under the procedure previously only used for approving statutory instruments. There is quite a range of views on the role and effect of this act. Geoffrey Howe (1973, p. 8), accepting Lord Gardiner's view that there 'is in theory no constitutional means available to us to make certain that no future Parliament would enact legislation to conflict with Community law' feels that the 1972 Act 'has tried to achieve the supremacy of Community law by more conventional and pragmatic means'. However, Street and Brazier (1981, p. 91) argue that 'this unique Act is a fascinating exercise in equivocation, a wilful manifestation of legislative schizophrenia . . . the United Kingdom Government has seated Parliament on two horses, one straining towards the preservation of parliamentary sovereignty, the other galloping in the general direction of Community law supremacy.'

These polarized views on the 1972 EC Act in part reflect the difficulties of making constitutional changes in the absence of a written constitution, and in part reflect the difference between a politician's and a lawyer's approach to the same problem. Howe's view (1973, p. 6) is that the Government (he actually uses the word Parliament) 'has identified an area within which Community legislative power will operate. Within that area Parliament [the Government] intends to refrain (as is required by the treaties) from exercising its own legislative power. The legislative area affected in this way is defined as that within which "in accordance with the Treaties" Community law is required to prevail.'

The 'pragmatic' solution to giving effect to EC membership is thus the presentation to Parliament of a Bill, very carefully drafted by Sir John Fiennes and other parliamentary lawyers. The 'conventional' means are allowing Parliament more than 50 days to debate the Bill and the Treaty of Accession. However, where this apparently reasonable and traditional method is deficient on the issue of EC entry is that the 1972 EC Act had to be so carefully drafted to give effect to EC membership that there was no room for Parliament to propose substantial changes. In other words, Parliament could talk (Howe estimates (1973, p. 8) that something like 2,400,000 words were spoken in Lords and Commons debates), but could not act, a problem that was exacerbated by the deep division in both main parties over EC entry itself. Such divisions would certainly have led anti-marketeers to seek if possible to have incorporated in the Act more specific safeguards for traditional British constitutional practices and arrangements. Tony Benn in fact tried (Usher, 1981, p. 34) to introduce a Bill to give the British Parliament the unilateral right to alter a legal rule made by an EC institution. Moreover, this sort of action was allowed in the passage of the European Direct Elections Bill, where a clause was inserted in the 1979 Act to provide that parliamentary approval would be needed for the Government to agree to any changes in the powers of the European Parliament. Although there may have been good party political reasons, and it was difficult to draft a workable Act, there is substance in Mackintosh's comment (1982, p. 62) that 'Mr Heath demonstrated what can be done by a determined Prime Minister when he drove through the Bill to carry Britain into the European Community in 1972 despite sufficient Conservative opposition to put his majority at risk.'

The problems in the Conservative party over internal opposition to EC entry, and the potential consequences for the government's Commons majority are well documented in Kitzinger (1973, chapters 6 and 13) and Norton (1978). Kitzinger notes the importance of Prime Minister Heath's personal commitment, which 'committed the Conservative party to pursue that application when on all evidence the majority of local associations and a very large section of the parliamentary party were distinctly cool or hostile.' The Conservative Government needed first to ensure a majority for the principle of entry on the terms negotiated. This was obtained by the vote on the declaratory motion on 28 October 1981, which gave the Government an overall majority of 112, although in that vote 41 Conservative MPs abstained.

Next the Conservative Government needed to ensure support for the Bill to implement, domestically, Britain's accession to the EC. Kitzinger (1973, pp. 375–80) suggests that the Government had to choose between the extremes of either the passage of two Bills: one on constitutional powers, and one to list and change every statute which was in conflict with EC law, or a simple one-clause Bill to give automatic effect and precedence to EC law. The first extreme would have been time-consuming, and the second could have proved politically dangerous, giving the impression of excessive 'steamroller' tactics. The Government selected a compromise Bill with a three-clause Part I, covering the constitutional problems and a nine-clause Part II, dealing with specific issues.

The Opposition was quick to note that in giving effect to pre-entry EC legislation, the Government was allowing into domestic law a mass of legislation 'which no parliamentarian would ever have time to read, let alone debate or vote on' (Kitzinger, 1973, p. 380). The Opposition also drew attention to the fact that the decision-making system in the EC was intergovernmental and bureaucratic, and thus allowed little scope for parliamentary involvement. They also pointed out the procedural inadequacies of Parliament's delegated legislation process which would be applied to most of the implementation of EC legislation.

Because of the Government's domestic unpopularity, during 1972 the Conservative anti-marketeers had the importance of party loyalty made very clear to them (Kitzinger, 1973, p. 387). Nonetheless, the Second Reading of the EC Bill, on 17 February 1972, was only approved by eight votes and during the Committee stage on some amendments the Government only secured majorities against the proposals of four, five and six. The Bill passed its Third Reading on 13 July 1972 with 301 votes in favour. Thus, as Kitzinger points out (1973, p. 396) 'the Government could not claim to have obtained the votes of half the House in favour of its implementing legislation.' No wonder the political controversies were to continue.

A most useful legal commentary on the 1972 Act is provided by Lasok and Bridge (1982, pp. 341–2), who make the point that: 'As far as the body of Community Law in force on the eve of British membership was concerned no difficulty was experienced. That law . . . will be given legal force in the United Kingdom by Section 2 (1) of the Act and that will have precedence over prior British law by simple operation of the rule *lex posterior derogat priori.*' But they recognize that 'the critical question is whether our doctrine of parliamentary sovereignty means that such restraints must always be voluntarily imposed by Parliament or whether they can be compulsorily guaranteed.' They argue that although there is a legal presumption that Parliament would not intend to break a treaty that is not sufficient to prevent Parliament from expressly passing a law inconsistent with treaty obligations.

What options are open to resolve this problem? Lasok and Bridge (1982, p. 342) cite the following argument of J. D. B. Mitchell: that as the Act of Union of 1707 created a new legal order with restraints on Parliament, so too may a new legal order be created by joining the EC. They also cite R. F. V. Heuston's argument: that Parliament may be sovereign in the area of its power but accept limitations on how that power is exercised. Other writers have suggested formal clauses in all statutes of the intent to avoid conflict with EC law, or a special clause in the EC Act. Lasok and Bridge also note the suggestion that the situation could be resolved by 'the gradual emergence of a constitutional convention by which it would be recognized that Parliament could not legislate contrary to Community law.'

Lasok and Bridge see the 1972 EC Act as having been carefully drafted to avoid radical solutions, procedural solutions and the reliance upon the emergence of constitutional conventions, an approach which also avoided raising, formally, politically controversial constitutional points. Basically the 1972 EC Act (Section 2 (1)) was drafted so as to give EC law effect in the UK and since the doctrine of the supremacy of EC law is part of that law, that doctrine is also given effect in UK law. The doctrine is further supported by Section 2 (4) which, in broad terms, means that later acts shall be subject to the rule of the supremacy of EC law. An example of this provision being used is given by the case (*re* Medical Expenses Incurred in France (1977) 2 CMLR 317) where the National Insurance Commissioner held that Section 2 (4) of the Act required him to read the 1975 Social Security Act as being subject to the 1971 EEC Regulations on Social Security for migrant workers. Moreover, Section 3 (1) requires the UK courts to defer to the Court of Justice on all matters of EC law.

These sections of the 1972 EC Act do not forbid Parliament to pass conflicting legislation. What they do, however, is to deny (Lasok and Bridge, 1982, p. 344) 'effectiveness to such legislation within the legal systems of the United Kingdom to the extent that it conflicts with Community law'. Thus Parliament's political and legal power to repeal the EC Act is not affected, and indeed it is accepted that there is no rule of law which could limit Parliament's power in this respect, a point noted by the Judicial Committee of the Privy Council when commenting on the 1931 Statute of Westminster (Section 4) which states that the British Parliament shall not legislate for a Dominion without that Dominion's request and consent. As Wade (Dicey, 1965, p. xlix f) comments 'The Judicial Committee accepted the view that as a matter of abstract law the repeal or disregard of the section was within the powers of Parliament but declared that this was theory and had no relation to reality – there then is an example of the sovereignty of Parliament being restricted by political considerations . . .'

However, the question has been posed as to whether the 1972 EC Act was sufficient to guarantee even the backing of the British legal system for the doctrine of the supremacy of EC law. Lord Denning, former Master of the Rolls, was cited as saying in 1975 that if a later Act of Parliament conflicted with the Treaty of Rome the courts would 'have to abide by the statute without regard to the Treaty at all'.[11] This problem was recognized earlier by F. A. Trinidade who argued (1972, p. 395) that the Act should have specifically directed the courts to hold British statutes invalid or of no effect if they conflicted with EC law. He suggested that 'the absence of such a declaration is not only striking but it also enables lawyers and politicians to believe that the traditional doctrine of the sovereignty of the United Kingdom Parliament has not been affected in the least.'

THE EFFECT OF THE 1972 EC ACT ON THE JUDICIARY

At the time of entry commentators speculated that the British judicial system would have difficulty in adjusting to the fact that Parliament was no longer the only law-making body for Britain, and that it was now the duty of the judiciary to give precedence to EC law if it conflicted with British law. In fact, Parliament (in practice the Government) has not sought, so far, deliberately to create problems by passing an Act which would conflict with an EC obligation. Therefore the judiciary has been able to make a smoother transition to the new legal regime than some anticipated, although this smooth transition has in turn raised a further series of issues.

The first case on the effect of the Rome Treaty on English law came in 1974 (*Application des Gas sa v Falks Veritas* (1974) Ch. 381). In that case Lord Denning stated (Street and Brazier, 1981, p. 114) that 'the Treaty is part of our law. It is equal in force to any statute. It must be applied in our courts.' In a more recent case before the Appeal court, the Court held that (Street and Brazier, 1981, p. 114) 'EEC law, and in particular Article 119 of the EEC Treaty, is supreme over United Kingdom law by virtue of the European Communities Act 1972 itself.'

A detailed discussion of the impact of EC law on the courts and tribunals has been provided in an article by J. W. Bridge (1976, p. 13) who notes Lord Denning's picturesque phraseology that EC law has been 'like an incoming tide. It flows into the estuaries and up the rivers.' Bridge's study was based upon 13 cases, including two before tribunals. He found that in the earlier cases there 'appears to be an unquestioning acceptance that Community law is now part of our law'. These included the case before Lord Denning cited earlier. However, Bridge feels that this acceptance of the EC law in English law showed a 'misconceived and somewhat naive attitude to the impact of Community law'.

Bridge points to the differing impact of regulations and directives, and notes that Vice-Chancellor Pennycuick was the only judge in reported cases to show an awareness of those differences. He also feels that in the two cases (Esso Petroleum and Aero Zipp) where judges concluded that conflicting English laws must give way to EC law, they failed to fully justify such a conclusion.

The final general question that Bridge addresses (1976, p. 13) is that of the 'mode of interpretation of Community law'. First, it is recognized that the European court is the final interpretative authority on EC law. Second, and more difficult to assimilate in the British legal tradition, is the fact that EC laws are not drafted in such detail as British statutes, thus allowing the courts in the EC states to fill in the detail in EC laws. A task which British judges are not normally supposed to carry out as filling in the detail is part of Parliament's legislative function. Faced with this new task of expressing in detail the purpose and intent of law, Bridge has found some differences in the practice of interpretation. Indeed, he argues (1976, p. 17) that 'there is also a serious risk that the uniformity of Community law may be undermined if United Kingdom Courts and Tribunals are allowed when interpreting that law, to go on voyages of discovery of their own without taking advantage of the navigational aids provided by the European Court.'

With the benefit of more experience of the impact of EC law on the English legal system, Bridge (1981, pp. 351–76) further developed his analysis of the differences in national legal tradition in this context. Bridge, pointing again to the differences in legislative style (the more general style of EC legislation contrasting with the more detailed format of Acts of Parliament), notes, however, that in interpretation British judges before 1973 have actually gone beyond simple literal interpretation. They have at times found it necessary to attempt a purposive approach to the interpretation of English Acts in order to avoid a particular Act being rendered ineffectual. Bridge has found that during the 1970s the courts have shown an increasing awareness of the need to use the guidance of the rulings of the European court. Moreover, it has become apparent (Bridge, 1981, pp. 372–3) that the Court of Appeal has been adopting in cases concerning EC law the methodology of the European court, the teleological approach; that is, attempting to give effect to the spirit of legislation if a dispute as to meaning arises. However, when Lord Denning, noted by Bridge (1982, pp. 375–6) as an enthusiastic interpreter of laws, attempted to use this approach on rules relating to a European transport treaty which were not rules of EC law, the House of Lords rejected this too sweeping approach.

So far there have been very few conflicts between British law and EC law which have caused a major problem to reach the European Court in the form of a case. Among examples from the 1970s was Case 141/78 *France v UK* (4 October 1979), where the European court held that Britain was in breach of a Council Resolution of November 1976 which had, under Article 5 (EEC) laid down a specific requirement for states to co-operate over the introduction of unilateral fishing measures by first seeking the approval of the Commission. Britain was in breach of its obligations by not seeking prior approval for the Fishing Nets (North-East Atlantic) Order 1977. During 1982 two cases involving Britain came before the court.[12] Case number 61/81 involved an action by the European Commission over a conflict between the 1970 Equal Pay Act as amended by the 1975 Sex Discrimination Act, and the provision of Council Directive number 75/117/EEC of 10 February 1975 on equal pay for work of equal value. The Court held that Britain had failed to fulfil its treaty obligations to permit the full operation of the equal pay for work of equal value principle.

In the second case, number 40/82, the Commission argued that Britain's curbs in 1980–81 on the imports of poultry, eggs and egg products, which were supposed to be for the protection of animal health (a permissible restraint on trade under EC rules) were in fact an unlawful measure of trade discrimination because imports continued to be allowed in from Denmark and Ireland. The Court agreed that the rules made under the Animal Health Act 1981 and the Importation of Animal Products and Poultry Products Order, meant that Britain was not fulfilling the treaty obligation to permit unrestricted intra-EC trade.

In general though, it appears that the problems for the judiciary itself and for the relations between Parliament and the judiciary, suggested at the time of entry, by writers such as Trinidade, have not materialized to any great extent. Partly the problem seems to have been avoided by careful drafting of subsequent domestic legislation both to give effect to EC law and avoid conflict with it unless overriding domestic considerations prevail. Also the judiciary seems to have accepted that entry into the EC did constitute a political fact from which legal consequences followed.[13] Moreover, other EC states have also experienced conflicts between their laws and EC laws so Britain's problems are not unique. Thus a *modus vivendi* seems to have evolved between the executive, legislature and judiciary on the issue of the supremacy of EC law in the United Kingdom. However, this does not mean that the constitutional issue of Parliament's sovereign law-making powers and the law has been resolved – it has merely been avoided, so far.

When the Labour Government was elected to office in February 1974 the deep divisions in the party on EC entry and the strength of the anti-marketeers produced a major political problem for the Government if Britain was to remain in the EC. Robins (1977, pp. 124–5) points out that at Labour's second special conference on the EEC, the party voted by 3,724,000 to 1,986,000 against membership, and that the parliamentary party voted against membership by 145 to 137 with 33 abstentions. Moreover, for reasons of party management the 1974 Labour Cabinet had an overall anti-market composition. At the very marginal level the party was held together by its 'twin policies of renegotiation and consultation' (Robins, 1977, pp. 124–7). But how, if renegotiation was successful, could the continuation of membership be formally confirmed? A general election was not really feasible as a pre-renegotiation general election keeping Labour in power had already been held in October 1974, only eight months after Labour had been first returned to office. However, the Labour election manifesto of October 1974 contained the promise that a Labour Government would 'give the British people the final say, which will be binding on the Government – through the ballot box – on whether we accept the terms and stay in or reject the terms and come out.' This promise was rightly interpreted as a pledge to hold a referendum on EC membership.

The referendum issue raised some important constitutional points. It raises the notion of popular sovereignty as something which can exist at other times than at general elections. Street and Brazier (1981, p. 107) consider that the divisions in the political parties made it very difficult to confirm a decision on entry by any of the normal means. They argue that the question 'could not be answered by a vote in the House of Commons or at a General Election because different answers would be given by members of the same

political party and of none.' In essence the referendum
provided a political solution to the issue of continued
membership of the EC which would have to be accepted,
whereas reliance upon a legal solution by way of the Treaty
of Accession and an enabling act could be more fiercely
challenged. However, in either case, under the British constitution both solutions can be altered at some future date.
Accession to the EC treaties could be abrogated and the 1972
Act repealed through the exercise of parliamentary powers
alone, or the exercise of these parliamentary powers could be
preceded by a referendum decision to leave the EC.

The 1975 referendum on staying in the EC has been
variously described: as 'a unique constitutional experiment'
(Street and Brazier, 1981, p. 107); a 'distinct innovation in
British constitutional practice' (Butler and Kitzinger, 1976,
p. 1); and 'the direct outcome of Labour's internal struggle
over Europe' (King, 1977, p. 55). There had been some
earlier advocates (King, 1977, pp. 56–7) of a referendum on
EC membership, such as Jo Grimmond and Tony Benn.
Douglas Jay also argued for a referendum because Parliament
would be yeilding power which might, in practice, be
difficult to recover. Prime Minister Harold Wilson was
reported (King, 1977, p. 59) not to be too enthusiastic about
the use of a referendum as it could be seen as abdicating 'the
role of political leader in a parliament-based system. It was to
say that the institutions which had made one, and in which
one had one's political being, were inadequate to the performance of some large national task.'

The key factor in determining the use of a referendum on
this occasion was the necessity for reconciling deep divisions
within the Labour party. Robins (1977, p. 128) comments
that 'the advantages of holding a referendum as far as the
party managers were concerned was that it made the EEC
conflict largely external to the party . . . they were hopeful
that the result of the referendum would be recognized as a
legitimate solution to the conflict by all sides – the type of
solution . . . the Labour party was unable to produce.'

The problems of party management in the Labour party
produced separate but related constitutional departures.
The constitutional convention concerning the collective

responsibility of the Cabinet has only been suspended three times since 1932 (Norton, 1981, pp. 151–2), and two of these occasions concerned controversy over EC membership: in 1975, over the conduct of the EC referendum campaign, and in 1977, on the second reading of the European Assembly Elections Bill. On the latter occasion the exercise of political control over constitutional matters was evident in Prime Minister Callaghan's comments (933 HC Debs 1977, Col. 552) on collective responsibility that 'I certainly think that the doctrine should apply, except in cases where I announce that it does not.'

It is evident that there is no constitutional or legal argument which can suggest that traditional understandings concerning the negative and positive aspects of parliamentary sovereignty are invalid. It is, as Hartley and Griffith have pointed out, a political problem. If Britain's membership of the EC becomes an undisputed and established political fact, then the 'doctrine of parliamentary supremacy will cease to be the bedrock of the Constitution' (Hartley and Griffiths, 1975, pp. 392–3). On the question of Britain's national sovereignty, doubt has now crept into what appeared to be a resolved issue. It is clear that British politicians view the Luxembourg Compromise/Agreement as providing an essential safeguard for national sovereignty, by giving expression to the political concept of a national veto on EC policies judged as harmful to the national interest, and where unanimity is not required by treaty. Therefore British governments and Parliament will obviously monitor the post-May 1982 EC approach to the 'veto' very closely for implications concerning national sovereignty. What might be called the 'sovereignty of the people' has been tested once in the 1975 referendum; will it be tested again? The overall impression is that constitutional issues are only issues when politicians wish them to be seen as such.

The one issue that does tend to unite politicians from all parties, though not always simultaneously, is the dislike of accepting the law-making powers of the European Community without attempting to exercise close executive and parliamentary scrutiny of the process. This again raises Street and Brazier's point about the 1972 EC Act, which, on the question of sovereignty, effectively seats Parliament on two horses, each going in a different direction.

NOTES AND REFERENCES

1. This chapter has been partly based upon two very useful sources: D. Lasok and J. W. Bridge (1982) *Law and Institutions of the European Communities* (3rd edn), London, Butterworth; and P. S. R. F. Mathijsen (1972) *A Guide to European Community Law*, London, Sweet and Maxwell.
2. This Van Duyn case was Case 41/74 *Van Duyn v Home Office* (1974) ECR 1337, reference Council Directive No. 74/221, as cited in J. Usher (1981) *European Law and National Law*, London, Allen & Unwin, p. 68.
3. Information on EC legislation, its progress and status in Britain can be pieced together from various sources, for example: *Encyclopedia of European Community Law*, Sweet and Maxell, European Communities (1980); *Register of Current Community Legal Instruments*, Vol. I, Analytical Register and Vol. 4 Chronological Index, Brussels and Luxembourg; the *Annual General Report on the Activities of the European Communities presented to the European Parliament by the Commission.*
4. See the discussions of sovereignty in international law in G. Schwarzenberger (1967) *A Manual of International Law*, London, Stevens, 5th edn, pp. 55–69.
5. The Treaty of Accession is to be found as 'Treaty concerning the accession of Denmark, Ireland, Norway, and the UK to the EEC and the European Atomic Energy Community', Cmnd 5179 *Parliamentary Papers*, Session 1972–73, Vol. viii; and Cmnd 5179 II, *Parliamentary Papers*, Session 1972–73, Vol. ix.
6. On Treaties and Treaty-making, see M. Akehurst (1982) *A Modern Introduction to International Law*, (4th edn) London, George Allen & Unwin, pp. 121–40.
7. There has been an effort to tighten up the principle of *rebus sic stantibus*, by the Vienna Convention on Treaties. See M. Akehurst, *op. cit.*, pp. 134–9.
8. See the report in *The Times*, 19 May 1982; also 'Community Voting Procedures', European Communities' Commission, Background Report, No. ISEC/B24/82, 3 June 1982.
9. See Case 232/78 *Commission v France*, 25 May 1979 as cited in J. Usher (1981), *op. cit.*

10. In addition to Lasok and Bridge, *op. cit.*, see particularly G. Winterton (1976) 'The British Gründnorm: parliamentary supremacy re-examined', *Law Quarterly Review*, 92, pp. 591–617; C. Dike, 'The case against parliamentary sovereignty', *Public Law*, 1976, pp. 283–97 and J. Usher (1981), *op. cit.*

11. Lord Denning's comment was cited by the Master of Gonville and Caius College in a letter to *The Times*, 29 Apr. 1978. This letter was part of a prolonged correspondence on the issue of the supremacy of EC law over national law prompted by the Simmenthal case heard before the European Court – see the useful discussions in 'Supremacy of European Community Law', European Communities Commission Background Report, ISEC/B40/78, 22 May 1978.

12. See the European Law Reports in *The Times*, 17 May 1982, and 26 July 1982.

13. Indeed it is now even being suggested that the British legal system may be moving towards monism in the relationship between domestic and international law. See F. E. Dorwick (1982) 'Overlapping international and European laws', *International and Comparative Law Quarterly* 31 (1), pp. 59–98.

CHAPTER THREE

Parliament and European Community Business

INTRODUCTION

A discussion of the effects on Parliament of Britain's EC membership has to be related to the existence of parallel changes that have occurred in Parliament and in Parliament's role in the political system. The discussion must also note that Parliament's methods of handling EC affairs have a dynamic character and thus some early criticisms are no longer valid. However, one can agree with David Marquand (1981, p. 220) that 'In Britain, the effect of the Community's decision-making process on Parliament, and in particular on Parliament's ability to hold the executive to account has always been one of the staple themes of the debate over EEC membership.' Moreover, as Kolinsky has argued, and as was suggested in the previous chapter, 'The more serious issue is not the potential restriction of political capacity implied in the phrase "national sovereignty", but the erosion of parliamentary powers as a consequence of Community membership.'[1]

However, lest too many tears are shed for Parliament's losses as a result of EC entry, it is useful to examine some alternative preliminary considerations regarding the role of Parliament today. Norton (1981, p. 146), notes in the context of a discussion of the Commons, decision-makers, and the EC that 'The House of Commons is no longer a major part of the decision-making process in this country', and there have been marked changes in the Commons during the 1970s. Thus, as these changes coincide with the period of EC membership, the analysis in this chapter needs to be particularly careful in assessing cause and effect.

In the 1970s Norton points out there were minority governments and 'a high incidence of intra-party dissent' (Norton, 1980a, pp. 334–48). Also significant is the fact that according to Norton's researches, there were only 34 government defeats between July 1905 and March 1972, there were 65 government defeats between April 1972 and April 1979, and many (Norton, 1980a, p. 334) 'were on issues of importance.' Some of the defeats were on EC matters, for example, the defeat on the devaluation of the Green Pound and the use of proportional representation in direct elections to the European Parliament.

Of particular relevance to this study is Norton's finding that 'Members who disagreed with their leader on the issue of entry into the EC were able to take their dissent further than many previously would have believed possible.' Moreover, what Norton notes as an 'increased unwillingness to accept that "the Government knows best"' may be considered to be a particularly healthy and helpful approach to EC affairs where, at times, the Government may be as confused as MPs.

These changes in what was happening in the Commons can also be related to the pressures for parliamentary reform. In particular those stemming from what is often described as the two-party adversary system which hindered the traditional functions of the House to monitor and influence the government of the day. Ideas for reform envisaged either changing Parliament's method of work, for example new select committees, or external reform via changes in the electoral system. In both of these specific areas Britain's membership of the EC has produced domestic consequences which could be seen as providing precedents. It has been pointed out that Commons' scrutiny of EC affairs could only be done by a select committee and that the European Legislation Select Committee was also something of an innovation in terms of its functions. Because of the nature of the EC decision-making process, the post entry European Legislation Committee (ELC or Scrutiny Committee) can involve Parliament before decisions are actually taken; as John Roper MP has said (Stevens, 1976–7, p. 273), it 'opens the way for backbenchers to be involved in policy-making'.

The long debate over the electoral method to be used for the first direct elections to the European Parliament was, in so far as it concerned the use of a system of proportional representation, also about domestic electoral reform.[2] The Liberals clearly supported proportional representation for the European Parliament because in part it would provide a precedent which could be used in domestic discussions of electoral reform. This was why proportional representation for Europe was resisted by members of both the other main parties.

The problems consequent upon EC membership required Parliament to experiment with methods for handling EC affairs. There is no detailed EC role for national legislatures under the Rome Treaty. They are barely mentioned and it is left to each member state to handle the processing of the domestic obligations of EC membership by its own national methods. In some states, such as France and Luxembourg, this function is mostly under the control of the executive. Denmark has by contrast a system more akin to the one developed in Britain, namely a stress on as much control as possible by the legislature. Indeed, the Danish Parliament's (Folketing) all-party Community Affairs Committee can prevent the Danish Government from agreeing to Community policies. This power was used on 30 December 1982 over a major EC policy development, the Common Fisheries Policy, to delay the Danish Government from participating, despite the fact that all other EC members supported the Fisheries policy. It has also been noted that this spectrum of varying degrees of national legislative control of EC affairs can be roughly correlated with a country's known degree of enthusiasm for EC membership, or its domestic political tradition in terms of legislative–executive relations.[3]

Because of Britain's late post-foundation entry and deep internal divisions on the issue of membership, Parliament has tended to display (Coombes, 1981, p. 238) a defensive conservative reaction to EC business. Stevens (1976–77, p. 269 and pp. 274–5) identifies two fundamental questions concerning Parliament (especially the Commons) and EC legislation: What relationship should ministers have to EC policies and legislation?; and, How and in what ways should ministers be answerable to the House for their activities in Brussels? Regarding the influence that Parliament might seek to exert over EC affairs, Miller (1977, pp. 45–66) identifies three possible forms of direct influence: modification, negation and delay. He argues that although Parliament might ideally like to have a direct modifying or negating role over EC policies, this is unlikely to happen, and he cites comments from ministers and civil servants to that effect. Miller also suggests that direct influence by 'delay . . . is the source of Parliament's greatest effect', together with Parliament's capacity for exerting 'indirect' influence. However, ministers would have to agree not to proceed to decisions in the Council of Ministers to make the delaying power effective.

Before examining how Parliament approached the task of handling policy proposals emanating from Brussels, it is necessary to note that EC legislation should not be too readily dismissed as being 'secondary' in character or completely akin to delegated legislation in Britain. Coombes (1981, p. 238) has pointed out that 'the enactments of the Community can be much broader in scope, and politically important in content, than delegated legislation made by Ministers in Britain.' Moreover, as a number of MPs and ministers have found, the political methods used in the EC are very different from those in the Commons. John Silkin, referring to EC's annual agricultural price review said (HC43–iii, 1977, p. 33) 'the bases of the price review, indeed of many of the decisions in the Community, are those of the consensus package at the end of the day.' Michael Foot, when Lord President of the Council, described (HC400 and 43–iv, 1976–7, p. 1) EC decision-making as 'a mixture of negotiations and legislation, and the two do not necessarily mix very easily'. Barbara Castle comments in her Diaries (1980, p. 279) that 'the EEC only works on the basis of tortuous compromises . . . It is government by the fractionalization of policy . . . Under such a system it is impossible to mandate anyone, but it is such a break with what we have been accustomed to under our parliamentary tradition of voting on clear-cut blacks and whites that most MPs don't yet realize what is going to hit them.'

Membership of the EC poses some particular problems for the British parliamentary system. It is nearly impossible for a government to present a comprehensive EC policy to Parliament. The EC covers too many diverse policy areas, some of which like the CAP, are governed by a wide range of long-established regulations. This means that EC policy, except on major issues like the Community budget and the CAP, tends to become blurred by being merged within the pre-membership responsibilities of government departments. Therefore the EC will only exist in Parliament as a single issue if a government chooses to present it as such, or when pro- or anti-market MPs or peers make their contributions. Otherwise, generally, MPs or peers are likely to simply include those aspects of EC membership which impinge upon their own personal or constituency interests. Finally, in many respects the EC is almost too 'technical' in many of its policies for the 'broad sweep' adversary politics of the Commons. This is particularly seen in the fact that many EC policies are given effect in Britain through Parliament's statutory instrument procedure, which is a form of procedure that does not give much scope for backbench influence. As with all other aspects of the legislative process in Britain, both the Commons and the Lords have their own particular functions in respect of EC matters, and a difference of political outlook has been evident (Miller, 1977, p. 49), with the Lords generally more pro-EC than the Commons. This makes close co-operation between the two Houses and the Lords and Commons EC Committees rather difficult and accounts in part for the recent lack of use of concurrent hearings. In addition there is an important difference in the two EC committees' functions. The scrutiny of EC matters in the Commons is limited to matters likely to be of political or legal significance and the committee acts (Coombes, 1981, p. 243) as 'essentially a political filter'. Indeed, in its early years, 1974–76, the Commons Committee was even restricted as to the type of EC document that could come before it for scrutiny. By contrast the House of Lords, working under less political and legislative pressure, has adopted a much broader form of scrutiny, allowing it to comment at great length at times on the merits of EC proposals. Both committees have, of course, been involved in a similar 'learning process' with Government, about what is required in terms of information, time and experience, to provide the most useful form of scrutiny service to Parliament as a whole.

Despite the decade or so of debate upon the merits or otherwise of EC membership for Britain, relatively little thought was given to the effect of membership on Parliament's work, until just before the actual entry. The first official and public proposal concerning a new scrutiny role for Parliament was made by the then Chancellor of the Duchy of Lancaster, Geoffrey Rippon, in the Commons in February 1972. The preparatory work for presenting a scheme for parliamentary scrutiny of EC affairs has been well described in Kolinsky (1975), Bates (1976), and Ryan and Isaacson (1974–75). The basis for parliamentary scrutiny of EC affairs was established by the findings of the Foster Committee in the Commons (HC 143 and 463, I–II, 1972–73) and Maybray-King Committee in the Lords (HL 67 and HL 194, 1972–73). These committees reported during 1973, having been appointed in December 1972. Their establishment may be regarded as the first stage in developing scrutiny procedures. In parallel, as a second stage, the information provided to MPs was increased. From February 1973 onwards, the Vote Office provided a wide range of EC documents and sent a 'yellow form' to MPs each Thursday on which they could order EC documents. The Commons Library established a European desk with an information service, began indexing all EC regulations and directives, and started to produce a monthly EC bulletin.

This new and large information flow produced the first EC problems for Parliament. Did MPs have the time, competence and interest to study EC affairs? Even if they did, there was confusion over ministerial accountability. Who was to answer for which EC issue? In part some of these problems were met by the recommendations of the First Report of the Foster Committee (HC 143) in February 1973. This report proposed that the legislative proposals from the European Commission should be accompanied by a government explanatory memorandum, setting out the legal and policy implications, the department responsible for that area of activity, and the date by which the proposal should reach the Council of Ministers.

However, even as early as 1973, two further problems became evident to Parliament. First, there was a difficulty in obtaining adequate information on Commission proposals. Some departmental memoranda were decidedly unhelpful to MPs; one MP described the contents of some memoranda as 'a general tendency to err on the laconic' (Bates, 1976, p. 31). Second, there was the problem of keeping track of ministers' activities in the EC which forms part of Parliament's more general problem of exercising control over Ministers involved in international negotiations (Richards, 1967). For example, in July 1973 the Commons was annoyed (Ryan and Isaacson, 1974–75, p. 203) when John Davies, Minister for Europe stated that the British had agreed in the Council of Ministers to a supplementary budget costing Britain over £35 million, without first informing the House. This was part of a wider issue as Ryan and Isaacson note (1974–75, p. 207): 'Legislation by the Executive branch of government is "expressly prohibited" in Great Britain.' Thus, ideally, MPs would like to commit a minister to a particular course in the Council of Ministers. However, ministers have pointed out that their participation in the 'negotiations' in the Council of Ministers would be hampered by having the British position too rigidly and publicly defined in advance. Ministers have also complained (Castle, 1980, pp. 279 and 302) that EC entry has allowed MPs to try and intrude into the, traditionally, executive area of relations with foreign states and even that the title 'EC' on a document has brought before the House matters, such as food content, that would, as purely domestic issues, have been within the prerogative of a Minister.

SCRUTINY BY SELECT COMMITTEE

The next stage in the development of Commons scrutiny came in October 1973 with the publication of the final report of the Foster Committee. The Committee proposed (HC

463–I, p. xviii) the establishment of a 'new and different kind of Committee . . . its essential role is participation in legislation.' The aim of the new committee was, in Foster's (HC 463–I, p. xiii) view, 'to restore to Parliament responsibilities for, and opportunities to exercise its constitutional rights . . .' in the domestic area of EC law making. The best that ministers would try and guarantee was stated on 4 November 1974, by Roy Hattersley as Minister of State at the FCO, when he said (880 HC Deb. Cols. 691–2) that the Government would try to ensure that no proposals, recommended by the scrutiny committee for debate, would be agreed to in the Council of Ministers until Parliament had debated the topic. In the same year the new Labour Government agreed to some of the more general Foster and Maybray-King proposals that there would be a place for EC questions on the question rota, and per session, four days for general EC debates, plus two days for the debates on the twice-yearly White Papers on the EC. Bates (1976, p. 25) suggests therefore that by 1974 'Parliament now had a scrutiny procedure; it still lacked a clear policy for its development.'

Before looking in detail at the work of the Commons EC Scrutiny Committee, a number of general comments have been made on the Commons and EC affairs which form useful preliminary guides to analysis. Most obvious is the fact that the 'pro and anti' EC debate continued after membership and affected the establishment and operation of scrutiny procedures. Miller (1977, p. 59), on the basis of interviews and comments from ministers and civil servants, expresses the view that Parliament is unlikely to be able to modify or negate EC policy-making in any way. These comments can be linked to Kolinsky's view (1975, pp. 61–2) that the Foster Committee reports allowed ministers 'discretion' in how they resolved conflicts of views between the Commons and the EC on EC affairs. Moreover, Kolinsky questions whether the balance between the convention of ministers being accountable to Parliament and the exercise of 'discretion' will always be satisfactorily maintained.

Miller lists a number of reasons (1977, pp. 57–8) why Parliament might be able to exercise more influence on EC policy-making than on domestic policy-making; the cross-party doubts on the wisdom of entry will ensure EC affairs remain contentious; even pro-EC MPs may wish to curb excesses of EC policy-making, especially over harmonization; EC draft legislation differs in form and origin to government Bills and therefore a government does not necessarily have to defend EC legislative proposals; interest groups may seek the support of the parliamentary Scrutiny Committee, and EC policy-making is more public.

However, there are some further points to consider. It has been noted (Ryan and Isaacson, 1974–75, p. 213) that if ministers do not actually try to defend an EC policy, how can Parliament really attack a minister who says, in effect, 'this is the best deal we could get'? Such an approach is a marked contrast to the tradition of domestic politics where ministers are expected to defend their own policies with some enthusiasm. Moreover, interest groups do not necessarily see Parliament or its EC Scrutiny Committees as useful allies in influencing the EC policy process. Some groups have felt that the deep divisions in the Commons on EC affairs would hinder the presentation of a particular case. Others, like the Road Haulage Association, have said that they believe the most useful ways to exert influence are through the British Government departments, and through the European Road Haulage Federation to the European Commission, MPs in general, having no direct EC links.[4]

The House of Commons scrutiny of EC affairs is now carried out in three ways; in the specialist scrutiny committee (the ELC) in the post-1979 departmental select committees and the standing committees; by debates on the floor of the House; and through members asking questions. These are reinforced by the MPs' activities in the various EC-related groupings of their parliamentary parties and through MP's extra-parliamentary links. In the next few paragraphs, the analysis will start with the specialist Scrutiny Committee, and then move to the more general activities of the House.

The Second Report of the Foster Committee contains two general comments on Commons' scrutiny of EC affairs. These are worth stating in full, for evaluation against the record of the Scrutiny Committee work. Foster noted:

It seems that there is no possibility of exercising in this field anything like the same degree of detailed control as is available to the House of Commons under the present process of enacting a Statute. *However, so long as the weighted majority rule in the EEC Treaty is in abeyance, and so long as the practice of unanimity is required* [my italics] it should be possible to exert at least as much control over this legislation as is currently available in respect of delegated legislation in the United Kingdom (HC 463–I, p. xv).

The sixteen member ELC was set up in May 1974 following the suggestions of the Foster Committee. It was given a good start to its work by having as the first Chairman, John Davies, MP. Davies had been Prime Minister Heath's Chancellor of the Duchy of Lancaster with special responsibility for EC affairs. The Committee's current order of reference is:

> to consider draft proposals by the Commission of the European Communities for legislation and other documents published for submission to the Council of Ministers or to the European Council whether or not such documents originate from the Commission, and to report their opinions as to whether such proposals or other documents raise questions of legal or political importance, to give their reasons for their opinion, to report what matters of principle or policy may be affected thereby, and to what extent they may affect the law of the United Kingdom, and to make recommendations for the further consideration of such proposals and other documents by the House (Standing Order No. 105).

The ELC has always interpreted its order of reference as a requirement to identify important documents and to make a report to the House based on its order of reference. Thus the ELC has taken the view that it is not its task but that of the House to offer opinions on the merits of EC legislative proposals or other documents. The only change in the ELC's terms of reference occurred in December 1976 when it was empowered to consider EC documents, such as the Tindemans' report on European Union, which might be extremely important, in the longer term, but raised no immediate legislative requirements. At the same time the Committee dropped the term 'secondary' from its title to avoid the possibility of confusing EC legislative proposals with domestic statutory instruments. It can be argued that the ELC is something of a hybrid type of select committee, in terms of House of Commons committee practice, as its scrutiny of many minor legislative instruments is similar to the work of committees on Statutory Instruments but it differs from those committees and is therefore similar to the new departmental select committees in that the ELC is involved in the preliminary stages of legislation or government policy-making. Moreover, ELC has also taken the Commons further along a form of committee development with precedents in the non-partisan pre-legislation committees examining issues such as violence in marriage. In March 1983 the Standing Orders (Revision) Select Committee (HC 244) proposed to change the Standing Order governing the ELC to give it the same status as Committees like Public Accounts in that it would have a permanent status by its inclusion in the Standing Orders.

The ELC has all the usual powers of Commons' select committees and it therefore takes evidence from ministers and civil servants as well as evidence from outside interest groups. However, it does have one unique problem regarding evidence. It is helpful sometimes for Parliament to have a greater insight into EC policy proposals than may be given by ministers or civil servants. However, under the 'Thomson Rules' the European Commission can only give off-the-record evidence on an *ad hoc* basis to national parliamentary committees. Usually the EC evidence is given by officials at the level of Director General. The reason for this 'distance' between the two bodies is because formally the Commission is in no way accountable to national legislatures.[5]

Initially the committee faced a considerable backlog of EC documents because of the delay in its establishment and the sub-committees it is empowered to appoint were used during the 1974–9 Parliament to expedite the scrutiny. These were of two types, a sifting sub-committee to identify major issues and Sub-Committees (A and B Jan–Dec 1976 and then I and II Dec 1976–April 1979) to take evidence on particular topics. The last evidence meeting of a Sub-Committee (I) was on the milk sector on 7 February 1979. In order to assist its work the ELC (or a sub-committee) is also empowered to 'confer and to meet concurrently' (Standing Order No. 205) with the Lords Committee (or Sub-committee) on the European Communities. This power is restricted to concurrent hearings of evidence.

The Committee decides whether an EC proposal requires further attention, partly through the development of its own general expertise in EC matters and its knowledge of those matters likely to be of concern to the whole House. An issue may also be identified by way of the 'scream' function of the Committee or, as Bates (1976, p. 27) puts it: 'In practice a Community proposal has been reported as raising a question of political importance where one or more members of the committee felt it was politically important.' Less obviously it is also an exercise of political judgement not to recommend a document for further study.

The Foster Committee (HC 463–I, p. xviii) identified the provision of adequate staff as being of crucial importance to the Committee if it were to function properly. Initially the Committee did not have all the staff suggested by Foster. However, this problem has been gradually remedied and now the ELC has the services of four officers from the Department of the Clerk of the House (the Committee Clerk and three Clerks who act as advisers to the Committee), a Documentation Officer, and a legal adviser (one of Mr Speaker's Counsels). The three clerks/advisers have all had considerable experience of working in Whitehall departments.

At the outset of an examination of the Committee's work it must be said that the Committee, at both MP and officer level, is very dependent upon ministers and civil servants to keep it fully informed about the development of EC policies. As Stevens comments (1976–77, p. 272), the Committee 'must act in expectation of Government co-operation'; and as

Roy Hattersley agreed in talking to the Committee, it needs 'the demonstration of goodwill on the part of the Government'. This relationship has naturally taken some time to develop and will never be entirely without friction. It must also be remembered that the Committee only becomes involved in the consideration of an EC proposal at a relatively late stage in its life and when the document has actually reached the Council of Ministers level.

Miller (1977, pp. 53–4) provides a very succinct statement on the committee's work routine.

> It settled into an efficient routine of weekly meetings at which from fifteen to thirty documents were considered. The formal sources of information – the documents themselves, explanatory memoranda for them from the departments, briefs prepared by the clerks, written and oral evidence from interest groups, and evidence from ministers, legal advice from the legal adviser – were of sufficient quantity and quality that MPs had the opportunity, when they chose, to consider documents in depth. The commentaries on reported documents took on some substance, though they remained brief . . . After each meeting, the Committee produced its report listing, inter alia, the documents it recommended for debate, the documents thought not important enough for debate, and the backlog of documents previously recommended but not yet debated.

This statement provides a number of useful headings under which the Committee's work can be examined.

By the end of the 1970s the Committee was considering about 700 documents a year. Government departments have developed the practice of producing, usually within two weeks of receiving an English language version of the EC document, an explanatory memorandum, signed by the minister, setting out legal and policy implications. However, these memoranda do not always arrive on time and this can hinder the ELC's work. Some government departments have found that their EC responsibilities involve them in a heavy work-load producing memoranda for the ELC. Gibbs (1977, p. 350) found that in 1974–5 the European Coordination Division of the Department of Trade and Industry had four staff working nearly full-time on producing these memoranda. Currently, the Department of Industry has estimated that they have to produce about one hundred memoranda each year. During the week in which a document will be considered by the Committee at its Wednesday afternoon meeting, the Committee staff produce an advisory brief on the documents. This brief sets out the aim of the document, provides an assessment of it and suggests a possible course of action for the committee.

Even assuming that there is information on the items before the ELC, its work is complicated by a number of factors. Some instruments may be slow-moving and return before the committee in an altered or a new form. This has led the Committee to identify the need for a 'second stage scrutiny'. Although the Government has accepted in principle that the committee should carry out this additional scrutiny, it cannot easily provide more information from confidential Council meetings unless the Commission provides additional published information. However, supplementary memoranda can always be provided with reference to changes in the government's position on an EC issue. Other instruments may be so fast-moving that the Committee barely has time to consider them before they are due for council consideration, and no official published text may be available. However, the Committee does not regard the absence of a formal text as a bar to discussion.

It is particularly in the context of these fast-moving documents that the Committee and the House have sought to have some control over ministers' actions in the Council of Ministers. However, it was not until October 1980 that the House was able to replace verbal promises by ministers to wait, if possible for the view of the House, by a formal resolution of the House. The resolution of 30 October 1980 states:

In the opinion of this House, no Minister of the Crown should give agreement in the Council of Ministers to any proposal for European legislation which has been recommended by the Select Committee on European Legislation for consideration by the House before the House has given it that consideration unless:

(a) that Committee has indicated that agreement need not be withheld, or

(b) the Minister concerned decides that for special reasons agreement should not be withheld;

and in the latter case the Minister should, at first opportunity thereafter, explain the reasons for his decision to the House (991 HC Deb. Col. 838).

The ELC is much smaller than the Lords' Committee (sixteen members compared with seventy-plus) and has a much more restricted function (identification of issues rather than examination of merits), and it usually meets in private session. Thus, it has a lower public visibility. However, in this context it must be remembered that, unlike the Lords' European Committee, the ELC's work is not directed towards giving explanations and opinions to a wide audience. The ELC's work is specifically related to providing the first stage in a scrutiny process involving the whole House. The reports of the committee can be divided into three categories: those concerned simply with recording the general sifting work and its attendant problems, those concerned with major EC issues such as the budget, CAP — including topical items like the fisheries policy; and reports aimed at developing a general understanding of EC policies. In general the reports provide specific comments on draft EC instruments, and a commentary, especially in the Minutes of Evidence taken before the committee, on the workings of the relationship between the Commons, ministers, and civil servants in the context of EC membership.

Information on the ELC's scrutiny process is provided by the Committee's reports, in particular those reports which contain evidence taken in public hearings. In 1975, having dealt with the backlog of scrutiny work, the ELC (HC 234, 1975–6, p. 6) was able to identify two opportunities for the Commons to attempt to exert influence on the draft EC instruments.

First, national parliaments can try to make their views known when the document is published by the Commission and is in the early stages; for example, being considered by the working groups. Second, when it is known that the instrument is actually going to come before the Council of Ministers, and therefore there may only be a little time gap ment, especially the responsible minister. However, the Committee points out that some instruments are 'fast moving', especially those for the Council of Agricultural Minister, and therefore there may only be a little time gap between the stages. The Committee set out, as its main future aim, to ensure that really important items arrive in the House in good time for a debate before the Council of Ministers' meeting. This it tries to achieve by a more rigorous selection of instruments backed by the assessment of the official and non-official evidence available to it.

It has become extremely important for the ELC to be able to identify the really major EC instruments for debate because there has been a persistent backlog, since the 1975–6 session, of instruments awaiting time for a debate. Indeed the ELC has regularly pointed this out in its reports and after the 1979 General Election the newly appointed Committee stated, in its first report (HC 159–i, 1979–80, para 10), that recommendations for debate did not lapse because of a dissolution and that 'every recommendation for debate outstanding from the previous Parliament should be regarded as continuing to have effect unless and until (the committee) themselves subsequently decide to withdraw it.'

Following its order of reference the ELC identifies and recommends documents of political or legal importance for debate by the Commons, under more recent powers, the ELC may recommend a document as suitable for consideration by a Standing Committee on EC Documents. For example, in Session 1981–82 the ELC (HC 21–xix, p. 6) recommended that the Standing Committee should consider a draft regulation which proposed to strengthen the controls over the operation of the CAP because it raised questions of political importance. In Session 1982–3 the ELC recommended (HC 43–i, pp. 8–10) that the whole House should consider one of the many proposals on the Community's

Fisheries' Policy because of the political importance of the fisheries issue.

Sometimes the ELC has to draw the House's attention to the need to consider the long term political and legal issues raised by proposals for future developments in the EC. In Session 1982–3 the ELC examined the 'Draft European Act' (HC 21–xxiii p. xx). This document covered proposals, put forward by Germany and Italy to the European Council, which dealt with questions of economic integration between the member states and under the heading 'European Act' proposed a political declaration regarding the programme to achieve the goal of a true European Union of the member states.

On some documents the ELC notes that it does not have to recommend further action, even though the subject matter is politically or legally important because a section of the 1972 EC Act has already made provision for the Commons to consider such a matter, for example, a draft trade agreement must be approved by an affirmative resolution of the House on the appropriate Order in Council (1972 EC Act I (3)).

The ELC may note on some proposals that no immediate action is being proposed and that further consultative stages are envisaged. However, even on these types of document the ELC may find good reason to express a measure of concern, to the House, in its reports. There was an instance of this occurring in the ELC's comments, in Session 1981–2, on the document titled 'Measuring Instruments', (HC 21–xiii, pp. viii–ix). This was a draft amendment to a draft Directive amending a 1971 Directive on the approximation of the law of the EC states relating to common provisions, for both measuring instruments and methods of metrological control. In this case the proposals were to refer the matter to the EC's Technical Progress Committee procedure. Under this procedure a committee of national representatives, chaired by a member of the Commission, could decide the issues by qualified majority. Moreover the issues would only come before a ministerial Council if there was a disagreement between the Technical Progress Committee and the Commission and the ministerial Council would only have three months in which to take action.

The ELC quite rightly expressed concern to the House in its report on three separate points. It pointed to the dangers of the above procedure being used over the range of consequent directives. The ELC also drew attention to the use of qualified majority voting procedures which could leave Britain in the minority on a particular decision. Finally, the ELC stressed that it expected the responsible government department, in this case the Department of Trade, to keep the Committee informed well in advance of a stage involving the Council of Ministers.

Finally, the ELC may note that whilst questions of political and legal importance are raised by an EC proposal the House does not need to consider the matter further. For example, regarding draft Directives on the 'Control of Motor Vehicle Exhaust Gases' (Session 1981–2, HC 21–xxix, pp. 5–6). The Committee took the above view because of the following factors. The draft Directive would not involve any changes in the existing British requirements for motor vehicles. The draft Directive gave member states the discretion to decide whether and how to implement the new standards. Moreover, the ELC was satisfied that in further negotiations on the draft Directive the responsible government department, Transport, would be taking account of the views of the relevant interest groups like the Society of Motor Manufacturers and Traders.

The current work and problems faced by the Committee are documented in its recent special reports. On average the Committee has to scrutinize about 700 instruments per year, and, for example, 134 were recommended for debate in session 1979–80 and 81 in session 1980–1. For a short time the Committee took advantage of its unique power to meet concurrently with the Lords' European committee to assist its work, avoid duplication and pool information. Even before the establishment of the new departmental select committees it was noted how useful some of the reports of the pre 1979 committees could be, such as the Expenditure Committee's report on fisheries policy and the Overseas Aid Committee's report on the Lomé Convention.

The committee has identified a number of particular problems encountered in the subject matter of its work. It felt that the European Commission's self-imposed rule against formally submitting evidence to national parliaments hindered the proper understanding of some of the Commission's objectives. Like the Lords Committee, the Commons Committee was concerned at the legal basis under the Rome Treaty, of some of the Commission's proposals for the approximation of laws in member states. In this context the committee was still finding certain deficiencies in the late 1970s in some departmental memoranda accompanying instruments. The Committee recommended that:

> in future the Departmental Explanatory Memorandum should, for any legislative proposal: (1) specify the Treaty power relied on; (2) state whether in the Department's opinion the proposal falls within that power; and (3) state whether or not they accept any statement of fact which is made in, or in support of, the proposal and which is a necessary condition of exercising the power (HC 642, 1977–8, p. 15).

The chief difficulty of scrutinizing the EC budgetary proposals was identified as being that of getting accurate and up-to-date information on the stages in the budgetary process. Here the Treasury has agreed to try and provide the requisite information. However, the main problems have been the shortness of time between the EC Budget stages and the accountability issue as the ultimate power over the EC Budget lies with the European Parliament over which the Commons has no control. The ELC also noted that particular scrutiny problems arose under the ECSC Treaty which gave greater legislative authority to the Commission than under the EEC Treaty.

In procedural terms the main issues relating to consideration of the draft instruments are those of access to a deposited document in time for scrutiny before it reaches the EC decision stage, and with the benefit of an adequate departmental memorandum. When the ELC does refer draft instruments for debate in the House members of the House have drawn attention to problems over the timing and the nature of the debates allowed. The ELC has noted that their remit does not include the responsibility for suggesting the format of debates. Also, there remains the important question of how the Commons can hold ministers accountable to the House for actions in the EC, after the House has expressed a view, or before it has had a chance of expressing a view.

A separate procedural issue is the relationship between the Committee and the European Parliament. It has already been noted that the Committee expressed a desire for closer and more open contact with the European Commission. However, in the case of the European Parliament, the Committee does not seek such a direct relationship. The 1977–78 special report noted (HC 642, 1977–78, p. 25) that an MP who was also a delegated MEP, Mr John Prescott, gave oral evidence to a concurrent hearing with the Lords Committee. In an earlier report the Committee did receive a memorandum (HC 41–xiii, and 76–i–iii, 1976–77, p. 44) from Mr John Evans MP, also a delegated MEP and chairman of the European Parliament's Committee on Regional Policy and Regional Planning. However, this memo was accompanied by a disclaimer that it was written in a personal capacity and not as an MEP. Despite these 'contacts' the Commons declined to participate in a Lords European sub-committee inquiry into relations with the European Parliament, although members gave evidence in a private capacity. The Commons as a whole has avoided seeking specific links with the European Parliament, partly because for a number of years the Labour party did not even send delegated members, and partly because the Commons does not want to see the status of the European Parliament raised to any form of equivalence to national parliaments. By contrast, the Committee has sought contacts with other national parliaments in order to evaluate their EC scrutiny procedures by comparison with those in Britain.[7]

As might be expected, the Committee has devoted a considerable number of reports to agricultural and budgetary matters. At the start of Britain's membership the Committee found itself in agreement with the Agriculture Minister Mr Peart, who said (HC 87–I, 1974, pp. 2–3) 'the CAP is basically the main organization which is functioning in

Europe' consequently it [CAP] produces a considerable flow of draft instruments. As well as considering annual issues such as the agricultural price fixing and the work of the European Agricultural Guarantee Fund, the Committee has considered a number of special agricultural topics such as the dairy sector, New Zealand butter, and horticulture and quite early in its work – Session 1974–75 – the Committee established contact with outside interest groups in this area.

The Committee's consideration of agricultural issues involves it in understanding many detailed and technical agricultural problems. It encounters similar difficulties in reviewing EC budgetary questions and there are also some problems peculiar to the EC budgetary process. In session 1974–75 the Committee identified the difficulties of the EC budgetary timetable and the Commons' session timetable. It was also advised by Mr Joel Barnett MP, as Chief Secretary to the Treasury, that the EC budget was only really a forecasting mechanism and therefore quite distinct from the policy-making and accounting functions of the British budget.[8] Currently, as the arguments in the EC over budgetary shares continue, it is evident that the Committee still finds the timing of consideration a problem, and notes the uncertainties about the figures used in EC budgetary forecasting, which consequently makes the task of scrutiny much harder.[9]

Apart from the obvious EC issues mentioned above, the Committee has reported on documents on other EC activities such as Regional Policy, the Steel Industry and Social Security. It has also reported on the long-running efforts of the EC states to develop a common fisheries policy. In all these areas the Committee is in touch with the relevant outside interest groups. The Committee's hearings on the European Regional Development Fund and the European Social Policy provided particularly interesting evidence for the House on the contrast between British expectations about EC membership and the realities.[10] In session 1976–77 the Committee scrutinized document (1664) R/1611/76 'First Annual Report on the European Regional Development Fund' (ERDF) and found that it raised important political questions. On the ERDF, the Committee found that it did not constitute a regional policy as that term was understood in Britain. Moreover, Britain had so championed the EC Regional Fund as a benefit of membership that the difficulties were not fully considered, and expectations were raised that were difficult to fulfil. First, the British local authorities cannot deal directly with the European Commission, and second, the UK had wanted EC aid but not EC interference in regional policy. Consequently the visibility of EC aid in this area has not been as high as was expected. A similar problem of the 'visibility' of EC aid is the sphere of social policy. Another problem the Committee discovered was the difference in the approaches to policy-making in the UK and Europe. In evidence, Mr Michael Shanks, a former EC official, noted that the British approach was to go from decisions on political issues to consider innovations to meet new problems. By contrast the continental countries tended more to refer back to the foundation treaties for guidance in resolving new political problems.

Thus one can say that the Scrutiny Committee performs two functions for the House; its assigned function of identifying documents raising important political and legal questions which should be debated; and, through its hearings, an educational function for the House through the discussions with ministers and civil servants and other contributors. In addition to its special reports already cited, a memorandum on the Committee's work was submitted to the Procedure Committee in July 1977 by the (then) chairman, the Right Hon. Sir John Eden Bt, MP. In this he commented (HC 588–i, 1977–8, p. 193) that 'the Committee are now satisfied that they have evolved a method of working which enables them to keep up with the flow of documents from Brussels without experiencing undue difficulty.' However, he did point out a number of issues which might warrant more general consideration by the House. The Committee is not empowered to scrutinize EC legal instruments which the Commission can promulgate under its own delegated authority. Although these are usually of a more minor regulatory nature they do total some 5,000–6,000 documents per year, as compared with the 700 odd per year the Committee does examine, and it does mean that a considerable volume of EC business is not being scrutinized by the Commons.

Of more substance is the fact that (HC 588–i 1977–8, pp. 193–4) 'the Committee have interpreted their order of reference to mean that they are not expected to pronounce on the merits of the Commission's various proposals' and consequently 'the work which the Committee offers to Members appointed to serve upon it is of a relatively routine and unglamorous nature.' However, Sir John Eden had to point out that, first, a 16-member committee was not large enough to pronounce on the merits of the number of documents likely to need that form of treatment. Second, the differences of views on EC membership between MPs would make it very difficult to produce agreed reports if the merits of proposals were to be considered. Similarly, this factor of differing views on the EC would make a joint Select Committee of the Lords and Commons an unworkable proposition. Currently the House would seem to have the appropriate committee structure. The European Legislation Committee can provide the necessary 'alarm' function quickly, and now more expertly, on the range of EC documents falling within its remit. The new departmental select committees can provide the detailed evaluation of EC matters falling within their remits as has happened in the Transport Committee's examination of an EC transport report (HC 466–v, 1979–80), the Agriculture Committee's Report on aspects of the CAP (HC 687 and 826, Sess 1979–80) and a Welsh Committee inquiry on the impact of the EC on Wales.

This point was recognized by the Procedure Committee in 1977 which clearly felt that the European Legislation Committee was performing an important role in a satisfactory manner. The Procedure Committee recommended that the Committee should continue in its present form, commenting (HC, 588–i, p. xl–xli) 'the work . . . is of a specialised nature which could not easily be devolved on other committees. The evidence given to us by the Committee's Chairman about the procedures in other national parliaments in the Community tends to reinforce this view.' Indeed, one could now say that the European Legislation Committee's work is not only of general help to the House, it can also be of help to ministers.

This fact was explicitly recognized during a debate in April 1982 in the Second Standing Committee on European Documents by the Under-Secretary of State for Health and Social Security, Mr Geoffrey Finsburg MP. Commenting on the 6th Report of the ELC (Session 1981–2) Mr Finsburg noted that the ELC has recommended the document before the Standing Committee (concerning Medical and Public Research) as one which raised questions of political importance. Moreover, he stated that he 'found the Select Committee session valuable as Hon. Members made a number of helpful and constructive points which have influenced our negotiating stand on this draft in Brussels.'[11]

In this context it may be noted that in their general questioning of ministers the members of the ELC are particularly interested in getting the Minister's views on the merits of a proposal, discovering how the Minister expects the discussion might go in the Council of Ministers and identifying any possible modifications that might emerge as a result of bargaining between member states. On occasion a Minister may be pressed very hard over the stand that will be taken in the Council of Ministers. For example, in Session 1974–5 (HC 45–xxiii and 87–vi) one member of the ELC, Mr Bryan Gould, MP said to the then Agriculture Minister, Mr (now Lord) Peart, 'If the House, following a debate in this topic and following representations made to individual Ministers by farmers in their constituency and by the NFU [National Farmers' Union], should take a view and should say to you, "This is a matter on which you must take a stand, you cannot allow this to happen". Would you feel able to commit yourself?' Mr Peart answered, 'I am in agreement with the criticism but I cannot say to the Scrutiny Committee, no, at this stage of the discussion . . . that I will block a certain section and veto. It would be wrong of one to do so because my objective will be to try and change that [issue] . . .'

This exchange illustrates two important points about the relationship between a Minister, the Commons and EC matters. Firstly, a Minister is involved in bargaining and therefore may need to be flexible. Secondly, a Minister does not go to a Council of Ministers as a delegate from the House of Commons but as a person responsible for carrying out government policy. The House may, of course, quite properly, express a view on a Minister's actions, after they have been carried out, especially if those actions were against any explicit view taken by the House on the matter at issue.

The reference previously to the Second Standing Committee on European Documents brings the study of the Commons and EC affairs to the point where consideration must be given to the matter of how EC affairs are debated by the House. As with the examination of the work of the ELC, one is here also looking at an evolutionary process on the floor of the House and in standing committee. A standing committee is a committee established to consider a bill or other legislative business and consists of 16–50 MPs.

EC affairs come before the House in a number of ways, apart from the work in the European Legislation Committee.[12] There is time for consideration on the floor of the House, in standing committee and through the medium of question time. As with all Commons business the timing of debates and the procedure followed is dependent on decisions by the Government. In the case of EC affairs, adequate scrutiny, in terms of the time allowed and the format of the debates, was not developed until 1980 after the Procedure Committee had reported on the inadequacies of the previous system.

Apart from full day debates on major topics such as the Community budget and the annual agricultural price proposals there are the debates on documents recommended by the ELC for consideration by the Commons. Generally the Government does not bring an instrument forward to the Commons for debate until it is also on the agenda for discussion and possible decision of the Council of Ministers. From 1973 until 1980 the instruments were either debated on the floor of the House under Standing Order No. 3 (1) for one and a half hours after 10 o'clock on a motion to 'take note' or before a standing committee, again limited to one and a half hours, and none of these arrangements were very satisfactory as they too easily equated EC business with Statutory Instruments business. It must also be remembered that the drafting of 'take note' motions are in the hands of the governing party and thus any additions to such a motion, known as an 'expanded take note' which '. . . calls on the Government to . . .' will normally reflect a position which a government is prepared to adopt. However, in the case where a minority party forms the government then the Commons can exert more influence on the content of such motions.

It might have been thought that with the election, in 1974, of a Labour government containing anti-EC MPs the Commons might have evolved procedures giving as tight Parliamentary control over EC affairs as in Denmark. However, there are a number of reasons why this has not happened. There is always a delicate balance to be maintained by any government between its desire to control the business of the Commons and the satisfaction of backbench MPs desire for influence. More specifically, in the period 1974–9 the Labour government lacked a secure majority and depended, in part, upon Liberal Party support, the Liberals being pro-EC. Also, as has been noted before, all MPs were involved in a learning process about the impact of EC affairs. In looking at EC affairs on the floor of the House the topic can be considered under the headings of procedural developments and the record of dissention in divisions.

From 1972–5 governments did little to help consideration of EC matters on the floor of the House, the Conservative government had little interest in the matter and the Labour government was really marking time to see whether Britain was in or out of the Community.

MPs faced a number of difficulties over EC matters during these early years. Many debates on EC topics were after the main business of the day after 10.00 pm, or at 4.00 pm on Fridays. Neither time is likely to attract anything like a full turnout of MPs. Also, in the early years of membership an

EC matter was identified only by the title 'European Community' and a number. Thus it was difficult for an MP to know whether the subject matter was important. In addition, the statutory instrument procedure used for implementing many EC obligations offers little scope for backbench influence. Also despite the fact that the treaties negotiated by a British government must be laid before Parliament 21 days before ratification (a practice which dates from 1924, known as the 'Ponsonby rule'), EC treaties, not being negotiated by a British government, were laid before Parliament with much shorter notice, and also dealt with under the statutory instrument procedure by a Definition of Treaty Order. Until more notice was taken by governments of some MPs' concern at the Commons' lack of meaningful scrutiny powers on EC matters, the procedure which had the most impact was the use of the procedure (in Standing Order 73B (3)) where at least 20 MPs rise in the Chamber to prevent an order going through to a Standing Committee without a debate and thus provoke further consideration of the order in the House.

After the establishment of the ELC to filter important EC matters to the whole House, the suitability of the House's procedures to debate and control Government actions was not considered in detail until 1975 (Coombes, 1977, pp. 244–9 and 256–9). After the two years of experience of the problems of handling EC business in the House the Procedure Committee (HC 294, Session 1974–75, pp. xviii–xix) was able to produce a detailed report and recommendations. The recommendations may be grouped under the headings of information for the House, procedure of the House, and the remit of ELC. For the better information of the House the Procedure Committee suggested that EC secondary legislation proposals should be laid on the table of the House, like Command Papers, that Government departments should prepare and publish lists showing progress of EC proposals and publish, for the House to consider, up-to-date explanatory memoranda on amendments to Commission documents which affect Britain.

On the procedure of the House the Committee recommended that Standing Order No. 3 should be applied to the consideration of Commission documents. This Standing Order allows various forms of extensions to the basic one and a half-hour consideration for statutory instrument types of business. It also allows that an objection by 20 or more members should defeat a motion to refer an EC document to a standing committee (cf. Standing Order No. 73A). Finally, the Procedure Committee recommended that a special standing committee on European Secondary Legislation should be constituted, and that the House debate a substantive motion rather than just a 'take note' motion.

The House's concern with the costs of membership and its own control over financial matters was reflected in the recommendation to enlarge the remit of the ELC. This would have allowed the ELC to report whether any Resolution of the House requiring a change in the EC budget had been complied with.

Although in November 1975 the (then) Lord President of the Council, Mr Edward Short MP announced that the Government would introduce proposals along the lines recommended by the Procedure Committee, this did not in fact happen at all during the period of Labour Government from 1974–79. In his speech in the debate on 28 November 1977, Mr Nigel Spearing MP pointed out that debates on the procedure for handling EC affairs had been held on three previous occasions: November 1975, May 1976, and April 1977 – with little result. Indeed, Mr Spearing felt (940 HC Deb. Col. 48) that it was 'coming to something' when the ELC itself had to table Early Day Motion No. 158 during the 1975–76 Session 'That this House deplores the inadequacy of consideration of important EEC measures, both in Standing Committee and on the Floor of the House'. The ELC expressed its concern with the timing, form and nature of the debates in the House.

At the end of the 28 November 1977 debate on the EEC the then Lord President of the Council, and Leader of the House, Mr Michael Foot MP, accepted that there was all-party concern that the procedures of the House for handling EC affairs should be improved (940 HC Deb. Col. 102). He also indicated that the Government was conducting an examination of the problems which included looking at the much closer control exercised in the Danish Parliament. During his speech Mr Foot suggested that ministers had adhered very largely to the letter and spirit of ministerial statements on how they would behave in the Council of Ministers with regard to not proceeding to decisions if a Commons debate had to be held on the matter. In the previous session over 100 EC documents were debated in the Commons, and Mr Foot pointed out (940 HC Deb. Col. 106) that on only about five EC proposals did ministers take prior decisions in the Council of Ministers and then came to the House afterwards to explain. In conclusion, Mr Foot, for the Government, accepted that new procedures ought to be introduced and undertook to bring them before the House as soon as possible. On the basis of that promise Mr Spearing allowed his motion to lapse.

There the matter rested until 27 July 1978 when, during Business of the House, Mr Foot in reply to a question on the introduction of better control of EC legislation, said that he had to ask 'the House to release me from that undertaking because I fear that I am not able to fulfil it' (954 HC Deb. Col. 1797). His justification for this position was that many representations had been received from MPs urging further consultation. In the event, the Labour Government did not bring forward any new proposals. The matter rested with the Select Committee on Procedure.

The Select Committee on Procedure in Session 1977–78 reported on debates on EC documents (HC 588–I) that:

> Whilst in some cases the time is adequate, complaints have been frequent, especially where a whole series of documents, often of a technical nature, need to be debated together. Other difficulties have arisen over the common use of the motion to 'take note'. Whilst amendments have from time to time been tabled, selected and, in some cases, agreed, the practicability of tabling them has depended as much on the approach of the Government to the proposal as on the merits as such. Since the Government's view of the proposals as distinct from the proposals themselves, is usually only known at the commencement of the debate itself, it is

not easy for members to make their views effective in
debate and in the division lobbies by the prior tabling of
appropriate motions.

The Committee felt that it was crucial for the House to be
able to 'express an opinion on the merits of the proposals'.

In this context the Procedure Committee also recommended that the Standing Committee procedure be replaced
(under Standing Order No. 73A) as it was not being much
used, so failing to alleviate pressure on the floor of the
House, because MPs felt it was not a satisfactory alternative
to debate in the House. The Procedure Committee recommended the establishment of standing committees on European Communities Legislation along the lines of an earlier
Procedure Committee Report (HC 249, 1974–75).

These recommendations were accepted by the Right Hon.
Norman St John Stevas as Leader of the House in 1980.
Standing Order No. 80 now governs the procedure of the
Standing Committee on European Community Documents.
The ELC can indicate documents suitable for the Standing
Committee but actual referral is on the initiative of the
Government. The debates take place on a government
motion, amendments may be moved and selected by the
Standing Committee chairman and up to a two and a half-
hour debate may be held. Currently the 'take note' debates
on the floor of the House have also been expanded to include
a general statement on British Government policy regarding
an EC proposal.

EC DEBATES ON THE FLOOR OF THE HOUSE

In making an overall assessment of debates on the floor of the
House and in Standing Committee, I have used the period
1975–81. This is the period for which whole year records for
debates are available.

It is evident that the peak years for debates were 1976–78
which coincides with the Scrutiny Committee coping with
the backlog dating from entry in 1973 and 'playing safe' in
the early years as it developed more expertise to discriminate

TABLE 3.1: Debates in the Commons, 1975–1981, on documents recommended for debate by the Scrutiny Committee and British Bills or instruments related to EC matters, and including more general debates which relate to an EC instrument.

Year	Total number of debates	General debates	Queen's speech	Friday debate	Debate on Bills etc.	'Take Note' motion	Amendment selected to a TN motion	Standing Committee	Adjournment
1975	21	1	1	1	—	14	—	2	2
1976	32	2	—	—	1	18	9	8	3
1977	40	—	—	1	1	32	2	4	—
1978	35	2	—	—	1	28	—	2	1
1979	11	—	—	—	—	11	3	—	—
1980	26	3	—	—	1	22	—	—	—
1981	26	5	—	—	—	17	—	4	—

Source: Information supplied by the Clerk to the European Legislation Committee

between documents. The figures also show the heavy reliance on the 'take note' procedure, and the relative lack of use of standing committees.

Going back over the chronological record of debates, a number of observations can be made. The first complaint over the shortage of time available under the 'take note' procedure came in December 1974 over two energy instruments. The debate was talked out by ministers, provoking angry complaints. However, in the same month, an adjournment debate on general EC topics produced a Government promise for time on EC budgetary issues. It was noted earlier that there were criticisms of the one and a half-hour restraint on 'take note' motions; however when a number of draft instruments were grouped together this could produce quite a long, if not very satisfactory, debate. For example, in November 1975 four instruments were debated for three hours on 'take note' motions. In December 1975 there was the first example of complaints about the shortage of debate time under the Standing Committee procedure. Then EC draft instruments were being referred to the Standing Committee on Statutory Instruments.

By the late 1970s it was evident that among the more common forms of debate in the House were those occasions when a collection of draft EC instruments on a single topic were scheduled for debate together. For example, in February 1977 the House spent five hours debating on a 'take note' motion, 19 documents related to the EC's Multi-fibre Agreements on textiles; in June 1977 the House spent five and a quarter hours debating documents relating to the Common Fisheries Policy – this debate was on a motion to adjourn – and in March 1978 the House spent five and three-quarter hours debating on a 'take note' motion, Milk Marketing, and the 1978 Agricultural Price Review.

Other debates provide examples of the House's efforts to maintain the convention of ministerial accountability. Some of the complaints relate to Government failures to supply adequate and timely explanatory memoranda and the timing of debates. On one occasion, 20 December 1979 (reference Document 5347/79 and ELC Report HC 10–XX, 1978–79 Units of Measurement), the debate on an amended document needed, at the Speaker's request, the department concerned to rush a memorandum into the Vote Office. Another example occurred in the debate on the 14 February 1980, when the Minister of Agriculture had to give a comprehensive apology to the House because two sets of proposals had been agreed to in the Council of Ministers before the House had debated them.

As Norton (1980b) and Wood (1982) have shown, the votes in the divisions from 1974–79 also record the continuing anti-market views of Labour MPs, thus making the Labour Government of the period very dependent on the support of Conservatives and Liberals. Overall (Norton, 1980b, p. 429) records show that during 1974–79 two principal issues caused serious divisions in the House: those of membership of the EC, and devolution. Fifty-six divisions in Parliament on EC matters showed dissenting Conservative and Labour votes with a much greater number of Labour dissenters. Some of the related debates included expressions of the kinds of concern with the Common's ability to control EC affairs that actually led to the 1980 procedural reforms.

In January 1975, when the Minister of Agriculture Mr Peart moved the House to 'take note' of three Commission proposals relating to agricultural price rises, Mr N. Buchan MP (Labour, Renfrew West) moved an addendum declining to approve, as the EC Council of Ministers held the powers to increase the price rises, thus overriding the Commons. In April 1977 the Under-Secretary of State at the FCO moved a prayer to approve the EC (Definition of Treaties Order, 1977). MPs expressed criticism of the lack of information on the documents, and the practice of putting several treaties in one order, and raised questions about the effects of the treaties on Britain. However, with Conservative support the prayer was carried.

Labour ministerial dissent is also evident from the debates examined by Norton (1980b). When, in February 1975, Mr D. Jay MP (Labour, Battersea North) moved a prayer to annul an Import Duties Order which would have raised food import duties on food from outside the EC area, the Secretary of State for Trade, Mr P. Shore, agreed that he did not like the EC import duties but that the government was bound by EC law. Rather more pointedly, in January 1979 during a 'take note' debate on EC documents relating to the steel industry moved by the Foreign Office Minister of State, another junior minister voted against the Government. Mr F. Hooley (Labour, Sheffield Keeley) moved an amendment to 'take note' but not accept proposals to curb aid to the steel industry. This amendment was voted for by the Parliamentary ·Under Secretary of State for Industry. Not surprisingly the two EC issues which caused the greatest dissent during this period were the referendum on staying in the EC and the enabling legislation for direct elections to the European Parliament.

OTHER CHANNELS FOR BACKBENCH INFLUENCE

Question time is one of the traditional means for MPs to elicit information from the Government, or to put pressure on ministers. Ryan and Isaacson (1974–75) carried out a survey of written and oral questions between February 1973 and February 1974. They found, generally, a low level of interest in EC affairs. Only 3 per cent of written questions and 1 per cent of oral questions were on the EC, and 64 per cent of MPs did not ask any EC questions at all. Of the written questions, 44 per cent were asked by only 11 MPs, nine of whom were anti-marketeers (four Conservative and five Labour). Ryan and Isaacson (1974–75, p. 207) comment, 'The object of both written and oral questions was to elicit information which could be used to show up the Communities in an unfavourable light.'

The responsibility for answering EC questions remains as it was laid down by the Leader of the House in 1974, that is, departmental ministers answer questions in the area of their department. In addition, the Foreign Secretary has the overall responsibility for supplying information to the House and answers the more general or political questions.

One of the problems with questions on EC affairs is that some count as 'FCO questions' and these may not be readily identifiable from Hansard. The FCO's European Community Department (Internal) has calculated from department records (letter of 9 February 1983) that, during the period January 1979 to December 1982, Peers and MPs asked an average of 215 questions (written and oral) per year which related to the FCO's interests in EC internal and external affairs.

Overall, however, current interest in EC affairs by MPs is at the same low level as identified by Ryan and Isaacson (1973–74) although the percentage of oral questions on the EC has risen. The information in the Polis Computer shows that in Session 1981–82 3.8 per cent of all written questions were on the EC and 4 per cent of the oral and supplementary questions related to the EC. Moreover, the computer print-out records that, with regard to Britain's membership of the EC, the largest categories of specific questions (both written and oral) relate to the Community Budget, British repayments and the CAP. In other words, the questions are concentrated on the most politically sensitive EC issues. Freida Stack (1983) has calculated, from the Polis 1981–82 figures of oral and supplementary questions on the EC, that 66 per cent were directed at the Foreign Secretary though, until the January 1983 reshuffle, usually answered by the Lord Privy Seal. She argues that the EC slot seemed to have become, like the Prime Minister's question time, a slot for MPs to range over a wide variety of topics.

Regarding members' interests it may be noted that in the most recent study of backbench specialisation in the Commons (Judge, 1981) the author finds little to say about MPs' specialising in EC affairs. Judge does note (p. 14) that MPs responses to questions on which members were considered specialists produced a view that there were more Conservative EC specialists than Labour ones. Also, with regard to the use of early day motions, although Judge argues (p. 121) that these were not very important for expressing backbench feelings he does cite Early Day Motion 335/1975. This was signed by 151 Labour members and warned the Prime Minister of their implacable opposition to continued membership of the EC.

Another less well documented channel of influence is provided by the backbench committees. Recently (Norton, 1983) published a survey of party organisation in the

Commons, including the committees. In the Parliamentary Labour Party, committees or groups tend to have been used more to express pro- or anti-EC feelings than to provide informed commentary on EC matters. As few Labour MPs were enthusiastic about the EC the European Affairs group was merged with the foreign affairs group. Members of the PLP are most likely to try and use sub-committees of the NEC or groups such as Manifesto and Tribune as forums for expressing opinions on the EC.

The Conservative Party in the Commons has a European Affairs Committee; however, it has suffered from some of the same problems as seen in Labour committees. That is the problem of becoming just a vehicle for the committed, pro- or anti-market MPs. It also did not attract a very high regular attendance – usually only eight or nine MPs. However, it did extend an open invitation to MEPs – indeed, at times, the number of MEPs attending could exceed the number of MPs. In the PLP it has been noted (Butler and Marquand, 1981, p. 5) that acess to backbench committees tends to be difficult for the MEP.

In the Parliamentary Conservative Party the most influential type of backbench committee on EC affairs is likely to be an existing specialist committee like the Agriculture, Fisheries and Food Committee. Indeed, it is a sign of the current Parliamentary Conservative Party dissatisfaction with aspects of EC membership that there has recently been formed a backbench European Reform Group containing about 40 Conservative MPs. This group's aim can be summarized as supporting EC membership but at the same time pressing for reforms in the EC, such as changes in the CAP.

THE HOUSE OF LORDS AND EC AFFAIRS

The House of Lords has in recent years been more the object of reforming schemes than the subject for major analyses of its actual contribution to the legislative process in Britain.[13] However, the two most recent major studies of the Lords (Bromhead, 1958; and Morgan, 1975), do provide starting points for examining the contribution of the Lords to the parliamentary scrutiny of EC affairs, a contribution that has even been considered to have had greater external impact than that of the Commons. Indeed, during a Commons debate in November 1977, on the scrutiny of EC affairs, Mr Neil Marten MP (Cons., Banbury) commented rather ruefully on the greater attention paid to the Lords' EC Committee reports: 'The reason is that the House of Lords serves up its reports in nice blue covers that are easily identifiable and read by the Press, whereas our criticisms of regulations are always made late at night when the Press has gone home to sleep' (940 HC Deb. 5S Col. 60). Mr Marten's point could have been illustrated by a reference to a report in *The Times* only a few weeks earlier (31 October 1977), which carried lengthy excerpts from a Lords Report ('Commercial Agents Aid', 51st Report, HL 267, 1977). In large type *The Times* reported 'Lords condemn EEC directives on commercial agents as inflexible and distorting competition'. Bromhead (1958, pp. 271–2) lists three inherent advantages that the Lords possess over the Commons in the scrutiny process. Firstly, the House of Lords in the face of external pressures has developed considerable 'vitality' and discusses a broader range of subjects in a more informed manner. This point is certainly applicable to the Lords scrutiny of EC affairs and is evident from even a cursory reading of the headings of House of Lords EC committee papers, for example: 22nd Report 'EEC Energy Policy Strategy' (HL 205, 1975); 37th Report 'The Lomé Convention' (HL 353, 1975); 2nd Report 'EEC Transport Policy' (HL 9, 1976); 48th Report 'Youth Employment' (HL 261, 1977); 28th Report 'International Mergers' (HL 159, 1978); 'Report on Spierenburg' (HL 133, 1979); and 39th Report 'Genetic Manipulation' (DNA) (HL 188, 1980).

Secondly, as a consequence of this more wide-ranging scrutiny, House of Lords proceedings contain useful advice and comments. This point has been specifically acknowledged by the Commons EC Committee (HC 642 1977–78, p. 21) which reported that it 'welcomed the opportunity of making use of evidence collected by the House to Lords Committee and, where appropriate, drawing the attention of the House to Lords Reports that are relevant to items for debate'. Thirdly, the Lords have the advantage that they can avoid strict timetables or classifications of business. In the context of EC business this has allowed the Lords to adopt a wider order of reference for their European Community Committee than was possible in the Commons.

The value which the Commons European Committee has placed upon the Lords EC work would seem to support Janet Morgan's comment (1975, p. 8) that:

> It is important to see how far the Peers' awareness of their political and public reputation is a constraint on their behaviour – for they have to be narcissistic in order to survive. Only by monitoring their own behaviour and remaining sensitive to their image in the world outside can they avoid infringing a web of sanctions, explicitly formulated or implicitly understood.

The Lords, by developing useful and generally acceptable areas of activity such as EC affairs scrutiny can, to quote Morgan again (1975, p. 221) 'assure the world that the Upper House has become an indispensable auxiliary to the over-burdened Parliamentary process'.

Is all the effort of the Lords to inform Parliament, the Government and the public worthwhile? Clearly the Commons EC Committee has felt it is valuable. However, the Lords still face a similar problem to the Commons – will a government listen, and even if it listens, has it the time or ability to act according to parliamentary advice in the EC? Indeed, Plaskitt (1981, p. 213) has suggested that 'Any assessment of the entire EEC structure within the Lords is bound to conclude that there is an impressive amount of manpower, time, paper and resources depending entirely for its effect on a less than entirely reliable plenipotentiary', that is, a British government acting in the EC.

It is a measure of the general lack of academic effort devoted to the Lords that one of the principle sources for the Lords and the European Community is an undergraduate dissertation by Caroline Moore (1979) of Hull University; another useful source is the article by Bates (European Law Review, 1976). The following paragraphs on the Lords EC

Committee are partly based upon Moore's study. The Commons EC Committee has underlined the nature of the Lords contribution by pointing out (HC 642, 1977–78, p. 24) that 'the House of Lords Committee, with its elaborate structure of sub-committees comprising a total membership of over 80 peers [cf. the 16 members of the Commons EC Committee] and without the responsibility of scrutinizing every Commission proposal, is able to devote far more time and manpower to its inquiries than is possible in the Commons.'

When the Heath Government was preparing to take Britain into the EEC in 1972, Parliament began to consider the issue of scrutinizing the expected flood of EC documents, many of which would have political or legal implications as a consequence of membership. Committees were set up in both Houses to examine this issue. In the Commons it was the Foster Committee (discussed earlier); in the Lords it was the Maybray-King Committee. The first report of the Maybray-King Committee (HL 67, 1973) recommended the establishment of a joint committee of both Houses to sift proposals for EC legislation. This innovative proposal was not acted upon, but there has actually been an innovation in parliamentary procedure which allows the Commons and the Lords EC Committees to hold concurrent hearings whilst being able to write separate reports on the same evidence. The power to meet concurrently was obtained by the Commons Committee in 1976, and the last concurrent meeting was in March 1978. Furthermore, as the Commons Committee has acknowledged (HC 642, 1977, p. 24) 'in other ways the two Committees have maintained a close and regular collaboration in order to eliminate as far as possible unnecessary duplication of effort and to pool evidence and information collected.'

When the Maybray-King Committee made its second Report in July 1973 (HL 194), it recommended a Select Committee similar to that recommended by the Foster Committee for the Commons, but with two important differences. First, the Lords Committee was to have a broader remit 'to consider all Community proposals whether in draft or otherwise, to obtain all necessary information about them and to make reports on those which in the opinion of the Committee, raise important questions of policy or principle, and on other questions to which the Committee feel that the special attention of the House should be drawn.' This broader remit was to allow the Lords, unlike the Commons, officially to consider the merits of a proposal. Second, the Lords Committee was empowered to appoint sub-committees which could co-opt additional peers for the work in hand.

The House of Lords Select Committee on the European Communities was first appointed on 7 May 1974, and had 23 members. By 1979 it had delegated work to seven sub-committees: (A) Finance, Economics and Regional Policy; (B) Trade and Treaties; (C) Education, Employment and Social Affairs; (D) Agriculture and Consumer Affairs; (E) Law; (F) Energy, Transport and Research; and (G) Environment. All members of the main committee serve on one or more sub-committees and the sub-committees involve other peers in the work.

The general committee procedure followed in the Lords is similar to that in the Commons, namely, sifting of proposals into categories, regular meetings (normally fortnightly), preparing reports and sending proposals for debate in the full House. However, it has been noted that less than 5 per cent of all proposals are actually reported as being suitable for debate. Unlike the Commons the Lords has a rather elaborate sifting system carried out by the chairman alone. List 'A' contains proposals requiring further scrutiny; List 'B', proposals already referred to a sub-committee for information, awaiting scrutiny or under scrutiny; List 'C', proposals referred to sub-committees but not reported on; List 'D', proposals reported for information; and List 'E', reports to be debated. Clearly the Committee chairman has considerable responsibility and quite a work-load; between June 1975 and December 1976, 959 proposals came before the Committee.

The general assumption that the Lords has a useful reservoir of people with knowledge and experience in many fields who can contribute 'expert' opinions on matters before the House is borne out by Moore's findings. She lists, as participating in the work of scrutiny, 17 former ministers, nine ex-civil servants, 18 academics, of whom 11 are scientists and eight farmers. The Law Sub-committee has included two Law Lords, a professor of jurisprudence and a criminal lawyer.

To date, the most detailed published study of the House of Lords work on this subject is by James Plaskitt (1981), who has examined the work of the Law Sub-committee (E). Plaskitt has concentrated upon the scrutiny of the Community proposals for directives on legislative harmonisation under Article 100 of the Treaty of Rome. The Lords Committee has taken the view that such harmonisation can only be in the context of the defined objective of the Community. As Plaskitt notes (1981, p. 203): 'The work draws attention to questions of Community powers, their impact on UK sovereignty and differing views of legal interpretation. The problems and the disputes that have arisen in this area since UK accession to the Rome Treaty in many respects represents the root conflict between the UK and its Community partners.'

Plaskitt's conclusions on the work of the Sub-committee E are to some extent valid for the work of the Lords in other areas where some form of harmonisation is contemplated. For example, Sub-committee C looked at European Social Policy and in the minutes of evidence to this report, Lord Alexander, commenting on suggestions that the EC might become involved in post-16 education and vocational training, noted that the DES was not very positive on proposals in this area, saying 'there is not yet a sufficiently clear understanding of the relative functions of the Community and the nation' (HL 60, 1976, p. 39). Plaskitt's more general findings suggest (1981, pp. 211–12) that the Lords' scrutiny of EC affairs has been too negative and conscious of the minutiae of proposals in its approach to the EC. However, he balances this by pointing out that the House of Lords' work on the EC is actually very much in tune with the approach to EC membership taken by successive British Governments, which have stressed the maintenance of British sovereignty to the greatest extent possible, and have adopted a 'leisurely process of assimilation'.

Moreover, when EC proposals are such as to involve substantial preparatory work by Government departments and private bodies, the reports of the Lords' EC Committees are considered as providing useful reference material and comment. It must also be remembered that, unlike the ELC in the Commons whose task is specifically to report to the House, the Lords EC Committee is not so tightly constrained and can therefore address its reports to a wider audience. A good example of this practice is provided by the Lords European Community Committee report ('European Institutions (Three Wise Men) and the Spierenburg Report', HL 172, Feb. 1980) on the organisation and workings of the EC. Furthermore, the Companies Division of the Department of Trade (1982) lists the Lords EC Committee report on 'Company Law: Scissions' (HL 206, Session 1979–80) as documentation relevant to the Draft Directive on that subject.

The British Bankers' Association cites, among background documents on the EC and banking, the Lords EC Committee Report (HL 42, Session 1981–82) on the Annual Accounts of Banks and Other Financial Institutions. Moore (1979, p. 24) specifically notes the use made of Lords EC Committee Reports by Government departments in explaining Community proposals, and the use made of the reports by EC institutions and committees. Indeed, the Hansard Society comments (1977, pp. 39–40) on 'the relevance and business-like nature of the results of the Lords' work in this field'.

Bates (1976, pp. 32–4) has identified two areas where the more politically relaxed atmosphere of the Lords EC Committee's broader remit has produced some interesting differences in practice, compared with the Commons. As early as June 1975 the Lords Scrutiny Committee was attempting to improve its consideration of published Commission documents by asking for information on the preliminary pre-publication stages of EC documentats, and for information on the proposals arising from European Council initiatives and from EPC meetings. On formal evidence to the parliamentary scrutiny committees Bates noted that in some early hearings before the Lords Committee, civil servants even gave information on negotiating positions in the Council of Ministers. By contrast, civil servants in attendance with ministers before the Commons ELC only give evidence on rare occasions.

It is generally agreed that the House of Lords' scrutiny of EC affairs performs a valuable and informative critical service to Parliament, Government departments and other interested bodies. However, the same question remains as with the Commons' scrutiny of EC affairs: can it influence Government action in the EC decision-making process? Discussions with civil servants suggest that a Lords Report can be influential in slow-moving areas of EC policy-making especially, as in the case of legal issues, when the Lords may have relevant expertise. Also the Lords' broader remit and more flexible timetable can be used to alert Government to the consequences of enacted EC legislation. Moore (1979, p. 19) quotes the 33rd Report (HL 326, 1975) which noted that Statutory Instrument 1975 No. 665 on the measurement of cereals regulations introduced to 'implement Directive 71/347/EEC on measuring of grain', was actually *ultra vires.*

When this matter was debated the Lord Chancellor expressed the view (House of Lords Debates, Vol. 386, Cols 413–17, 17 February 1976) that this report well illustrated 'the role of the Committees which are set up in maintaining the oversight, the control of Parliament over this aspect of Directives'. However, Stevens (1976, p. 274) raises an important point about the possible constitutional impact of this extensive and intensive activity by the Lords, and notes 'Should it increase this type of activity it is likely to impinge upon domestic as well as Community policy, and may acquire an investigatory function which goes beyond any which the House of Lords has previously enjoyed. This extension the Executive are likely to attempt to resist.'

CONCLUSIONS

Currently the points raised at the beginning of the Chapter concerning the effects of EC membership, development of select committees and electoral reform, are open issues. The

ELC, in its character and function, looks less unique in its involvement in EC policy discussions. In the area of the European Legislation Committee's (ELC) work, some of the other post 1979 Select Committees of the House of Commons, for example, agriculture, industry and trade, can provide more detailed studies in their fields to complement the initial identification of issues by the ELC. Before 1979 detailed studies on EC related matters were only carried out by the European Committee of the House of Lords and, exceptionally, by earlier Commons Select Committees such as the Select Committee on Science and Technology.

The proportional representation system for elections has recently surfaced again as an issue in British politics. In March 1982 the European Parliament approved a uniform proportional representation electoral system for all member-states for the second direct election for the EP, due to be held in June 1984. The proportional representation system proposed is based upon the regional list system which involves dividing the member-states into electoral regions, electing between three and 15 MEPs. Britain would probably be divided into 13 such regions. Under this system seats would be allocated on the basis of the order of names on the voter's list rather than on the number of votes for each candidate. However, for the scheme to become operational it has to be approved by the Council of Ministers and then the necessary national enabling legislation must be enacted. Given the known attitudes to proportional representation of the Conservative and Labour parties and the SDP/Liberal Alliance, a safe forecast is for a prolonged parliamentary battle, as happened on the previous occasion. Conservative and Labour MEPs have already opposed the PR system in the European Parliaments vote in 1982 on the issue when PR was approved by 138 votes to 74 with 24 abstentions.

Therefore, in terms of Norton's discussion of the changing House of Commons, two very visible effects of membership – the need for adequate scrutiny of EC affairs and the development of the representative nature of the European Parliament do not seem to have produced wholly new pressures for internal or external reform in the parliamentary system. At most they could be considered to have performed a sort of catalytic function, most obviously over the issue of electoral reform.

What EC membership has done is to add a range of new problems to a legislature that already felt itself to be staggering under the pressure of domestic legislation and executive domination. These problems can be broadly summarized under the headings of differences in the style and content of decision-making, differences in institutional procedures and the added personal workload for MPs.

NOTES AND REFERENCES

1. M. Kolinsky (1975) 'Pariamentary Scrutiny of European Legislation', *Government and Opposition*, 10 p. 47. See also similar comments by A. Stevens (1976–77) 'Problems of parliamentary control of European Community policy', *Millenium, Journal of International Studies*, 5 (3), p. 270; and T. St John N. Bates (1976) 'The scrutiny of European secondary legislation at Westminster', *European Law Review*, 1, p. 22.
2. For a good general study of this issue see D. Butler and D. Marquand (1981) *European Elections and British Politics*, Longman, London and New York.
3. Information about the methods used by other member countries legislatures to handle EC affairs can be found in the Memorandum of the Foreign and Commonwealth Office to the *Report from the Joint Committee on Delegated Legislation*; HL 184 and HC 475, Session 1971–72; and the Annex to the *44th Report, European Legislation Committee*, HC 256–I and 256–II, Session 1977–78; and M. Kolinsky *op. cit.*, pp. 46, 48 and 59–60.
4. This point has received further confirmation from Freida Stack's researches on interest groups and EC affairs. The role of those EC wide interest groups is also noted in the *28th Report of the House of Commons Select Committee on European Secondary Legislation*, 'VAT', HC 272–i–iv, Session 1975–76, HMSO, pp. 57 and 62. See also M. Ryan and P. Isaacson (1974–75), 'Parliament and the European Communities' *Parliamentary Affairs*, 28, pp. 203–4.
5. Comments on these points and the Thomson rules are to be found in *13th Report Select Committee on European Legislation*,

'European Regional Development Fund', HC 41–xiii and 76–i–iii,
Session 1976–77, HMSO, Introduction and p. 7.

6. See D. Englefield (1981) *Parliament and Information*, London Library Association, pp. 72–3.

7. See T. Bates, *op. cit.*, p. 33; and HC 336, 53–v, *op. cit.*, pp. 6–7 and EC 642, *op. cit.*, p. 24.

8. *Twelfth Report Select Committee on European Secondary Legislation*, General Budget, EMU', HC 45–xii (and Minutes of Evidence), HC 87–iii and iv, Session 1974–75. *The 35th Report*, 'EEC Budget', HC 45–viii, Session 1974–75 and *3rd Special Report* 'General Budget', HC 613, Session 1974–75.

9. See for example, *29th Report, Select Committee on European Legislation*, 'Preliminary Draft Buget 1978', HC 41–xxix, Session 1978–79, and *7th Report* 'Reference Paper on Budgetary Questions', HC 159–vii and HC 255–i, Session 1979–80.

10. *Thirteenth Report, Select Committee on European Legislation,* 'European Regional Development Fund', *HC 41–xiii and 7–i–ii (Joint Sitting with Lords Sub-committee A), Session 1976–77; and 11th Report* 'European Social Policy', HL 60, Session 1976–77.

11. *Second Standing Committee on European Documents*, 6 Apr. 1982, p. 3.

12. The general information on EC affairs and the Floor of the House is derived from information kindly supplied by the Clerk to the ELC (including a summary of debates July 1974–Apr. 1981). D. Brew 'National Parliamentary Scrutiny of European Community Legislation: the case of the United Kingdom Parliament, in V. Herman and R. Van Schendelen (1979) *The European Parliament and National Parliaments*, Farnborough, Saxon House; M. Ryan and P. Isaacson, *op. cit.*, pp. 204–7; and A. Stevens, *op. cit.*, pp. 274–5.

13. A useful review of this topic is provided by S. Bell (1981) 'How to abolish the Lords' Fabian Tract 476, London.

14. 'Euroform', *Europe 82*, No. 7, July 1982, p. iii.

CHAPTER FOUR

The Imperatives of Participation
Freida Stack

It is argued by a number of political scientists that the state has in the second half of the twentieth century come to be seen by its citizens as impersonal and remote, and as losing legitimacy and authority, trends which are for European states accentuated by membership of the European Community (Bogdanor, 1979). The authors of the Memorandum of Dissent to the Royal Commission on the Constitution writing in 1973 predicted that membership of the Common Market would:

(a) remove important areas of decision making still further away from the British people;
(b) further weaken the doctrine of ministerial responsibility
(c) increase even more the power of officials (Cmnd 5460–1, 1973, para. 106).

Certainly the British could be said to have had an essentially reactive approach to EC policies. This is partly because Britain entered a Community which was already fully operative in key fields – agriculture and customs in particular – and had therefore to implement policies which she had not participated in making. Second, and more importantly, the EC is unique among political institutions in having its major policy objectives laid out in the Treaty of Rome. What will be considered in this chapter is how civil servants and ministers have organized themselves to cope with the EC as a major source of policy initiatives.

ORGANIZING WHITEHALL FOR EUROPE[1]

When Britain entered the EC in January 1973 certain sections of the executive were quite familiar with the workings of the Communities. Britain had after all made a number of attempts to negotiate entry and had after the Accession Treaty was signed sent observers to some Community meetings. Those Departments likely to be most affected by entry – FCO, MAFF, and DTI – had supplied negotiators and had made efforts to improve their understanding of the EC. The other Departments largely relied on their External Relations divisions to keep a watching brief. Helen Wallace points out Whitehall's slowness to adjust to probable entry and attributes it to its unwillingness to anticipate the parliamentary vote in October 1971 (Wallace 1974). Two key departments were however already working on policies which would smooth entry; needing the changes for internal reasons they had in fact chosen options which would fit in to the Community regulations. MAFF had for financial reasons to reconsider their agricultural pricing system, and implemented one which approximated closely to that used in the CAP. Customs and Excise, given the brief by the new Conservative Government of 1970 to replace Selective Employment Tax and purchase tax, proposed a Value Added Tax, and in a form similar to that of the EEC Second Directive because 'there was evidently a possibility that we might be obliged to conform with the provisions eventually and there was no point in wilfully setting off in a diametrically opposite direction' (Johnstone, 1975, p. 17).

CENTRAL CO-ORDINATION

Once entry was definite, one of the questions facing the executive was whether to have a Minister for Europe, preferably in the Cabinet, with a department to handle all European matters or at least to co-ordinate them. Helen Wallace (1973, chapter 2) describes the models that Britain had available to her among the member states. France had a co-ordinating mechanism, separate from the leading finance and foreign ministries, in the SGCI (*Secrétariat Général du Comité Interministériel pour les Questions de Coopération Economique Européene*) which was technically responsible to the Prime Minister. In Italy, the Netherlands and Belgium the foreign ministry took the lead in EC matters, and in West Germany the role was shared by the Foreign and Economic Ministries. Only one of the countries had a Minister for European Affairs – the Minister of State in the West German Foreign Office, newly appointed in the 1972 Government. Belgium had from 1964–68 a similar minister, but the post was discontinued because his junior rank provided him with insufficient standing among his colleagues. It is worth noting that the suggestion that the responsibility should be taken by the Belgian Deputy Prime Minister was turned down because it was felt to be too threatening to the other departments, in particular the Economics and Foreign Ministries (Wallace, 1973, p. 26).

During the pre-entry period the Chancellor of the Duchy of Lancaster was placed in the Foreign Office and given responsibility for negotiations. The post was held by George Thomson in the Labour Government (raised to Cabinet rank in October 1969) and in the Conservative Government briefly by Anthony Barber, then by Geoffrey Rippon until November 1972 when John Davies took over. The negotiating team of senior officials from the key departments (FCO, Treasury, MAFF and DTI) was led by Sir Con O'Neill, Deputy Under-Secretary at the FCO, and serviced by a European Unit in the Cabinet Office under its Permanent Secretary, Sir William Neild (Wallace 1974b). When John Davies became Chancellor of the Duchy in 1972 he was placed in the Cabinet Office heading the European Unit, which came formally into existence under Sir John Hunt and then P. D. Nairne (later Sir Patrick Nairne). John Davies, a close associate of Mr Heath and a noted Europeanist, was the nearest that the British Cabinet has come to having a 'Minister for Europe'. Harold Lever who became Chancellor of the Duchy in the 1974 Labour Government had a floating brief for economic and financial advice to the Prime Minister, and responsibility for the oversight of European matters went to the Foreign Office Ministers. There is in the British system of ministerial responsibility for departments and collective decision-making in Cabinet no place for a minister without a secure departmental base to supervise or co-ordinate effectively. Even if the Conservatives had won the 1974 election it seems unlikely that the post would have continued.

What Britain did, then, was to give EC work to those departments which were already dealing with the relevant domestic policy areas, and to assign a central co-ordination role jointly to the Foreign Office and the Cabinet Office in what can be interpreted as a British equivalent to the French model.[2]

The Foreign Office set up two European Integration Divisions (now the European Community Divisions): EID (External) to deal with 'Questions involving the EC's relations with third countries and European political co-operation', and EID (Internal) to deal with 'Questions relating to the internal working and development of the EC parliamentary and legal aspects of Community membership' (*Civil Service Yearbook* 1974, col. 344). These divisions have been staffed by people with a good deal of experience in the EC field in the European embassies, in UKREP, or as in the case of David Hannay (head of EID 1981–83) in the *cabinet* of a Commissioner. It is worth noting, however, that the FCO feel that they can no longer offer their staff the kind of wide experience of EC negotiations that many home civil servants are getting in departments like MAFF or Trade.

The FCO carries out the mechanical functions of receiving all material from Brussels and distributing it throughout Whitehall. In the very early days of British membership when everything arrived in French it employed a team of translators. All written material to Brussels similarly passes through the FCO, which acts as a reference point for communications with UKREP. It is directly responsible for the political co-operation machinery and for the briefings for European Council meetings. It also has the duty of advising departments and the Government on the EC implications of proposed policies and decisions. This has given rise to the suspicion, particularly among ministers, that the Foreign

Office is interfering in domestic policy-making from which it has traditionally been very separate. The responsibility for the co-ordination of policy was therefore given to the Cabinet Office, but the European Secretariat has been very small and has depended on the close co-operation of the European Integration Departments who provide much day to day back-up support.

The European Secretariat has always been a small group. In 1975 there were ten administrative staff and 18 clerical staff; in 1982 there were eight administrative staff – a Deputy Secretary, an Under Secretary, two Assistant Secretaries and four Principals. These people are recruited from departments on two-year secondments. The four senior staff are people with long EC experience, but the Principal positions seem to be regarded as career postings for high-flyers who have not necessarily worked on European policies. Since 1975 the heads of the European Secretariat have been men with long, outstanding careers in the EC field. Sir Roy Denman, Second Permanent Secretary 1975–77, came from the Department of Trade and had been a member of the negotiating team 1970–72. His successor, Sir Michael Franklin, had represented MAFF in the negotiating team and was Deputy Director-General (Agriculture) in the Commission, from 1973 to 1977. He was appointed at Deputy Secretary level, as have all subsequent heads of the Secretariat. David Hancock, who headed the Secretariat from 1981–83 had worked for much of his career in the Treasury becoming a Financial and Economic Counsellor at UKREP between 1972 and 1974 and returning to a post in the Treasury with major European responsibilities. The current head is David Williamson, a MAFF official who followed Sir Michael Franklin in the Commission from 1977 to 1983.

The European Secretariat acts as a co-ordinating mechanism on EC matters. Its major tasks are to facilitate the resolution of any differences between departments over policies or tactics, and to keep a watching brief on areas where difficulties might occur. Much of this work is done informally by telephone but there are a large number of committee meetings which the Secretariat services by arranging times, circulating papers and taking the minutes.

At Cabinet level there has been a relatively similar committee structure under the 1974 Labour and the 1979 Conservative Governments. There is a slot for the EC in the weekly Cabinet meeting, but this is to report rather than to stimulate discussion. Most EC business that requires attention at Cabinet level is taken to a committee chaired by the Foreign Secretary; under Labour this was called EQ and it is currently called OD(E). Ministers from a wide range of departments attend (including junior ministers if their area of responsibility is under discussion), and the Foreign Office is represented by another Minister, in the 1979–83 government often the Lord Privy Seal. Under Labour it met when necessary (Gibbs (1977) says about once a month) to discuss important specific issues, for example preparation for a Council of Ministers meeting.

As with other Cabinet committees these are shadowed by official committees. The current arrangement is that EQ(S), a group of officials at Deputy Secretary and Under Secretary levels from the major departments, prepares for OD(E). It takes major EC issues and is chaired by the head of the European Secretariat. EQ(O) takes the many run of the mill issues, meeting frequently (often several times a week) and having a large circulation list. The European Secretariat is anxious that all interested parties in Whitehall should come to these meetings in order to avoid complaints later about decisions taken. The membership therefore varies according to what is on the agenda. It is chaired by the Under Secretary in the European Secretariat. Under Labour there were subcommittees of EQ(O) – EQO(P) on the mutual recognition of professional qualifications and EQO(L) on legal questions. There is still a standing committee on legal questions. Specific areas, for example the electoral system for elections to the European Parliament, may be dealt with in one of the MISC committees.

Much work is done in interdepartmental meetings, arranged between a small number of departments. Where there is one main department, for example MAFF on fisheries, they will organize the meetings, but where, as on the budget, there are two key departments (FCO and Treasury) or where there is no leading department, the Secretariat arranges them.

In all such meetings the aim of the Cabinet Office is to secure the resolution of differences between departments over policy or tactics or the co-ordination of instructions for those members of UKREP, Ministers, or officials who are due to negotiate in Brussels.

Desk officers of UKREP attend about 85 per cent of these meetings, and it is clear that UKREP, unlike its counterparts in Brussels, is closely integrated into the Whitehall decision-making system. There is a regular Friday meeting at the Cabinet Office of the Permanent Representative and the Permanent Secretaries from the departments working in the EC field. The meeting receives a report on the previous week's business in Brussels and goes on to discuss current issues. The Permanent Representative may also meet ministers for discussions.

It is evident that the central co-ordination of British policy on the EC is effective at the day-to-day level, ensuring that policy ends and means pursued by one department do not conflict with those of another, or of the Government as a whole. It is evident too that the European divisions in the Foreign Office and the Cabinet Office work well together. However, two major problems remain: the responsibility of Foreign Office Ministers for European affairs, which can cause problems with their ministerial colleagues; and the very small size of the European Secretariat, which allows it too little time in which to do any forward thinking on policy.

EC WORK AND GOVERNMENT DEPARTMENTS

The absorption of EC work into existing departments had a number of advantages from the British point of view. First, it presented EC work as an extension of domestic policy-making, rather than as foreign policy. Second, it distributed responsibility throughout Whitehall (though very unevenly, particularly at first), in the hope of encouraging everyone to 'think European' (see Soames, 1972). Third, it sought to make the best use of the rather short supply of available expertise on Community affairs in the Civil Service. Fourth, it diffused EC work making it less politically obvious; given the difficulties in both major parties over membership, it suited their leaders to avoid the easy target of a European ministry.

The workload was inevitably spread unevenly throughout Whitehall. Four departments were affected immediately and substantially. In MAFF most of the commodity and food divisions had an increased workload, and indeed MAFF was the only department to have to set up a new offshoot: the Intervention Board for Agricultural Produce, with 422 staff and the duty to administer in the UK the market support arrangements of the CAP. The (then) Department of Trade and Industry had, in addition to its policy responsibilities, the duty of providing information on the EC to industry. The Treasury was concerned with Economic and Financial affairs, including the Budget, and both the Treasury, and Customs and Excise Department were involved in the taxation and customs policies of the Community.

Three policy departments – Environment, Transport and Energy – together with the three geographical departments – Scotland, Wales and Northern Ireland – were drawn slowly into European work, although they were to be fairly heavily involved by the mid-1970s. The DoE has dealt largely with the two important fields of environmental pollution and regional policy (including the administration of the Regional Fund). The other two policy departments have been involved with the controversial common transport and common energy policies. The three geographical departments have been heavily involved in a number of areas, notably agriculture where they work closely with MAFF and are represented on the Intervention Board, and where they have made use of the Agricultural Fund, particularly under the category of the less-favoured areas directive. The Scottish Office have been active on fisheries and all three departments act as administrators of the Social and Regional Funds.

Of the other policy departments, Health and Social Security and Employment have limited fields of policy interest in the EC, though Employment does administer the Social Fund. Finally, the Department of Education and Science has been dealing with the contentious area of education where the directive on migrants' education and the regulation on student awards have created a good deal of work despite the fact that education is not mentioned in the Treaty of Rome and that member countries emphasize that policy-making in this area is co-operative and not compulsory in nature. All meetings are, therefore, at an informal level and are stated to be outside the EC framework but the Education Committee can make proposals directly to the Council of Ministers.

Lastly, there are two groups of departments which have had to adapt, sometimes quite radically, to EC membership. The first group, consisting of the Inland Revenue, the Indirect Tax Division of the Treasury, the Treasury Officer of Accounts, the Export Credits Guarantee Department and the Office of Fair Trading, have been concerned with harmonization, mainly of taxes and revenue. The second group: the Exchequer and Audit Department, Central Statistical Office, Civil Service Department (now split between the Cabinet Office and the Management and Personnel Office), the Lord Chancellor's Department and the Treasury Solicitor, provide services to the rest of Whitehall, and have established and expanded their expertise in the Community field in the collection of statistics, or in the legal implications of membership.

Within departments, work was assigned to those divisions already dealing with the policy area, with one division (often in International Relations) having responsibility for the co-ordination of EC work. This co-ordination is mainly at the organizational rather than the policy-making level. Thus the EC division in MAFF acts as a point of reference for those civil servants currently negotiating in Brussels and arranges their regular Thursday meetings; it does not itself make the policy but seeks to ensure that the departmental viewpoint is a coherent one. The division receives from the Foreign Office all the material from Brussels and sends it on to the relevant divisions. In the DHSS, for example, a group of women with low Civil Service status but with a lot of expertise sift through to see what will affect the department and then 'flag' it for transmission to the various parts of the department's empire.

It is to these divisions that the Cabinet Office makes requests for the departmental viewpoint on an issue, for example the request in the autumn of 1982 for departments' views on the priorities set in their areas by the Danish presidency. In response to such a request the co-ordination divisions ask for short statements from the policy divisions and then carry out a sub-editing job, collating the replies and ensuring that they are in a form acceptable to the Cabinet Office. The Assistant Secretary then represents the department in the follow-up meetings, taking along two or three people from the policy divisions to explain technical points. The co-ordination divisions thus act as a point of reference within their departments and within Whitehall. They also liaise with Parliament, in particular with the two EC Committees. These divisions arrange for written and oral evidence to be given to the parliamentary committees, a considerable task in some departments, Industry claims for example to supply about a hundred explanatory memoranda a year. Gibbs (1977, p. 350) describes how the co-ordination division in the Department of Trade and Industry had to obtain explanatory memoranda from their technical divisions on the texts before Parliament, clear them with other interested departments and get them to Westminster within 14 days. This formed a large part of the work of four full-time officials. Finally, the divisions act as a point of reference to outsiders. This is particularly evident in the Trade and Industry group where there is a joint EEC Information Unit, staffed by a Chief Information Officer, and with a separate, listed phone number recommended by a leading businessman to his colleagues as 'the most useful telephone number for business in the Community' (Drew, 1979, p. 99).

In most departments, though not MAFF, the EC division is also the repository of the department's negotiating expertise, the staff often having had many years experience of EC work. The Assistant Secretary or Principal (sometimes the Senior Executive Officer) may go to Brussels as a departmental negotiator along with representatives of the policy divisions concerned. This happens particularly where the department has a limited amount of EC work and the policy staff are not used to negotiating in Brussels. In the DHSS the Principal in charge of the branch covering Health talks to any staff due to go to Brussels about negotiating techniques, and accompanies them on the first two or three visits until they have enough confidence to operate alone.

What is striking about these civil servants in the main-stream of EC work is their outward-looking stance. The classic portrait of the senior civil servant is of one who is insular both in a domestic and an international sense, yet many of the civil servants who were interviewed for this book claimed to speak and read French, sometimes both French and German. A DHSS Principal, explaining how to be an effective negotiator, said it was essential to understand the domestic political problems of the other delegations and for that reason read *Le Monde* every day. It is enthusiasm and energy of this kind which has turned MAFF, once a low-profile department in Whitehall, with a minister in the Cabinet largely for historical reasons, into a very strong EC team. The Minister, Peter Walker, in a BBC interview, told Hugo Young:

> It is quite a tribute to the Civil Service that a Depart-ment which was, I suppose, the most inward-looking and domestically-orientated department in Whitehall until we joined the Community, now probably has the best negotiating team (I'm talking about officials, no flattery to ministers) in Brussels of any member country (Young and Sloman, 1982, p. 74).

A few departments, like Trade, run their own language courses, but some of the credit must go the Civil Service College set up only three years before entry. In its first year, 1970–71, it ran two courses in which the EC was an element. In the following year it established courses which were more clearly preparation for entry including two for staff at Assistant Secretary/Principal level and one (heavily over-subscribed) for lawyers. Nine civil servants went on an intensive French course at Leeds University. In all, 99 took EC courses; in the next year, when entry was certain, this total jumped to 502. The numbers rose again in the following year and did not fall off in the mid-1970s as much as had been expected. The demand came largely from the departments most affected by entry, although even very small departments like the Charity Commissioners sent one or two staff during the early years.

The courses covered general and specific aspects of the EC, with a particularly strong demand from lawyers. The language training at Leeds University has continued as have exchange programmes with the French and German and now the Dutch civil services. Staff on these programmes undertake intensive language study and visit the political institutions of the country; they also have lectures, usually in the foreign language. Training in international negotiation techniques is an expanding part of the College's programme. In one such simulation exercise – based on the EC sugar negotiations of Autumn 1979 – participants are assigned roles as members of national delegations to the Council of Agricultural Ministers, of the Commission, and of pressure groups. The groups have three hours in which to prepare their briefs from material supplied and must then begin negotiating. Many civil servants with experience of negotiating in Brussels who have participated in this, or earlier exercises, have expressed their surprise at how well the atmosphere of negotiations can be recreated in such an exercise (Erridge 1980, p. 5).

What is not entirely clear is how far EC experience is a factor in promotion. More research needs to be done on the changes that entry into Europe has made to the promotion prospects of civil servants who may now not only be promoted upwards in their home departments, but may also move to UKREP and into the Commission. In MAFF these days it would be difficult not to have done EC work, and certainly the appointments at Permanent Secretary level since entry have been of people with extensive EC experience. In the Department of Industry, however, the view is that the EC work helps a person's promotion as far as Assistant Secretary level, but that wider experience is needed to rise further.

Willis (1983) has produced valuable information on the British civil servants who join the Commission or the Council Secretariat. At the time of entry, the Civil Service Department agreed with the unions that such staff would be guaranteed reinstatement after up to five years away. However, as she points out it was 'rarely demonstrable to the able and ambitious that service in the Commission actually enhanced career or even job prospects on return to Whitehall, and quite often the reverse seemed to be true' (Willis, 1983, p. 80).

Departments had ambiguous attitudes towards promotion partly because some people had been promoted on going to Brussels and partly because Commission officials were not subject to the annual reports on performance which were carried out at home. 'The official view was that "time spent doing one thing was time not spent doing another", reflecting a perception that the work done in the Commission, for example, was not necessarily relevant to the Civil Service' (Willis 1983, p. 80). Thus, British civil servants recruited into the Commission tended to stay there. It is the rising numbers of *agents temporaires* seconded to the Commission who bring back with them to home departments a valuable understanding of how the EC works, and a wide range of professional contacts. Willis (1983, p. 83) found that departments were increasingly aware of the benefits of this and that these officials were felt to be picked out for fast promotion.

Finally, membership of the EC may bring a closer integration of the home civil service and the foreign service through closer working relations in Whitehall and in UKREP. Certainly the move of Sir Donald Maitland to be Permanent Secretary of the Department of Energy in 1980 was an unprecedented one, since his career had been almost wholly in the Foreign Office, and he had been the UK Permanent Representative from 1974 to 1979.

NEGOTIATING IN EUROPE: CIVIL SERVANTS

Membership of the EC has added massively, albeit unevenly, to the work of departments. In 1980 MAFF estimated that they sent 2,500 civil servants to attend 1,200 meetings, the Departments of Trade and Industry together say they send about 1,200 officials a year, the DHSS send two or three a week, the Home Office sent 67 civil servants to 51 meetings in 1980 and the DES say they send not more than 30 in a year. EC work is slow in that it takes place over long time periods, but at various points it takes place at speed. In MAFF the work is constant and always at high pressure because the Special Committee on Agriculture meets on Monday and Tuesday every week. The agenda is available only the previous Wednesday, so other interested departments are merely notified and a time-consuming inter-departmental meeting called only if there is a real problem. Peter Pooley, formerly Minister (Agriculture) in UKREP described his weekly routine in Brussels. On Sunday he picked up his briefs from MAFF for the Monday and Tuesday Committee Meeting. On Wednesday he reported the outcome to MAFF and to other interested parties, and on Thursday he flew in to London for the weekly departmental meetings where it was decided 'what form of briefing we need for the next Monday or Tuesday Council of Special Committee; what lines need to be cleared with other departments and with the Minister before we put pen to paper on the instructions; and how we shall handle the thing tactically' (Young and Sloman, 1982, p. 76).

A similar momentum exists in areas of trade policy but most departments are working at a much less frenetic pace as proposals work from the Commission to the Council of Ministers via the expert working groups and bilateral negotiations which form most of the civil servants' work in Brussels. Before they go these, the department must have a clear view of the British standpoint on an issue. To obtain this they have, as in many areas of domestic policy-making, to discuss not just with other Whitehall departments but also with interested parties such as industry, pressure groups, or local authorities, since it is often they, rather than the Government, which will have to implement any decisions.

It is in fact possible to view the Government as playing different roles in EC negotiations, according to the type of policy area under discussion. In the agricultural field the National Farmers Union and MAFF have if anything become closer allies since entry. Richardson and Jordan (1979, p. 115) report that: 'One minister has told us that the union knows 99 per cent of the British information and arguments . . .

This means that when an agreement is reached not only does the Minister have to get it accepted in Cabinet, but the interest group leadership has to "sell" it to its own membership. In this important first area the Government is acting as partner.

In the second category the Government must negotiate the policy, but implementation is largely in the hands of the industry concerned. In the areas of company law, banking, consumer credit and misleading advertising the British tradition has been one of self-policing by the industry, and in EC negotiations the government can be seen as agent. In this role its negotiating position is directed towards securing regulations which are acceptable to the industry concerned and which the government would be willing to police.

The third category concerns issues such as water pollution, the environment, energy and regional policy, where the interested parties are other public bodies. The Government here is acting as a sort of public sector guardian. Finally, there are issues such as social security and taxation, where the Government is the actor, subject to pressure from interested groups and from the public, but responsible for both the decision and its implementation.

These categories are of course not watertight; it is easy to think of issues which can be placed in different categories, according to differing viewpoints, or which fall between categories. The increase in the axle weights of heavy lorries could be seen to fall into the second category, although some who view the Department of Transport as having been captured by the Roads Lobby would want to place it in the first category. The local authorities who had the responsibility for the upkeep of roads and bridges felt strongly that the Government had not paid enough attention to the problems that would be caused to them, that is, it had not paid enough attention to its role as public sector guardian. In all these situations, however, what the Government and the Civil Service are doing is seeking to mitigate, through negotiation and compromise, the effects on Britain of the Commission's proposals.

Before civil servants go to Brussels they are briefed by the Cabinet Office on the form to be followed and the phrases

which may (or may not) be used along with their meanings.
One group of expressions are the reserves which range in
strength from the *réserve du fond* which indicates that consultation with the home Government will be required at the
highest level through to the *réserve d'attente* which means that
time must be allowed for the domestic parliament to be
consulted. The difficulty for the negotiators is in having clear
but flexible instructions and in maintaining accountability to
ministers and to the Cabinet. Civil servants who have
worked in Brussels say that they aim for the 'broad course
that ministers wanted' and in cases of doubt refer back to
London (Young and Sloman, 1982, pp. 77–8). Sir Donald
Maitland, Britain's Permanent Representative from 1975 to
1979 describes the procedure:

> I myself used to find in Brussels that there were times in
> a debate when my instructions left me in an intolerable
> position. In which case I would ask for a period to
> reflect on this and I would ask the chairman 'Could we
> come back to this item later in the day?' A lot of
> telephoning between Brussels and London would then
> take place, and I would hope to receive a message later
> in the day saying 'The Minister agrees to amend your
> instructions in the following respect.' And when we got
> back to this item, the chairman would say 'I wonder if
> you have completed your reflection by telephone?' as it
> is called euphemistically there, and then we would be
> able to proceed (Young and Sloman, 1982, p. 78).

Not all ministers are happy to provide the go-ahead for
modifications in their department's position. Brian Sedgemore, Tony Benn's PPS at the Department of Energy in 1977
and 1978, felt that the 'pressures that came from these
committees and from Foreign Office and Department of
Energy civil servants were always for the Minister to give
way a little'. He remembered Tony Benn 'writing three
times on a minute "NO, NO, NO", when Sir Donald
Maitland advised making some concessions on oil refinery
policy, supplies of energy to our EEC partners in times of
crisis over coal' (Sedgemore, 1980, p. 94).

What the civil servants and Permanent Representatives are doing is preparing the ground for ministers. They aim to agree as many areas as possible, political issues being referred to COREPER. Peter Pooley makes a distinction between technical and political issues. Thus farm structure subsidies:

> were issues of the sort that did not involve a major political dimension, and had we left that issue to ministers, they would have really had a struggle to arrive at agreement on it. As it was, the special committee spent four or five hundred hours, I should think, arguing over these issues. Ministers spent four or five hours, and it was settled. So there we prepared the ground and I did a job that Peter Walker could not have done. Equally on New Zealand lamb and mutton, a great deal more political an issue, he did a job that it was absolutely inconceivable that I or any other official could have done (Young and Sloman, 1982, p. 79).

TABLE 4.1: *Council Meetings 1975–81*

	1975	1976	1977	1978	1979	1980	1981
Foreign Affairs	14	15	15	13	12	12	12
Finance/Budget/Economic	13	12	15	13	15	15	14*
Agriculture/Fisheries	15	13	15	21	15	20	18
Social Affairs	2	2	2	2	2	2	3*
Transport	2	2	3	2	2	2	2
Environment	2	1	2	3	3	2	2
Energy	2	3	4	3	6	2	3
Development Co-operation	2	2	3	3		1	3
Research	1	3	2		2		1
Public Health			1				
Industry/Steel						2	4

Source: Biannual White Papers on Developments in the European Communities

*1 Joint Council Meeting of Employment, Economic and Finance Ministers

The agenda of the Council of Ministers is divided into two parts with 'A' items expected to go through on the nod and 'B' items requiring the kind of political weight and expertise that only ministers can provide. 'B' items also cover those areas which present a problem to more than one government.

It is clear from tables 4.1 and 4.2 that some ministers are frequent visitors to Brussels. The Council of Agriculture Ministers met 117 times in the years 1975–81, and the British Minister of Agriculture attended all but one of these. The Foreign Secretary and the Chancellor of the Exchequer attended about half of their respective Council meetings. Such ministers have a good deal of experience in negotiating, but where the Councils meet only two or three times a year ministers cannot have the expertise of their civil servants.

TABLE 4.2: *Total of ministerial-days spent in Council Meetings 1975–81*

	All ministers	Cabinet ministers	Per cent
Foreign Affairs	320	166[1]	52
Finance, etc.	117	45[2]	38
Agriculture/ Fisheries	454	269	59
Social	29	7	24
Transport	31	9[3]	29
Environment	17	1	6
Energy	35	19	54
Development	16	—	—
Research	17	2	12
Public Health	1	1	100
Industry/Steel	6	—	—

[1]Of which Foreign Secretary 86
          Trade Secretary   43
[2]Chancellor of the Exchequer only, no addition has been made for the two years, 1977–79 when the Chief Secretary was in the Cabinet. The Chief Secretary and Financial Secretary spent 32 days in Council meetings during this period.
[3]Minister of Transport not in the Cabinet 1979–81

Source: Biannual White Papers on Developments in the European Communities

MINISTERIAL WORKLOAD

Table 4.1 shows the number of meetings held by each Council in the years 1975–81 (figures for 1973 and 1974 are incomplete), and table 4.2 computes the number of days spent by ministers at such meetings. Table 4.2 shows clearly the heavy load that MAFF ministers carry, though it should be added that the Secretary of State for Scotland has attended three-quarters of all Fisheries Council meetings. At the meetings of the Finance and Economic Councils, the Chancellor of the Exchequer usually heads the British delegation, while his second Minister (the Chief Secretary under Labour, and the Financial Secretary in the 1979 Conservative Government) is responsible for negotiations on the annual budget. Foreign Office ministers (including the Lord Privy Seal in the 1979 government) have accounted for 62 per cent of the days spent in the Council of Foreign Ministers and the ministers from the Department of Trade have added another 21 per cent, but over the years ministers from eight other departments have been required to attend.

Much EC work in the other departments is the responsibility of junior ministers. It is not that it has been specially assigned to them but that issues like water pollution in the DoE are of a type traditionally entrusted to junior ministers. The Secretary of State for Environment has in fact only once attended the Council of Environment Ministers and that was during the 1977 British Presidency when he had to take the chair; the Junior Minister took the chair in the 1981 Presidency. The attendance of senior ministers at Council meetings depends partly upon the political quality of the agenda and partly upon personal preferences. In 1975 Barbara Castle decided to make her EC debut at the Council of Labour and Social Affairs Ministers, largely, it appears, to disconcert her civil servants. 'There was nothing of any importance coming up, so the Office had assumed that we would be sending a Parliamentary Secretary. Alec Jones's transfer to the Welsh Office gives me an excuse to announce that I will go myself' (Castle, 1980, p. 418). She made a rousing speech defending Britain's decision not to equalize the retirement ages of men and women, and then departed leaving her Junior Minister to handle the subsequent negotiations. By contrast, the Secretary of State for Energy attended more than half of the Council of Energy Ministers meetings in each of the years in question. This was due in part to ministerial interest but mainly to the highly political nature of the evolving energy policy and to Britain's perception of her special position as an oil producer.

Tables 4.1 and 4.2 cover only the time spent in meetings, the additional time used in briefing for these varies according to the individual minister concerned, and no generalization can be made about this. Some ministers have formal briefing sessions and some are briefed as they walk into the meeting. There are also informal meetings of EC ministers. Some of these are called at the discretion of the current president and allow proposals to be discussed in a general way rather than in the narrow confines of negotiation. Foreign Affairs ministers have had informal meetings to discuss political co-operation since the early 1970s, and the Economic and Finance ministers have met since the late 1960s to discuss issues on which they do not want to commit themselves, or for which they require complete confidentiality.

In the Labour and Social Affairs field ministers (normally junior ministers) have to attend the meetings of the Standing Committee on Employment, a group consisting also of representatives of the Commission and of employers and trade unions. It meets regularly twice a year, though it met four times in 1980 to consider the worsening employment situation in Europe. In 1977 and 1978 in response to trade union demands for discussion with finance ministers as well there were meetings of the Tripartite Conference. These meetings are very large, last only for a day and seek to discuss broad economic issues. As far as ministers are concerned, what they provide is a forum to speak to their own industry and unions in a European context.

Finally there are the unilateral discussions that take place with the Commissioner, with fellow ministers from the other member states, or with the current chairman of the Council. In his first four weeks as chairman of the Energy Council in January 1977, Tony Benn had a meeting with every Energy minister in the EC and with the Commissioner. His chief aim was to discover the objectives of the member states for the next six months and to discuss the Council's method of working, but he also discussed the question of external links in the energy field. Ministers usually use such meetings to discuss policy and possible concessions, that is, as part of the negotiation process.

THE BRITISH PRESIDENCY

The British have held the Presidency twice, in the first six months of 1977 and in the last six months of 1981. Preparation for the first Presidency began in 1976 with officials looking at the experience of the other governments who had held the chair, and at the additional workload involved. The FCO set up a special Presidency Secretariat to co-ordinate the work, and a Conference Secretariat to make the arrangements for this and for the meetings of the NATO Council and the Commonwealth Prime Ministers Conference which were also to take place in London that year. Edwards and Wallace (1977) point out that the British were not so daunted by the Presidency as were Ireland or Denmark because they had fairly extensive experience of running international conferences. They indicate however that ministers took rather longer than civil servants to focus on the Presidency. The resignation of the Prime Minster, Harold Wilson, in March 1976 brought the Foreign Secretary, James Callaghan, to the position, and new ministers, some with very little Community experience, to key posts. The two most important positions – Foreign Secretary and Minister of Agriculture – were filled by Anthony Crosland who was ambivalent about the EC, and John Silkin who was a well-known anti-marketeer. An additional difficulty was Crosland's death during the Presidency and his replacement by David Owen who was pro-market but an inexperienced negotiator. One helpful factor, however, was that the Presidency of the Commission was held by Roy Jenkins, until recently a member of the Labour Government. The split in the Labour party over EC membership meant that the tone of the

Presidency was necessarily rather subdued; Edwards and Wallace (1977, p. 78) describe it as pragmatic rather than enthusiastic, with the British arguing that 'the primary and indeed dominating role of the Presidency was the competent management of business, and that flirting with grand initiatives was naive and doomed to failure.'

The British therefore aimed for efficiency in Council meetings and in the preparation of business. The Minister of State for the Foreign Office, Frank Judd, appeared before the House of Commons Select Committee on European Legislation on 13 July 1977, and justifiably claimed some success in this area. First, COREPER had been instructed not to bring issues before the Council of Ministers until they had been properly prepared, and that had in time produced a more disciplined approach to the agenda. Second, the meetings of the European Council were divided into two parts: general political issues being discussed in the first half, and specific decisions taken in the second half. Finally, the procedure to secure political co-operation had been improved to ensure greater co-ordination with EC business.

What was more difficult for the British was the list of issues due to be discussed. Many of them, for example, VAT, Social Fund, transport regulations, economic and monetary co-ordination, would require a lot of work, but three in particular – Joint European Torus, the agricultural price review and the fisheries policy – were too close to British interest[5] to be capable of mediation by British chairmen. Fisheries did not prove such a contentious issue as expected, but on JET and agricultural pricing the British were extremely partisan. This alienated their partners, in particular the smaller states, and was one of the reasons why the British Presidency was felt not to have been a success. It is hard, however, to see in what way the country holding the Presidency can be expected to behave. All the member states have fundamental national issues at stake in many EC negotiations and, as Frank Judd pointed out, 'What was misunderstood about the Presidency amongst some commentators and others is the notion that we could go into a six-month period during which we suspended national interests and just became technical chairman' (HC 43–VI, 1976–77, q. 330).

The second British Presidency came in for similar criticisms and indeed had very similar problems. The Prime Minister carried out her first major Cabinet reshuffle in the middle of the six months which brought new ministers to all the Councils except for the key ones of Agriculture, Finance and Foreign Affairs. The Cabinet was much less pro-European than previous Conservative administrations, and led by a Prime Minister who was very dissatisfied both with the CAP and the British contribution to the budget, areas of disagreement which she was unwilling to put into abeyance during the Presidency.

The Secretary of State for Foreign Affairs made the customary speech to the European Parliament in July setting out the objectives of the British Presidency. He stated that the first obligation of the country holding the Presidency was 'to ensure that business is despatched with the maximum of efficiency and the minimum of fuss' (Cmnd 8525, 1981–82, p. 54). He then listed the areas of current concern to the Community and divided them into the problems of renewal, of enlargement and of identity. Referring back to these in his speech to the European Parliament on 12 December 1981, at the end of the UK Presidency, the Foreign Secretary bemoaned the lack of progress in some areas.

> It is not to the Community's credit that after six years of discussion and five meetings of Foreign Ministers during our Presidency alone we have not been able to agree on the non-life insurance services directive; nor that Foreign Ministers have been unable to agree on important measures in the field of telecommunication because of the disagreement over one word (Cmnd 8525, 1981–82, p. 71).

Progress had been made in some areas – in the structuring of energy needs away from oil, in the budget and on fisheries – but agreement had yet to be reached. It is difficult for the country holding the Presidency to achieve a great deal in six months (especially in the second half of the year when effectively there are five months and some claim only four); any agreements in Councils will have been in the pipeline for months.

Where the President can influence matters is in pushing ahead with issues already being discussed, or in placing issues on the political agenda. The London Report on political co-operation owed much to the determination of the British to capitalize on the agreement under the Luxembourg Presidency to produce such a review of the EPC machinery, and to the hard work done under the Dutch Presidency. The Report reflected a strengthened commitment to joint action in foreign affairs, set out the agreed procedure for convening meetings quickly in a crisis, and recognized that extra support was needed for the Presidency in its increasingly demanding role in this field. In the second area, that of placing issues on the political agenda, the British had something of a success in obtaining from the Commission a report and a draft directive on the liberalization of European air fares. The British Government and British pressure groups had been keen for some time on raising this but had failed to interest their national or Community counterparts in the issue as a priority. There had been some activity at Community level including a request from the Council of Transport Ministers in June 1980 for a report on air fares and a report from the Transport Committee of the European Parliament in October 1980. When Lord Carrington discussed priorities with the President of the Commission in May 1981 he referred to the importance of making progress in this area (HC 431–I, 1980–81, para. 11). He was supported in this by a quick report from the House of Commons Industry and Trade Committee which reiterated its dismay over the Community's dilatoriness in this field and saw the UK Presidency as 'a real opportunity to put the issue firmly on the Community's agenda and to swing the argument in favour of a much more liberal regime in European air transport' (HC 431, 1980–81, para. 15). The question now remains whether the British can keep up the pressure for action when they are no longer President.

NEGOTIATING IN EUROPE: MINISTERS

Ministerial teams are generally accompanied to Council meetings by the relevant Deputy Secretary from the department and by the minister from UKREP. These two officials sit on either side of the leading minister to provide respectively the national and the *communautaire* response to negotiations as the progress. Behind them sit an official at Principal level from the department and from UKREP, plus, perhaps, the Assistant Secretary from the co-ordinating branch. The usual procedure is for the President to call for a *tour de table*, that is for the delegations to state their positions. Where there are one or two recalcitrant countries the President may well call for a *tour de table* at regular intervals as the meeting wears on into the night, so as to isolate these countries and break down their resistance to a compromise. In such circumstances the contribution of officials is made in meetings in the corridors or the coffee rooms where an acceptable deal is arranged and announced to the Council as having been made 'in the margins'.

The difficulty in negotiations is the degree to which ministers can move from the position agreed in the Cabinet. Under Labour there was a small group of ministers – the Chief Secretary to the Treasury (Joel Barnett), the Minister of State at the FCO (Roy Hattersley and later David Owen), the Minister of State for Prices and Consumer Affairs (Shirley Williams and later Roy Hattersley) – who were to oversee negotiations on agriculture. Evidently this was only partially successful as a controlling mechanism. Fred Peart, the Agriculture Minister, was in deep trouble with his colleagues in March 1976 over the deal he had agreed on skimmed milk powder. Criticism came not only from those such as Barbara Castle who wanted ministers mandated, but from pro-marketeers like Shirley Williams. She reminded the Foreign Secretary who was attempting to defend Peart that there 'had been a meeting of EQ [the Cabinet Committee] . . . which had laid down "precise negotiating objectives"' (Castle, 1980, p. 685). The next Agriculture Minister, John Silkin, although an anti-marketeer, was also distrusted by his colleagues, among them the Chief Secretary to the Treasury, Joel Barnett, who later wrote

> In the Cabinet Committee itself, John Silkin was always the very essence of sweet reason in putting forward a negotiating tactic he should be authorized to deploy at a meeting of the Council of Ministers in Brussels or Luxembourg. Yet neither David Owen, Roy Hattersley nor myself was entirely happy with him. After we had all agreed, including the reluctant John himself, that he could go so far and no further, we still could not relax. He would phone from outside the Ministerial Conference Chamber at 2 or 3 o'clock in the morning, and we, in David Owen's room in the House of Commons, or in our separate beds at home if the House was not sitting, would be put in the position of agreeing to what we had strongly opposed, or risking an unplanned confrontation. It was a difficult area for all concerned, for while we might win the argument in Cabinet Committee, the actual negotiations were in John's hands (Barnett, 1982, pp. 158–9).

Individual ministers are not always as powerful in negotiations as this would imply. Barnett (1982, pp. 156–8) precedes this complaint with a description of a crucial Budget Council meeting he attended in November 1978, following which the small but important successes achieved for Britain were whittled away by his own and the Foreign Office civil servants, who persuaded the Prime Minister to give precedence to the policy of resisting any increase in the powers of the European Parliament.

However, this area of Cabinet control of negotiating ministers, remains problematic. Certainly for the individual minister there is an advantage in being able to negotiate within a flexible framework, bound neither to specific instructions from the Cabinet as German ministers are, nor to strict accountability to Parliament as are the Danes.

The relationship with the House of Commons is also difficult. Barbara Castle records James Callaghan as Foreign Secretary grumbling about the backbenchers' querying of policy in advance of Council decisions, and claiming that they were trying to alter the relationship between Parliament and the executive. '"They want to give ministers instructions before they go to Brussels." But the whole essence of negotiations, he continued, was that Ministers must be given a free hand and then face the music afterwards' (Castle, 1980, p. 279). The House has never been able to instruct ministers in this area, and clearly at a formal level it has only a limited impact on policy-making in this area. It does have a degree of influence at an informal level. Groups of backbenchers do see ministers on specific topics; Fred Peart, as Labour Minister of Agriculture, regarded as important his meetings with a group of Conservative backbenchers with agricultural constituencies.

Efforts have been made to accommodate the wish of the House of Commons (and in particular the European Legislation Committee) to be kept in touch with developments and not simply presented with *faits accomplis*. Governments cannot argue that this is impossible because of the Danish example, although the UK is active on a wider range of issues than Denmark. The problem with negotiating is that the final positions of the participants cannot be revealed publicly without pre-empting possible solutions. Until we entered the EC this occurred largely in the areas of foreign affairs and defence, areas traditionally in the power of the executive. The difference now is that it occurs in a wide spread of domestic policy issues. The House of Commons is only too aware of its limited powers, and membership of the EC has moved policy-making even further from the control of the House. The real restraint on ministers in this field therefore may be their unwillingness to remind the House too clearly of its powerlessness.

There were also tensions in the Labour Government over the role of the Foreign Office. Harold Wilson 'was concerned that if all the official work were concentrated in the Foreign Office we should run into serious difficulties with ministers since it was widely suspected that the Foreign Office was so committed to membership of the EC that they would tend to use their position to override the interests of other departments' (Wilson, 1979, p. 54). It was for this reason that he retained the European Secretariat in the Cabinet Office, although he did put ministerial responsibility back in the FCO. Tony Benn feels that 'the Foreign Office influence on Whitehall is now quite pernicious because the Foreign Office can properly claim that every bit of economic policy, industrial policy, social policy, is now European policy and has to be fed through them' (Young and Sloman, 1982, p. 80). This is a view confirmed by Roy Hattersley, Minister of State in the FCO 1974–76 and during that time very heavily involved in EC business: 'The Foreign Office has been transformed by our membership of the EEC. It now interferes in and is concerned with subjects which were not its proper province ten years ago. Foreign Office civil servants are interfering in agricultural prices; they're interfering in economic policy; they're interfering in energy policy' (Young and Sloman, 1982, p. 81). He sympathizes with the Secretary of State for Energy over this interference, but attributes the Foreign Secretary's position to a natural desire to ensure that someone has an overall view. He adds that if even Mr Benn were Foreign Secretary he would enjoy his role in this respect.

The problem is, however, much more difficult than Hattersley's description of it. Benn was extremely annoyed by the Foreign Office's insistence in 1975 that he could not publish his Industry Bill until it had been approved by the Commission. 'I absolutely declined to agree and the Bill was published. But I've no doubt that that Bill had been shown to the Commission before it was shown to the House of Commons' (Young and Sloman, 1982, p. 74). In fact, member countries must notify the Commission within two months of any financial aid which they propose to give their industry in case it infringes Community rules on unfair competition. Part of the Bill was clearly affected by this obligation, something that the Department of Industry should have pointed out to their Minister. What this example demonstrates is less the insidious power of the FCO than the fact that membership of the EC has radically changed the traditional autonomy of the Cabinet minister. Politicians and parties can no longer freely invent policies, they must do so within the framework of Community rules. It is not just civil servants who must 'think European'.

One duty of the Foreign Office is to ensure that domestic policies do not infringe EC commitments. This seems to be something which bothers ministers (in the Labour Government at least) more than civil servants. Indeed, the Foreign Office see themselves as having a decreasing role to play in this respect since civil servants in the home departments now have a great deal of expertise and experience in European affairs, more indeed than their FCO counterparts.

CONCLUSION

The Civil Service organized itself quickly and effectively for Community work, making use of the scarce expertise available at the time of entry and offering training to key staff in language and negotiation skills. It has also established co-ordinating arrangements at both departmental and central level which have maintained some kind of control over policies being agreed in the EC by officials. This control is less obvious in the case of ministers who are accountable to the Cabinet and the House of Commons but not mandated by them. Many British ministers have resisted the mandate arguing that they must have greater flexibility in negotiations than it would allow. It is worth asking however, whether more stringent instructions would not in fact strengthen the position of ministers in the negotiations.

NOTES AND REFERENCES

1. I am extremely grateful to Helen Wallace for reading this chapter and making very helpful comments. The most useful references on this area are the writings of Helen Wallace (see bibliography); Sir Christopher Soames, 'Whitehall into Europe', *Public Administration*, vol. 50, 1972, pp. 271–9; Hugo Young and Anne Sloman: *No Minister*, BBC, 1982, pp. 73–85; and Juliet Gibbs, 'The French and British National Administrations and the European Community', Unpublished M.Sc. thesis, University of Bristol, 1977.
2. Information for this section was derived from interviews with British officials. Gibbs, *op. cit.*, (1977) was also used extensively.

CHAPTER FIVE

The Community Dimension to the Machinery of Government

In the preceding two chapters the effects of EC membership were considered in relation to Parliament and the executive and administrative branches of government. This chapter covers the various roles that British officials and politicians can play within the institution of the EC or those associated with the EC. Meyer (1974) examined the roles of British civil servants working for Britain in the EC and Britons working in the EC for the Commission. He considered that the two groups could be distinguished by simply viewing the British civil servants as carrying out their normal duties with the additional requirement of working with other national civil servants, Commission officials in Brussels in the regular working groups, and management committees. The British civil servant would continue to owe loyalty as before to Britain. However, Meyer viewed the Britons working for the EC as a separate group owing loyalty to the Community.

This neat theoretical distinction tends, however, to become blurred in practice. Britain, like other EC countries, not only positively seeks to maintain a certain general level of national presence in the EC, but also tries to put forward candidates for vacant Commission senior grade administrative officer posts. This policy has the dual advantages of maximizing British influence in the Commission and providing British officials on leave of absence with first-hand experience of the EC system.

In addition to official level links British politicians can work in the European Parliament. The nominated British MEPs provided from 1973 to 1979 a link between Parliament and the EC. This was the period when MEPs (MPs or Peers) were delegates from the Commons and Lords. These nominated MEPs also provided the electorate with an indirect representation in the EC. Since 1979 the existence of a directly elected EP has largely broken the link, always somewhat tenuous, between Westminster and the EP. The directly elected MEPs do, however, provide the means for a closer relationship to exist between the interests of British voters and the EC policy process.

Direct elections to the EP have also been a cause of the continuing British political conflict over the desirability of EC membership. Direct elections cause political conflicts because they raise the spectre of EC institutions having federalist aspirations, and because the implication of a uniform EC electoral system is the introduction of a proportional representation voting system in England, Scotland and Wales.

The Community dimension to the machinery of government will be examined by looking firstly at the British delegation to the Community, known as UKREP. This delegation or embassy is the focus for Britain's official links with the EC policy process. Secondly, the British 'quota' of Commission officials will be considered. This 'quota' provides opportunities for unofficial and indirect links between the British and EC systems. Lastly, the work of the MEPs and their domestic political links will be considered. The MEPs can provide both direct and indirect links between Britain and the EC.

UKREP

The permanent official British link with the EC, UKREP, acts as a channel of communication with the EC for Whitehall. Communications go formally through the FCO to UKREP. UKREP officials participate in the average of 100 days of COREPER meetings per year. COREPER itself works at two levels; COREPER I is the meeting of deputies to ambassadors. COREPER II is the meeting of the full ambassadors who discuss foreign affairs and politically sensitive Community business. When Britain holds the EC Council presidency the British ambassador to COREPER becomes the chairman of COREPER and then 'he is a crucial figure in the handling of all Community business' (Henig, 1980, p. 33). The conduct of the more routine COREPER I business has been described by Bill Nicoll, a former British Deputy Permanent Representative. He states: 'We, around the table, speak to our instructions . . . Most of the time, therefore, we are engaged in what the Belgians . . . call the policy (or politics) of "little steps"' (Drew, 1979, pp. 15–16).

The staffing level of UKREP has remained fairly constant since 1973 at around 40 officials. The Whitehall departments which have been most affected by EC entry are represented at a senior level in UKREP. Overall the posts in UKREP are filled roughly on an equal numerical basis by diplomats from the FCO and officials seconded to the FCO from the home Civil Service. However, the post of Ambassador has always been filled by a senior diplomat from the FCO. To date the ambassadors have been Sir Michael Palliser, Sir Donald Maitland and now Sir Michael Butler. Sir Michael Palliser was an obvious choice as the first Ambassador because he had considerable experience of EC affairs. He had been Minister at the British Embassy in Paris and Private Secretary to Prime Minister Wilson. The deputy to the Ambassador does not have to come from the FCO. In April 1977 when Sir Donald Maitland was appointed Ambassador, his deputy was a senior official of the Department of Trade. Sir Donald made some interesting comments on his post, remarking: 'The tariff has taken over from the gunboat as the main instrument of diplomacy, and in Brussels we are in the front-line of a revolution in the nature and conduct of British foreign policy. I feel myself much more an extension of London than an Ambassador' (*The Times*, 25 April 1977). This point was reinforced by the regular presence of UKREP officials at meetings in Whitehall.

The issue of being an 'extension of London' has been noted as part of a more general problem for the administration of Britain's EC policy. Helen Wallace (1973, pp. 92–3) has argued that although there is a 'basic infrastructure in Whitehall of expertise and of procedures for handling the requirements of membership', there remains a problem of how to alternate personnel between service in the EC and in the home departments. Staff have to be found to man EC-related positions at home, in UKREP, and to fill vacancies in the Commission.

An adequately staffed and expert 'European' element in the Civil Service is very necessary because UKREP cannot handle all the EC business. The many working groups of the Council of Ministers need a British Civil Service representation and many civil servants who are experts on such topics as exhaust emissions, veterinary regulations, petrodollars and company law etc. have to go to Brussels each week. In this context Michelman (1978, pp. 32–33) has noted that UKREP really forms part of a triangular policy-making relationship between itself, the Commission and the government departments at home. UKREP does of course have a special separate responsibility for the operation of the EPC machinery for Britain when the EC is preparing foreign policy on matters outside the treaties.

In the EC policy, although the Commission's policy proposals go through COREPER where UKREP officials are present, the Commission first consults directly with officials and experts in member states. In fact this is really the most important policy preparation link between the EC and Britain's machinery of government. In fact, in major areas of EC policy, such as the CAP, there will be continuous dialogue between British officials and Commission officials. Even in the slower moving areas, such as harmonization proposals, there may still be continuous dialogue.

BRITONS IN THE COMMISSION

With such a close working relationship existing between member states' government departments and the Commission the placement of nationals in potentially influential Commission posts can be seen by states as contributing to their influence in the EC. Although, officially, such a relationship between the Commission and member governments is not supposed to exist. Indeed, Hull and Rhodes (1977, pp. 2–3) in their study focusing mainly on local government relations with the EC, comment that the EC also 'has effects (impacts *and* participation) on sub-national units of government'.

British governments have taken great care in the selection of nationals to fill the two Commissioner posts in their nomination. As was mentioned earlier these appointments are made by the exercise of the patronage power of the Prime Minister. The first Commissioners were Sir Christopher Soames and Mr George Thomson, and both were obvious choices to represent the major parties in British politics. Sir Christopher Soames, a leading Conservative politician, had been Minister of Agriculture 1960–64, and consequently played a part in the negotiations with the EC of that period. Subsequently he was Ambassador to France 1968–72, during the final period of negotiations. George Thomson was a leading Labour politician and as Chancellor of the Duchy of Lancaster, he had special responsibility for European affairs and was the Labour Government's chief negotiator on entry. Edward Heath, as Prime Minister, appointed both men; George Thomson's appointment was made after consultation with the Leader of the Opposition (Harold Wilson).

This policy of filling the Commissioner posts from politicians of the two leading parties has been continued. In 1977 Roy Jenkins was appointed to succeed George Thomson. However, it is important to remember that the power of appointment does rest solely with the Prime Minister, and the Prime Minister is under no obligation (or constitutional convention) to consult with the Leader of the Opposition, or take the advice from such a consultation. For example, in November 1976 when a successor to Sir Christopher Soames had to be appointed, Margaret Thatcher, then Leader of the Opposition, was considering among others either John Davies (former Minister for Industry), or Sir Peter Kirk (Leader of the Conservative delegation to the European Parliament). However, Prime Minister James Callaghan offered the appointment to the Conservative MP Christopher Tugendhat. Two reasons were suggested for this appointment; firstly, a desire to have as the second commissioner a young rising politician as opposed to one with a distinguished past. Secondly, Christopher Tugendhat had become an expert on the oil industry and energy problems. Energy was becoming an important EC topic and one in which Britain was taking a keen interest. The Labour Party, after some selection difficulty given the Party's attitude to the EC, put forward Ivor Richard, who had been a Parliamentary Under-Secretary for Defence (Army) and UK representative to the UN 1974–79, to succeed Roy Jenkins in January 1981.

Each Commissioner has his own *cabinet* and the Civil Service takes an interest in the people chosen by the Commissioners for their *cabinets*. This is because the cabinet is responsible for 'managing communications between member state and commissioner', and acting as 'political trouble-shooters particularly as this relates to contacts with national sources' (Michelman, 1978, p. 18). Moreover the *cabinet* also has an important role in trying to arrange the nationality balance in the Commission.

Below the Commissioner level, Britain has a 'quota' of some 20 per cent of other Commission posts. However, this 'quota' is unofficial and is really contrary to the spirit of the personnel statute of the Commission which 'recognizes no fixed percentage of representation from any member state' (Michelmann, 1978, p. 27). Nonetheless the 'quota' is operated, although Britain has had difficulties in filling its quota share even in the top policy-making 'A' grades.

This area has recently been researched in depth by Virginia Willis (*Britons in Brussels*, 1983), and the following paragraphs are based upon her study. In general her findings confirm the view, taken in this book, that the controversies over membership affected all facets of EC entry. Willis (p. 25) comments on the general under-representation of Britons in Commission and Council secretariats: 'in the general climate of uncertainty, long-term career prospects in Community institutions whose functions were anyway barely understood and whose representatives were less than dynamic were unlikely to have widespread appeal.' In the key 'A' policy-making grades in 1974 Britons filled only 14.9 per cent of the posts (cf. France 18.5 per cent, Germany 18.7 per cent, Belgium 13.1 per cent); and by 1980 the position was actually slightly worse, at 14.3 per cent (cf. France 20.4 per cent, Germany 18.8 per cent, Belgium 13.3 per cent). In numerical terms Willis (p. 17) estimates that Britain needs another 91 nationals to fill 'A' grade posts. Britain is also under-represented in the lower grades.

In Britain, the initial post-entry recruitment to fill the British quota was carried out by a special unit in the Civil Service Department with the Cabinet Office exercising oversight. An important early problem was that 'Within the Civil Service jobs in Community institutions at any level had no widespread appeal [thus] . . . there was no question of the British contingent in Brussels consisting of 75 per cent civil servants, as had been supposed by the CSD [Civil Service Department]' (Willis, (p. 32). To persuade civil servants to go to Brussels it was necessary to devise a scheme to allow them to return to their UK posts after a few years. The quota therefore could only be even partly filled by going to the private sector for recruits and, apart from Europhiles, as with the Civil Service, there was notable lack of enthusiasm.

National interests in EC posts were identified by ministers at the time of entry: 'They decided that first in order of importance were economic and monetary policy, industrial policy, external trade relations, regional policy and agriculture. Ranked second priority were transport (later upgraded), science and technology, and aid to developing countries' (Willis, 1983, p. 39). In the five key areas the Government aim was to have a Briton as Director-General or at least Deputy Director-General. Whitehall departments were also considering lower level posts likely to be of special interest.

Initially, in the 'A' grades civil servants accounted for about one-third of the British contribution. Somewhat predictably the largest numbers came from departments most closely involved with EC matters, MAFF, Customs and Excise, Inland Revenue and Trade and Industry. However, with reference to placing Britons in posts closely related to the Government's interests, Willis (1983, p. 17) suggests that this did not really happen until 1977 when Roy Jenkins became Commission President and Christopher Tugendhat took on the Budget, Financial Institutions and Personnel and Administration Portfolios. It was then possible for Britons to hold the External Affairs and Energy Directorates, and thus 'The range of A1 posts held by Britons was appropriate for an energy-rich nation dependent on external trade, with an interest in these areas and experience and expertise to offer.'

Commenting on the response in Whitehall to the issue of arranging adequate British staffing in the EC, Willis writes:

> Though by the end of the decade of her accession the UK had developed seemingly satisfactory machinery and methods to deal with the differing aspects of Community staffing, some problems might never have arisen in the form or extent that they did had there not been the period of uncertainty and near disengagement so soon after entry.

In fact Willis contends that after the initial efforts to fill EC posts the Civil Service took no significant interest in British postings until about 1977–78. Interest in these opportunities for Britons to serve in the Commission is important because, except for some very senior 'A' posts, nomination or 'parachuting' nationals in is no longer generally acceptable to the Commission. Therefore nationals need to be encouraged to apply for junior 'A' grade posts in order to qualify for promotion to the senior grades. Since 1978 ministers and ambassadors to the EC have also urged (Willis, 1983, p. 77) upon the Commission a policy of positive discrimination in favour of British candidates to raise the British element to a comparable size with France and Germany. Not surprisingly the Commission has resisted this pressure.

There is now an official policy of supporting Britons as candidates for vacancies in the Commission or Council Secretariats. The candidates may be civil servants, Britons already in the Commission or from the public sector. Reports from UKREP are important in providing full information on vacancies and when a candidate is proposed support may be sought through UKREP to the EC Director-General or Director level or from ministers to Commissioners. The policy is operated by 'Euro-watchers' in government departments, usually officials with considerable EC experience, keeping a close watch on the Commission for suitable vacancies. Vacancies and potential candidates are then considered by an inter-departmental 'Euro-staff committee' consisting of departmental representatives, representatives from the old Civil Service Department (now Management and Personnel Office) and the European Secretariat of the Cabinet Office. It is Willis's contention that this system can 'favour recruits from within the Civil Service who are most accessible to the Management and Personnel Office and whose suitability is most easily verified by known, i.e. Civil Service criteria' (Willis, 1983, p. 78).

In addition to permanent appointments there are opportunities for temporary appointments (*agents temporaires*) (Willis 1983, pp. 81–3) and on a similar basis, for experts from national administration to go to the Commission for periods from three months to two years 'under arrangements made precisely to develop better relationships between the Commission and public administration'. Britain in 1979 and 1980 sent the largest number of experts to Brussels of any member state. Britain has also taken advantage of an exchange scheme where civil servants go to the Commission for short attachments. Under this arrangement the officials who go to Brussels tend 'to be single and to be at Higher Executive Officer 'A' or Principal level and they come most frequently from Customs and Excise, the Ministry of Agriculture, Fisheries and Food, the Department of the Environment, Employment and Industry and the Nationalized industries' (Willis, 1983, pp. 82–3).

Overall, the official British policy towards EC posts is to maintain a fair balance of British officers in the Commission to help ensure that Britain's view is understood and fully taken into account in policy-making. Also Whitehall departments now appreciate the benefits of having officials with recent experience of working in the EC returning after short secondments. However, Willis, (1983, p. 94) is quite correct to contend that the maximization of British influence in the EC would be helped by 'the establishment of a political climate more generally favourable to the Community and Britain's part within it'.

BRITAIN AND THE DELEGATED EUROPEAN PARLIAMENT

In the preceding discussions of the relationship between the
political system in Britain and the British portion of the EC
system, distinct and officially supported links are evident.
However, when the relationship between the British political
system and the European Parliament is considered, no such
clear links exist. The relationship between the European
Parliament and the British political system can be said to
include the contribution of the European Parliament to the
more general national parliamentary function of scrutinizing
EC affairs, the role played by MEPs in the domestic political
system, and the link between 'Euro' political parties and the
national political parties. Care must be exercised in drawing
conclusions on the relationship because of the time periods
involved.

First, from January 1973 to June 1979, Britain was participating in a delegated European parliamentary system where
MPs and peers from Westminster were simply delegated to
serve in the European Parliament. Moreover, within this
period the British party system was not always fully represented, as from January 1973 to July 1975 the Labour party
refused to nominate any delegates to the European Parliament as part of the protest at EC entry being carried out on
Prime Minister Heath's terms. Second, the period of experience with a directly elected European Parliament is quite
brief, dating in terms of sittings only from July 1979.

In the next few paragraphs there is an examination of the
period of full British delegated representation in the European Parliament, from July 1975 to June 1979, the period
since June 1979, with directly elected MEPs, and the issue of
a uniform electoral system for the European elections.
Although the period of delegated representation is now
mostly of historical interest, it does provide some information on the contribution that can be made by elected
representatives with EC experience to the evaluation of EC
affairs in Britain.

This contribution has been well analysed by David Brew
(1979, pp. 238–60) using data from interviews with 17 MPs,

eight of whom were MEPs and 11 peers, five of whom were MEPs. He makes the important comment that 'it is not reasonable blithely to assume that (Westminster EC) scrutineers and British MEPs have a community of interest in pursuing the same goals.' A major factor mitigating against close ties is the sheer physical problem that existed for the delegated MEP, of coping with the conflicting time demands of Westminster, the European Parliament, the constituency, and home life. Another problem was the difference in attitude between the political parties to their MP/MEPs. The Labour party particularly did not make many active efforts to utilize the knowledge of its MP/MEP. It has already been noted that MEPs who did assist scrutiny committees did so in a personal capacity, not wearing a 'MEP hat'. Indeed, the Commons Scrutiny Committee did not see its task as including efforts to develop links with the European Parliament. Interviewees were unanimous in seeing 'a need for thorough national scrutiny for a long time after direct elections' (Brew, 1979, p. 248).

The Labour party's eighteen-strong delegation was studied in depth by Kevin Featherstone (1979), who provides some useful material to supplement Brew's analysis. Featherstone's interviewees' references to the value of participation in the European Parliament are particularly interesting. They felt that the EP provided another forum in which British representatives could attempt to influence EC policies. Also, the EP could provide a forum for debates on topics on which a British government may not wish to allocate parliamentary time. In particular, MEPs found that the EP's committees provided an opportunity for a much closer questioning of ministers from the Council of Ministers and officials from the Commission than would be possible in a Westminster Select Committee. However, the majority of Labour MEPs felt that '"the means available" to pass on their knowledge from the European Parliament were unsatisfactory' (Featherstone, 1979, p. 95).

Probably the most important conclusion from the Brew and Featherstone studies is the sheer human and occupational problems of a legislative system involving representatives holding dual mandates as MPs and MEPs. Featherstone finds that the data 'shows that the average Labour MEP took part in only half the number of Commons' divisions entered into by his typical Labour (non-MEP) colleague'. This, as Featherstone further notes, 'suggests a dilemma for the future: the present system of the dual mandate encourages a feeling of distance and thus a lack of accountability between the national and European bench – precisely the arguments used against its abolition.' Probably the most that could be said for the dual mandate system was that the MP/MEP had the opportunity, time permitting, to make a contribution at Westminster, in the various ways open to an MP, on the basis of deeper knowledge of EC affairs.

THE ISSUE OF DIRECT ELECTIONS TO THE EUROPEAN PARLIAMENT

Before considering how the Government and Parliament reacted to the issue of holding direct elections to the EP, it is necessary to examine the arguments about the likely effect upon the role of the EP of its members being directly elected. This is because the main political parties had a strong dislike of any EC institution developing a federal role, and there was specific concern that the EP could come to overshadow national legislatures in the scrutiny of EC affairs. Herman and Lodge (1978, p. 73 f) cite five possible arguments against direct elections that particularly relate to the generally critical attitude of British political parties to the EP. These arguments concern

(1) potential loss of national parliamentary sovereignty;
(2) waste of time, given the limited powers of the EP;
(3) lack of saliency of EP affairs to national voters;
(4) logistical problems of conducting a supranational campaign;
(5) dispersal of political talent between national parliaments and the EP.

David Marquand (1979, p. 115) succinctly summarizes some of these problems in his statement that: 'A prerequisite of a people's Europe is a parliamentary Europe: a prerequisite of a parliamentary Europe is a party Europe.' European political parties, as political parties are understood in Britain, are at present far from being established.

The immediate significance of direct elections was recognized by Helen Wallace (1979, p. 281) who argued that 'the mere fact of the election being held at all is an event of considerable significance, precisely because the member governments have accepted that the EC are qualitatively different from any other international organization to which they belong.' This comment relates to a key problem identified by Herman and Lodge (1978, p. 75) in examining the justifications for direct elections, namely the issue of how states view the political legitimacy of the EC. Do states want to increase the 'democratic legitimacy' of the EP and the Community, and would an increase produce conflicts of interest with national legislatures?

This question of conflicts of interest can only be answered by looking at the record of the directly elected EP and making speculations about its possible development. The former task is quite easy; the EP has not shown any signs of actively wooing voters' allegiances from their national political system, nor have the EP's powers of scrutiny developed in any way that has made Parliament's scrutiny less necessary. Indeed, at times the EP has been seen to be involved in very parochial issues, such as the site for its sittings and questions relating to MEPs' expenses.

Among speculations about how the directly elected EP could influence the EC policy process, is Helen Wallace's (1979) view that the EP could be a form of lobby, perform an educative function for other EC institutions on how citizens feel, and articulate 'more explicitly the overtly political dimensions of the policy options which member governments are engaged in exploring'. Roger Morgan takes a more expanded view of future tasks that the EP might perform. He suggests (1979, pp. 401–2) that the EP must carry out an effective representative function between the EC and the electorate, make an effort to control the work of the Commission and Council of Ministers, endeavour to 'think ahead' about EC development, and participate in the EC's external relations. Geoffrey and Pippa Pridham (1979, p. 63) consider that as any formal changes in the EP are unlikely given the attitudes of some member states to EC institutions developing new powers, it is necessary to look at the possibility of developments in the transnational party groups which play 'the dominant role within the Parliament'. Moreover, the practical reduction of dual mandates makes the party group a potentially important link between the EP and national parliaments. The party group is also important (G. and P. Pridham, 1979, p. 63) as an agent to assert 'the European Parliament's validity as a representative institution', and as a proponent for '"democratizing" the structure of the European Community, this being the principle argument for holding direct elections'. However, the Pridhams (1979, pp. 64–5) find that the party groups have only achieved a very limited amount of progress towards party political integration. Thus none of these speculations about future developments for the EP seem to suggest that it is actually likely to diminish the powers of Parliament. Nor does it seem likely that the voters will see the MEP as a more important representative than the MP.

In Britain the period of preparation for direct elections began in November 1975 when the Foreign Secretary, Mr James Callaghan, outlined to Parliament (899 HC Deb. Cols. 946–7) what he considered to be the main issues for discussion. The discussions did not end until 1978 when a Bill to provide for direct elections to the EP was finally passed and the Boundary Commission's proposals for the new Euro-constituencies were approved by Parliament. On this period 1975–78, Butler and Marquand (1981, p. 2) argue that while the actual EC entry, the associated controversies and the questions about EC laws '. . . had left little obvious mark on the everyday working of Parliament or the political parties. Direct elections penetrated further and more obviously into the working of the system.' They further note that preparing for direct elections involved a number of significant events in British politics, a government advocated the use of of proportional representation in national elections, the collective responsibility of the cabinet was waived on the issue, direct elections played a part in the Liberal–Labour pact and the the parties had new political, administrative, ideological and personnel problems.

It has already been shown that the controversies over EC membership affected the pre-entry period and the post-entry conduct of relations with the EC. It can also be demonstrated that these controversies affected the British approach to direct elections.[1] The Wilson Labour Government response to critics of direct elections was that Article 138 (3) (EEC), regarding the holding of elections, was a mandatory obligation which now had to be implemented because the referendum had decided the issue of principle for EC membership. However, the Government did not believe that it could be ready to meet the EC's target date for the first elections of June 1978 because of the political and administrative difficulties which were involved.

Foreign Secretary James Callaghan, whose department was responsible for the handling of the issue, suggested to Parliament that the major issues for Britain in preparing for direct elections the EP were:

(1) the preparation of the electoral roll;
(2) the franchise for the election;
(3) the method of election;
(4) the entitlement to be a candidate;
(5) whether MPs could or should also be MEPs (the question of the dual mandate);
(6) the constituency boundaries;
(7) the financial arrangements for the elections.

The initial Community proposals on direct elections were based upon the report of a Dutch member of the EP, Mr Scheldo Patijn. Patijn's proposals were for an enlargement of the EP from 198 members to 355, all to be directly elected initially by each state's national electoral system; members were to serve for five years and could also be members of their national parliaments; the allocation of seats was to be related to the population of each country with a weighting in favour of smaller states – this would have given Britain 67 seats. Under Patijn's proposals the 'big four', Britain, France, Germany and Italy would have had different sized representation in the EP. In addition Patijn's report proposed that the second direct elections should be under a uniform EC-wide electoral system.

As the debate in Britain proceded the main arguments tended to centre on five questions:

(1) Was a directly elected EP a challenge to Parliament's powers because of 'federalist' implications?
(2) Could or should MEPs have some form of dual mandate?
(3) What were the political implications of the boundaries of electoral districts?
(4) What number of seats should be allocated to the regions of the United Kingdom?
(5) Could Britain come into line with the other EC states from the beginning and adopt an electoral system based upon proportional representation?

In one respect, the distribution of seats, Britain was helped by the other major states in the EC. Under the nominated MEP system each of the 'big four' had 36 seats. This equality of treatment they clearly favoured as in July 1976 the European Council revised Patijn's proposals to enlarge the EP to 410 seats[2] and give each of the 'big four' an allocation of 81 seats. British politicians had been unhappy with the original allocation of 67 seats because of the difficulty of satisfying regional aspirations, given the rise in support for the Scottish and Welsh nationalists. In September 1976 the Council of Foreign Ministers signed the legal instrument for direct elections but they left the election date unfixed. Both France and Britain had expressed doubts as to whether they could complete their national preliminary arrangements in time for elections in June 1978.

Among the political parties the Liberals gave unqualified support for direct elections and were able from March 1977, via the Lib–Lab pact, to 'impose the early introduction of legislation, as promised in the 1976 Queen's Speech and favourable consideration of the Liberal views on PR' (Fitzmaurice, 1978, p. 76). The Conservatives too supported direct elections but with somewhat less enthusiasm although they were still keen to appear to the electorate as the major pro-EC party. However, for the Labour party, the issue of direct elections was to raise again the strong feelings, pro- and anti-EC, that had long existed in the party. As Joel

Barnett (1981, p. 128) commented: 'mention of the three letters EEC opened all the old wounds.' He also considered the exchanges in the cabinet on direct elections were 'the worst I had seen on any subject.' The opponents of EC direct elections in the Labour party were concerned not to appear to strengthen the political legitimacy of the EC, and to discourage federalist tendencies in that body. They believed that the use of PR in EC elections could only only fuel pressures for PR in the Westminster elections.

The Government opened the debate in February 1976 with a Green Paper 'Direct Elections to the European Assembly' (Cmnd 6398) prepared by the Home Office. This was followed by the consideration of the issue in the Commons and Lords. The Lords EC Scrutiny Committee was able to make the report on direct elections because of its wider remit. In the Commons, because of the narrower remit of its EC Committee, a special Select Committee had to be appointed in May 1976. Of its 13 members only two were known antimarketeers. Fizmaurice (1978, p. 81) points out that 'It was unusual in having a government minister as a member (Mr Roy Hattersley) and in that its composition had been the subject of fierce debate.'

The House of Lords Report on direct elections (HL 119) favoured the availability of an optional dual mandate for MEPs, i.e. that they could also be MPs if they were so elected. The Lords Report also favoured the use of PR, to bring Britain into line with the rest of the EC states and to avoid unrepresentative results. For example, it was clear that the simple majority system would work to the disadvantage of the Liberals. The Report suggested that the single proportional vote system used for the Northern Ireland Assembly provided a precedent for the use of a special electoral system in special circumstance. The first Report of the Commons Select Committee (HC 849, 1976) also advocated the optional dual mandate. The Committee's second Report (HC 515, 1976) suggested that electoral procedure should closely follow the Westminster elections procedure, including the simple majority system, and that all UK citizens (including peers) should be eligible to vote. Also because constituencies were to be larger, the Committee suggested changes in the

financial arrangements of the election, increased deposit
(£1,000) to be forfeit unless 12.5 per cent of the votes were
won.

During the spring of 1977 the deep split in Prime Minister
James Callaghan's Cabinet led him to modify the application
of the constitutional convention of Cabinet collective responsibility for legislation. However, the Cabinet was warned
(Barnett, 1981, p. 128) that he would end his leadership if the
party came out against direct elections. Thus ministers were
allowed to vote against the principle of direct elections but
not speak against the Bill. The Government's Direct Elections Bill (Cmnd 6768, 1977) contained a choice for Parliament: either the adoption of a regional electional system
incorporating an element of PR, or the normal simple
majority electoral system. However, the Cabinet formally
indicated its preference for the PR system. The system
recommended was the d'Hondt system which works by
allocating seats to the party with the highest average vote/
seat in order of highest averages. Under the regional list
system the parties would have put forward a party list of
candidates for each region and each voter would cast one vote
for their chosen candidate. If Parliament chose to use the
Westminster electoral system then boundaries would be
drawn for single-member constituencies, each constituency
equalling two plus Westminster constituencies. The Bill
recommended that Britain's 81 seats be distributed as follows: 66 to England, eight to Scotland, four to Wales and
three to Northern Ireland.

The debates in the Commons in autumn 1977 on the
Direct Elections Bill centred on the issue of the allocation of
seats to the regions of the UK, the choice of the electoral
system and the introduction into the Bill of a 'political' clause
declaring limits to the extension of the powers of the EP.
Finally on 13 December 1977 the Commons rejected the PR
clause by 319 votes to 222. The Bill was reintroduced in early
1978 without the PR clause but with a clause to require a
future government to obtain an authorizing Act of Parliament before it could agree to any changes in the powers of
the EP which might encroach on the powers of Westminster.
The Bill did not forbid MPs from standing for election as

MEPs, thus allowing the optional dual mandate, but the Conservative leader Mrs Thatcher let it be known that she did not favour this, and the Labour party was positively against MPs being MEPs.

Why the vote against PR? It was after all due to be introduced for the second round of elections to the EP. Butler and Marquand (1981, p. 39) note that the Government had advocated PR, not just to keep the Liberals happy but also 'because it would make the result in seats less disastrous for Labour and because it could be introduced at once, without the delays involved in a Boundary Commission'. However, some of the Labour opposition was in fact to the system proposed as they feared that it would only lead to more conflicts between candidates of the same party. Otherwise the bulk of the opposition to PR (Labour 147 for, 115 against; Conservative 61 for, 198 against) seems to have been on the traditional grounds that if used as a precedent for reform of the Westminster electoral system it could spell the demise of the two-party system and produce unwanted coalition governments.

The European Assembly Election Act received the Royal Assent on 5 May 1978 and the proposals of the Boundary Commission were approved in December 1978. The new Euro-constituencies were designed to cover as nearly as possible a number of Westminster constituencies, to produce an equality in electoral areas of one MEP to 516,436 votes (UK votes divided by the number of seats). Northern Ireland was an exception, being considered one electoral district and voting under PR. Elections for the EP were to be conducted under the same regulations as Westminster elections, with minor modifications. The candidate's deposit was to be £600, forfeit if the candidate polled less than one-eighth of the vote. Election expenses were fixed at £5,000 plus two pence per elector; as an example, in a 500,000 voter constituency up to £15,000 of expenses would be permitted. At one stage it had been proposed to establish some sort of uniform MEP salary; however, this was resisted, especially in Britain, as it would have meant greatly increasing the British payment to representatives to meet higher continental salaries. Thus, in December 1978 the Council of Ministers agreed that MEPs should receive the same salary as their respective national MPs. Because not all the EC states had been ready for direct election in 1978, June 1979 was fixed as the date for the first direct election.

One important issue was not settled in Britain before the direct elections, nor indeed has it really been settled since then. This was the nature and status of the MEPs in relation to Westminster. The problem was considered by the House of Lords in a Report (HL 256) published in August 1978. The Report was especially concerned that the natural direct links which existed when MEPs were delegated MPs and peers would no longer exist, except in a very few instances where MPs or peers opted to stand and were elected as MEPs. The Report advocated the establishment of a 'Grand Committee' to consist of the 81 MEPs and the members of the Commons and Lords Scrutiny Committees, which would meet at least three times a year. It also advocated formal links between the parliamentary Scrutiny Committees, the MEPs and the committees of the European Parliament. However nothing was done about the Report at the time, and in the Commons the matter was referred, eventually, to the Commons's Services Committee.

THE FIRST EP DIRECT ELECTION

In the following analysis of the British preparation for the EP election campaign, it must be remembered that by chance the timing of the European election came only a few weeks after the surprise April 1979 general election which ousted James Callaghan's minority Labour Government in favour of a Conservative Government under Mrs Thatcher, with a clear working majority. Consequently, conclusions about the Euro-election campaign and the results can only be of a tentative nature.

Once European direct elections were evidently going to occur the parties had to prepare their selections of candidates for them. Martin Holland (1981, p. 28) has argued that 'the emergence of a directly elected European Parliament has caused all three major parties to develop new approaches and procedures.' So far in this study it has not been necessary to deal in any detail with the political parties except to note where the views of a particular party on EC membership affected the conduct of government. However, as it is now being pointed that there is a new dimension to British government with an EC portion, the new representative element in this must be considered in some detail. It should be noted that the MEP is not, except where he or she is also an MP or peer, formally part of the domestic political system. The MEP represents us in the Parliament of the EC and can, in effect, be considered to give the voter an alternative way of having interests represented, particularly as the EC's area of interest is now quite broad, even if in some cases the EC only possesses very general powers. The MEPs themselves will also usually want to be part of the domestic political system, principally because they will usually be members of one of the main parties. They may well be young politicians who see being an MEP as a sort of apprenticeship for being an MP, or they may be former or sitting MPs who view being an MEP as a new career or a new part of an existing career. The MEPs will also need to try and make a domestic impact if only to improve their chances of re-election. This could take a number of forms: maintaining a highly visible presence in the constituency, developing links with their parliamentary party, and trying to ensure that EC issues are properly handled by the British government. This last activity will involve developing relations with the Civil Service.

The political parties' preparatory work for direct elections has been researched by Butler and Marquand (1981), and by Holland (1981); the following paragraphs are based on these researches. The parties will be examined separately. For the Labour party with its strong anti-EC lobby, the first hurdle was to accept the desirability of fighting the election under at least a broad EC socialist group manifesto. However, as each country's socialist party was free to draw up its own national manifesto, the Labour Party's National Executive Committee (NEC) was able to fill the vacuum in the party structure because there was no formal machinery for preparing the Euro-election manifesto. The NEC was pleased to do this as it then had the opportunity to reflect its anti-market bias and make the manifesto an uncomfortable platform for Labour pro-market MEPs. For example, the manifesto commenced by saying 'The promises and forecasts of the benefits that joining the EEC would bring had been shown to be false.' (Butler and Marquand, 1981, p. 59). However, the NEC did not exercise such a tight control over the selection of candidates, in particular there was no 'centrally compiled list of approved candidates' (Holland, 1981, p. 37) as the other main parties had. The NEC did retain the ultimate power of not endorsing a candidate. In each Euro-constituency a European Selection Organization was set up, containing representatives of the constituency Labour parties. These voted for candidates in the capacity of delegates, thus: 'The rigid nature of parliamentary selections was replicated for the European dimension' (Holland, 1981, p. 40). Of Labour's 78 final candidates, Butler and Marquand (1981, pp. 65–6) comment 'just over 30 . . . could be classed as pro-Marketeers [and] the remainder divided evenly between "hard" and "soft" anti-Marketeers'. They were also 'a very white collar contingent'; 29 of the 78 were either teachers or lecturers.

Unlike the Labour party, direct elections were no threat to the Conservative party because, as has been shown already, 'Europe was a Conservative issue' (Butler and Marquand, 1981, p. 162). As early as 1976–77 it was arranged that the National Union of Conservative Associations should run the direct elections. Central Office, through the Standing Advisory Committee on European Candidates (EuroSAC) produced a list of some 200–250 approved candidates; from these Conservative Euro-councils in the Euro-constituencies could make their choice. Unlisted candidates could be selected by constituencies but they had to be approved by the EuroSAC. By contrast with the Labour party the Conservatives did see an advantage in having just a few MPs holding dual mandate as MEPs. Although 'the preliminary stages in the recruitment process paralleled the Westminster experience almost exactly', the type of candidate enlisted was significantly different: 'industrialists, diplomats, administrators and those from the business sector predominated' (Holland 1981, p. 34).

Overall, Holland (1981, p. 45) believes that Euro-elections did give the Conservative and Labour parties the chance 'to experiment with a limited form of participation' in their selection processes. The selections produced an election result that meant that 'The standard blue-print Euro-MP has a business or professional background.'[3] This further confirms the observable trend since the 1960s of the EC being an issue dominated by the élite groups in British society.

It has been acknowledged that the direct elections campaign for the EC as a whole was disappointing, and the overall 61 per cent electoral turnout less than the expectations of around a 70 per cent turnout. In fact Britain had the lowest electoral turnout of 33 per cent. Butler and Marquand (1981, pp. 124–5) feel that, whilst the results of the April general election certainly had a deadening effect on campaigning and voters' interest, the direct elections campaign had its own particular problems. Firstly, it was a different type of election, voters were not being asked to elect a government. They were in effect being invited to register an opinion about the EC. Secondly, some voters felt that they did not really have an informed opinion to express via the ballot box.[4]

At the polls the 81 seats were contested by 283 candidates. Apart from the Scottish and Welsh Nationalist parties, 16 other minor parties fielded candidates on platforms related to the EC in one way or another. The results, after correction for a subsequent by-election, were that the Conservatives polled 50 per cent of the votes and gained 59 seats, and Labour polled 33 per cent of the votes and gained 18 seats. It has been estimated that if PR had been used Labour would have gained 27 seats. The Liberals polled 13 per cent of the votes and won no seats, and the remaining seat was won by the Scottish Nationalist Party. In Northern Ireland one seat each was won by the Democratic Unionist party, the Social Democratic and Labour party and the official Unionist party. Only four of the new MEPs were also Westminster MPs.

Overall the direct elections produced (Fitzmaurice, 1980, pp. 233–4) a slight shift away from the political left to the political centre and right in the European Parliament (from 42.2 per cent of members on the left to 40.9 per cent). In arithmetic terms, therefore, the centre right European parties have a majority in the directly elected parliament. The British MEPs sit as follows: Conservatives with the European Democrats which is almost, as Fitzmaurice (1980) puts it, a 'uninational' party being composed of 61 British MEPs (Conservatives and Unionist) and three Danish MEPs. The Labour MEPs and the SDLP MEP sit with the Socialist group. The Scottish Nationalist MEP sits with the European Progressive Democrats. There appears to have been only one subsequent change from these arrangements in that Lord O'Hagan, listed in June 1981 as a Conservative, describes himself in October 1981 as sitting with the small Independent group.

THE MEPS AND THE MACHINERY OF GOVERNMENT

Butler and Marquand rightly comment (1981, p. 166) that 'the impact of the elected Parliament on British opinion and British politics will depend overwhelmingly on the conduct of the British MEPs themselves.' They suggest that if the MEPs were to have a domestic impact then they need to be able to make constituents aware of interests that can be helped by MEPs, to show their domestic political parties that their job is important to the parties, and the MEPs need to have the organizational ability to build political power bases in their consituencies. Related to the second of these is the issue of the status of the MEP as compared with the Westminster MP.

The status of the MEP at Westminster can best be described as 'lowly'. It took a year for MEPs to get passes to the closed parts of Westminster and they did not receive free papers until November 1979. The relationship was discussed by the Conservative Government but in a rather desultory fashion. It was only with the publication of the Commons Services Committee Report in Session 1979–80 that any formal basis for MEP relations with Westminster can be said to have been formulated.

The Select Committee on House of Commons (Services) reported that there was no problem in MEPs who were either MPs or former MPs gaining access to Parliament. However, the rest of the MEPs were treated as 'strangers' or ordinary members of the public. The general problems faced by MEPs in seeking to have access to parliamentary facilities were examined in the Sub-committee on Accommodation and Administration, Catering and the Library. In producing its final report the Select Committee noted that the Recommendation of its Sub-Committees (HC 461, 1979–80, pp. vii–viii) fell 'far short of meeting all the wishes of the European Members, because all three Sub-Committees had in mind the over-crowding in the Palace and the demands already being made on the limited services available to our own Members'. The Select Committee also took account of the fact that the EP would be acquiring its own London offices.

The Select Committee recommended that MEPs should have the following rights and privileges: the grant of a special pass, MEPs to be allowed access to the Upper and Lower Waiting Halls, the main Committee Corridor, the offices of the European Legislation Committee in Parliament Street and the Norman Shaw (North) Branch Library. Furthermore, the MEPs were allowed a limited use of the Strangers' Cafeteria except between 12.30 pm to 2.30 pm, and four seats were to be reserved for MEPs in the Strangers' or special galleries for listening to debates.

Of these proposed concessions that of the right of access to the main Committee Corridor is important as it would help MEPs to attend meetings of party backbench committees. In this context two MP/MEPs, James Scott Hopkins (Conservative) and Barbara Castle (Labour) stressed the value of having informal contact at Westminster. Baroness White, MEP, giving evidence, stressed that she had found the House of Lords to be much more hospitable to MEPs than the Commons. Her comment has proved to be prophetic as the Commons have taken no action, so far, on the Services Committee recommendation on facilities for MEPs.

With regard to the roles of MPs and MEPs in the EC policy process Ann Robinson (1983, p. 288) has pointed out that 'we have two layers of elected representatives each with a degree of influence, but not power, over European policy. What is now missing are formal links between the two layers.' In addition Ann Robinson has argued (1983, p. 296) that 'one reason why British MPs have shown themselves slow to develop relationships with MEPs is that they are unfamiliar with the open policy making process of Europe in which decisions are finalised only after lengthy public discussion'.

The parliamentary political parties varied in their attitude to the MEPs. The Parliamentary Labour Party (PLP) was not particularly keen to have MEPs at their party committee meetings. In fact at the start only the PLP Foreign Affairs Committee invited MEPs to attend its meetings. In this instance there was a personal factor involved as the PLP Foreign Affairs Chairman, Tam Dalyell, had been a delegated MEP. By contrast, the Conservative MPs have accepted contacts with their MEPs. However, Butler and Marquand question whether MEPs, as they gained experience, really wanted closer Westminster contacts. They suggest that MEPs began to see their role as much more related to the EC institutions. Indeed MEP Lord O'Hagan observed that 'the elected European Parliamentarian knows that he has no genuine political ally apart from his colleagues.'[5]

During the Commons Services Select Committee hearings, Barbara Castle noted (HC 461, 1979–80, pp. 4–5) that, as well as some access to Westminster, MEPs needed links with ministers and their departments in order to fully represent the interests of their constituents and the country as a whole in the Community. Barbara Castle indicated that ministers were briefing MEPs on matters concerning the UK which were coming before the EP and that ministers were giving MEPs access to parliamentary papers.

The Cabinet Office has confirmed Barbara Castle's personal experience as being general policy.[6] Departments are responsible for briefing MEPs in a factual way on any significant implications for Britain of proposals referred to the EP. If government policy on an issue has been made public the briefing would reflect that policy. Any MEP may request a factual briefing on a particular subject. If more detailed information is needed an MEP may have an oral briefing from the relevant minister. The written briefings are made available to all MEPs, even a briefing on the result of an individual request. In addition MEPs are supplied on request with free copies of government publications and the Government has agreed that letters from MEPs on EC matters will, where possible, be answered by ministers. Thus MEPs do now have a reasonable degree of access to the legislative, executive and administrative branches of government. However, because the EP has only limited powers in EC policymaking, the MEP can generally only provide a politically lightweight and low-level of input into the EC policy process. MPs seek to exert influence on EC affairs through ministers, the departments have their EC and other member state contacts, and interest groups tend to rely upon departments to exert influence on their behalf.

HOW MEPS SEE THEIR ROLE

The European Commission publication *Europe* has provided a forum for MEPs to express their views on their role and problems and their comments provide useful information on the work of an MEP.[7] Since the first issue in January 1981 eight British MEPs have written articles containing reflections on their activities; five were Labour and three were Conservative, and their comments provide a small sample of the opinions of MEPs. Richard Balfe, MEP (London South, Labour), confirms Butler and Marquand's (1981, p. 168) general observations and the more general observations of Ann Robinson (1983, pp. 284) in that he says the major part of an MEP's activities consist of 'being lobbied by groups with different interests'. He suggests that lobbyists of MEPs should keep their papers short, non-technical, and make it clear why the MEP should be interested. On the latter point an MEP will be interested if a matter affects constituents, relates to the MEP's work on an EP committee or relates to an MEP's personal interests. Although Michael Gallagher, MEP Nottingham, Labour, notes (July, 1981, p. 12) that many letters in his post bag show great ignorance of the EC's activities, he does give an example of what an MP would consider a normal constituency 'surgery' case which, in this instance, could be helped by an MEP. This case consisted of helping a Pole in his constituency get compensation for being interned by the Nazis.

The question of how MEPs can become effective depends upon both their domestic political influence and the influence they can assert via the EP. It has been noted that government departments were treating MEPs in a similar way to MPs in terms of contacts, and Butler and Marquand (1981, p. 6) note that at times, for example over budgetary conflicts, governments may see MEPs as useful allies. Joyce Quinn (MEP, South Tyne and Wear, Labour) argues (November, 1981, p. 13) that for an MEP to be effective in a committee of the European Parliament the MEP must consider three basic questions about an EC proposal: Which countries are affected? Who benefits? and Who pays? In her case, as a member of the Agricultural Committee, she was able to be a member of its Fish Stock Working Group and thus directly to represent the fishing industry's interests of her constituency. In a different way, Ann Clwyd (MEP Mid and South Wales, Labour) was able (May/June 1982, pp. 26–7) to mobilize Dutch workers' support against a multinational seeking to transfer work from a firm in Wales to one in Amsterdam. This was achieved through the help of a Dutch Socialist Group MEP. Two Conservative MEPs, Ben Patterson, (Kent West) and Derek Prag, (Hertfordshire), point out (June 1981, p. 15; and July 1982, p. 15) that the EP is gradually learning to exploit more of the powers available to it, such as holding up the Council of Ministers' work until an opinion of the EP has been presented, and edging upwards the percentage of the budget under the influence of the Parliament.

Thus the MEP's voice can have an effect in the working of the Community. Indeed, given the important role of EP committees, British MEPs are quite well placed to exert influence. Lord Bethell is Vice Chairman of the Political Affairs Committee; Sir Henry Plumb (NFU) is Chairman of the Agriculture Committee; Mr Basil de Ferranti is Vice Chairman of the Economic and Monetary Committee; Michael Gallaghar and Tom Normanton are Vice Chairmen of the Energy and Research Committees; Sir Fred

Catherwood is Chairman and Mr Barry Seal is Vice Chairman of the External Economic Relations Committee; Mr Amedil Turner is Vice Chairman of the Legal Affairs Committee; Dame Shelagh Roberts is Vice Chairman of the Transport Committee; Mr Ken Collins is Chairman and Mr Stanley Johnson is Vice Chairman of the Environment, Public Health and Consumer Protection Committee, and Mr Peter Price is Vice Chairman of the Budgetary Control Committee.

However, these opportunities for influence within the EC may not always be used to promote the domestic political view of Britain's interests in the EC, but rather in a less partisan and more '*communautaire*' attitude. Thus MEPs may be seen, from a national perspective, as rather uncertain political allies, particularly as the British MEPs cannot hope to control voting in the EP. For example, it must be somewhat hard for British politicians to understand that the vote in the EP in December 1982 to withhold Britain's budget repayments was not directed against Britain, but was rather a form of pressure directed at reforming the EC's budgetary system. Therefore the most useful policy-making link between Britain and the EC is that provided by the official level working groups and parties reporting to the Council of Ministers. These bodies, manned by civil servants, currently provide the best forum for the articulation of British interests derived from inputs from the Government, Parliament and interest groups. If the issues are too contentious for national officials to resolve even through COREPER, then the task must be left to British ministers at the Council of Ministers.

NOTES AND REFERENCES

1. On this topic see also J. Fitzmaurice (1978) *The European Parliament*, Farnborough, Saxon House; V. Herman and M. Hagger (1980) *The Legislation of Direct Elections to the European Parliament*, Farnborough, Gower and J. Lodge and V. Herman (1982) *Direct Elections to the European Parliament*, London, Macmillan.
2. With Greece now a member of the EEC, the size of the EP had

been increased to 434 seats with the allocation of 24 seats to Greece.

3. See the very useful documentation of the Euro-elections in *The Economist*, Vol. 271, 16 June 1979, pp. 25 f. and C. Cook and M. Francis (1979) *The First European Elections*, London, Macmillan.

4. See the findings of the ITN/ORC Poll of 8/9 June 1979.

5. *Europe 81*, 10 Oct. 1981, p. 13.

6. Letter to the authors from Mr G. Stapleton, European Secretariat, Cabinet Office, 14 Oct. 1982.

7. The dates of references in the text from this point refer to issues of *Europe 81* or *Europe 82*.

CHAPTER SIX

EC Policies: British Perspectives

This chapter discusses the implications for Britain of EC policies developed under the authority of the Community treaties. The EPC foreign policy co-ordination activities are not considered as these take place outside the scope of the treaties, and are therefore entirely voluntary in character. By contrast, policies developed under treaty provisions may be obligatory in character. In Britain, outside the scope of the EC treaties, a British government is the source of policies on such matters as the rates of taxation, defence, housing, hospital building and the provision of education. However, as has been pointed out, Community policies are, formally, initiated by the Commission, discussed by national officials and agreed by ministers in the inter-governmental forum of the Council of Ministers. Moreover, the decisions on EC policies in the Community have been identified by British politicians as involving a negotiating and bargaining process, seeking national advantage but recognizing that in the end the resultant policy will have involved compromise in the search for consensus. The compromise may be within a particular policy or involve 'horse-trading' across a range of policies. One senior civil servant likened his training of junior colleagues to negotiate, in Brussels, a British position, to teaching them to sell a car before the wheels fell off.

The literature on policy-making looks at policy making as involving planning, strategic choices and rationality. That is, as containing a statement and evaluation of objectives and means. The activity of policy-making has also been seen as either an élitist or a pluralist activity. With some modifications these concepts are valid in relation to policy-making in the EC. The method of EC policy-making is predominantly

élitist in character because the powers of the representative
institution, the EP, are limited and thus the policy process is
dominated by ministers and civil servants from the member
states. However, in some cases the policy process may be
more pluralist, with the necessary involvement of interest
groups, both nationally and on a community wide basis, in
such matters as agriculture, company law, consumer affairs
and work practices.

Research suggests that as the EC policy-making chain is
relatively long, interest groups have good opportunities to
make an impact.[1] These groups can be divided into producers or commercial organizations, such as the Confeder-
ation of British Industry (CBI) and the Bankers' Association
who may be greatly affected by EC policy proposals. Then
there are groups concerned with consumers, social or
environmental issues who may be seeking legitimacy as
commentators on the effects of policies. Lastly, local government has an interest in the EC policy process as a recipient of
grants, being responsible for implementation of EC legislation on food standards and the effects of lorry weights on
road bridges.

Groups have made contacts with Brussels but this can be
expensive, especially for a group without much financial
support, if an attempt is made to maintain an office in
Brussels. The most important requirement for interest group
involvement is knowledge of the EC agenda. This can be
done both formally and informally in approaches to the
Commission especially as some Directorates-General need
the support of interest groups to bolster their own standing.
The Economic and Social Committee can sometimes be a
useful channel of information and influence in this area.
Domestically, the links between interest groups and Whitehall departments regarding EC affairs are now quite highly
developed and involve regular meetings between officials and
interest group representatives. The officers or members of
pressure groups may be co-opted into Brussels committees
such as the standing committees on employment questions
or the Consumers' Consultative Committee.

Because Britain was a late, and not completely enthusiastic,
entrant to the EC, and because she also entered with a stated

interest in changing certain EC policies (notably the CAP and budgetary system), there have been certain inescapable features of Britain's approach to EC policies. As Helen Wallace (1980, p. 29) has pointed out 'other dimensions of the continuing debate over EC membership within the UK mean that the budgetary issue has high political salience, both symbolically and because of its substantive repercussions.' Indeed Lord Carrington has agreed that the British preoccupations with the Community Budget and the CAP has inevitably made Britain seem to have only negative interests in the EC and to be a particularly non-*communautaire* member.[2] In particular, over the issue of budgetary contributions Britain has not been disposed to take a broad long-term view of the advantages and disadvantages of EC membership but rather to insist on a *juste retour* as Sir Geoffrey Howe proposed, at the Finance Ministers Council in September 1979.

The nature of British participation in EC policy-making will be considered from a number of perspectives. First, as the reaction to pre-entry politically important policies, the form of the Community Budget. Secondly, as participatory in the also politically important, but only recently concluded Common Fisheries Policy (CFP). Thirdly, the varied forms of the involvement in the numerically largest number of EC legislative proposals which relate to what may be matters of much less national political significance, and may thus seem purely 'technical' in character, like vehicle regulations or food packaging. However, some policy proposals of this type may have important sectoral impacts in Britain on workers, industrial processes or consumers, and even on hobbies or other personal activities. Many proposals in this category come under the general term 'harmonization' even if not under the specific Article 100 (EEC) on the necessary approximation of laws. Carol Twitchett (1981, p. 1) has aptly remarked that:

> Many of the most persistent myths prejudicing the Community's image in the eyes of the British people stem from rumours of impending harmonization measures . . . Despite EEC and British government denials, the horrific prospects of 'Euro-bread' and

'Euro-beer' (firstly measured by the kilo and secondly by the litre) are further evidenced as incipient threats to the so-called 'British way of life' resulting directly from participation in the harmonization process.

Finally, Britain's non-participation in the Community's European Monetary System (EMS), developed since Britain joined the EC, will be considered.

The effective representation of Britain's national and sectoral interests in the EC policy process is somewhat complicated by the fact that, as politicians and civil servants have agreed in interviews, EC policy cannot be considered as something which can be expressed with anything like the precision of national policies on the Health Service, or industrial relations. This is simply because the EC is not an inter-governmental organization with a single area of responsibility, but rather it is an organization with powers in many areas. Thus British policies may have to be considered from the perspective of possible conflict with an area of Community competence or interest, as happened with Tony Benn's proposed Industry Bill. Also the machinery of government needs to be able to respond, by activating, co-ordinating or consulting interest groups, to EC policy proposals. Sometimes on major or even minor issues Britain may have a very clear policy line to put forward, as was the case with fisheries. As an example of the recognition of the Community dimension in government: not only does the European Secretariat of the Cabinet Office act as the Secretariat for those Cabinet Committees specifically devoted to an EC issue, such as the Community Budget, the European Secretariat will also act as the Secretariat of other non-EC Cabinet Committees if they are discussing an item which has significant EC implications.[3]

Parliament's role in the relation to EC legislation has already been shown to offer little scope for the involvement of the Commons as a whole. In terms of legislative activity as part of the policy-making process this is particularly true. For example, in 1975 the European Community Committee of the Lords (HL 115) reported on the consequential legislation that might be required in the UK as a consequence of the 240

EC proposals then considered. Of the 95 draft Regulations proposals, 41 concerned agriculture, 39 customs and external trade and 8 transport. None was in conflict with an existing Act of Parliament and only 18 would require subordinate UK legislation. This new subordinate UK legislation would be required because the Regulations were either incomplete or in conflict with UK subordinate legislation.

Among the 240 proposals there were 50 Directives and of these the Lords Committee considered that 32 would need UK Legislation and in three or four cases the Lords Legal Sub-Committee felt an Act of Parliament would be needed. However, the Sub-Committee also noted that some consequential legislation might be inserted into a Bill or other legal instrument being used for another purpose. An example of this practice occurred over Council Directive 78/933/EEC of 17 October 1978, which dealt with 'Lighting and Light Signalling Devices of Agricultural and Forestry Tractors'. This was proposed to be put into effect in the UK within the framework of a Consolidation of Revision of the Road Vehicles Lighting Regulations.

THE BRITISH CONTRIBUTION TO THE EC BUDGET

How Britain acts in respect of Community policies, and to what extent, will in part be determined by the importance, to Britain, of a particular issue, and in part it will be determined by the treaty powers relating to that issue. Although British governments have made no secret of the fact that the size of our budgetary contribution is a major political issue and have suggested that Britain might seek to block the development of Community policy in other areas if this issue remains unresolved both in terms of the size of rebates in the short-term and in the sense of agreement for the long term reform of the Budget system and the CAP. However, in seeking changes in this area British governments are faced with a major problem, as Helen Wallace (1980, p. 74) has pointed out, because:

The budgetary process itself is rather tightly structured, in that it depends on precise rules about the operations

of individual institutions and their interactions. Thus
decision-making is much more systematically organized
than in most areas of Community activity . . . [and]
. . . the budgetary process stands alongside the bargaining on the CAP and negotiation of external trade
agreements as a prime example of a highly articulated
Community process.

In other words Britain is seeking to bargain for national
advantage in the most highly *communautaire* in character
policy achievement of the EC.

  It can simply be stated that Britain has not achieved any
actual fundamental change in the EC budgetary process,
despite ten years of effort. It has taken a great deal of negotiation even to achieve agreement on the size of annual
rebates. The issue of rebates has become more politically
important than long-term budgetary reform because the
period of transition to full membership obligation produced a
situation where the size of Britain's budgetary contribution
remained artificially low until the late 1970s. For example, in
1973 Britain's net contribution to the EC budget was £111
million, but by 1978 it had risen to £822 million. Changes in
the EC's budgetary system, especially the introduction of a
new EUA (European Unit of Account – based upon a basket
of currencies) in 1978, which helped to produce a rise in
Britain's contributions, produced the first major post renegotiation clash between Britain and the EC on the size of our
contributions. The Labour Government in 1978 sought ways
of easing the rising budgetary burden, and a modest short-
term solution was produced. However, in the process the
Labour Government encountered problems, illustrative of
the difficulties of policy-making in an inter-governmental
organization pursuing many different policy goals. Germany,
in particular, objected to easing Britain's contribution as she
(Germany) would have to assist in making up any budgetary
shortfall. Britain blocked the initiation of the new EUA, but
Germany countered by blocking development of the Regional
Fund which was, to date, partly the result of Britain's most
positive policy input into the EC, and moreover a fund from
which Britain hoped to derive great benefit.

Despite the problems encountered in the EC over reducing Britain's budgetary contribution, British politicians made it into such a major domestic issue, because of Britain's economic difficulties. Indeed, Prime Minister James Callaghan, in his speech at the Lord Mayor of London's Banquet in November 1978, raised the status of the issue to the level of another renegotiation of the terms of entry.[4] Britain drew attention to the magnitude of the problem at meetings of the European Council in December 1978 and March 1979. However, at this time the other members had been pre-occupied with the new European Monetary System (EMS) about which Britain had been unenthusiastic, and declined to join when it came into operation in December 1978 and no long-term solution to the budgetary problem was then forthcoming.

The Conservative Government, led by Margaret Thatcher, has been, for a supposedly pro-EC party, particularly strident in its demands for a reduction in Britain's budget contributions and for long-term changes in the EC Budget system and the CAP. At the start, Mrs Thatcher at the Strasbourg European Council of June 1979 was both *communautaire* and politely threatening. Concessions concerning the EMS and farm policies were made, but the other EC states were warned of the costs to them in increased budget shares if Britain had to leave the EC because of the burden of budget contributions. On this occasion the Commission was instructed to report on the equity of the budgetary system and financial mechanism. During the autumn of 1979 the Chancellor of the Exchequer, Sir Geoffrey Howe, at the Council of Finance Ministers, and Mrs Thatcher, before the Dublin European Council, both stressed the British aim of a board balance between payments and receipts and a permanent resolution of the issue.

The other EC members were divided over the form and degree of response that could be made to the British position. Among possible solutions were various levels of offers related to the British demand, and the search for a package of concessions by the other states and Britain on such matters as the CAP, the proposed CFP, energy and the EMS. Nor did the Commission's Report produce an easy resolution of the issue.[5] The Commission suggested that Budget restructuring was a long-term exercise, that Britain could only expect temporary relief, and that she could not expect the Community to accept *juste retour*.[6] The Commission did, however, propose various forms of refunds and additional EC spending in Britain.

The Dublin European Council of November 1979 produced no agreement on the size of refund for Britain which the British had suggested as one billion pounds. In the spring of 1980 the British position hardened and included talk of obstructive policies, including the withholding of VAT payments to the EC. by the Treasury.[7] The Luxembourg European Council of April 1980, was also unable to produce agreement, although the gap between Britain and the other EC states was narrowed. In part the proposals failed because the other members did not offer Britain enough in refund, moreover the refund was temporary and linked to Britain being prepared to make concessions in the CAP. The 1980 settlement was eventually reached partly through the General Council (foreign ministers) and partly with the help of the Italian President. However, the settlement was only for refunds in the years 1980–83 and involved Britain in conceding farm price rises, working towards the CFP and promising non-intervention in the French lamb market.[8] For the long-term, the Council of Ministers agreed to review the EC budgetary system.

Although a settlement was agreed in 1980 the payment of the annual refunds has not proceeded without dispute. These disputes have revealed that the British Government not only has to bargain for British interests in an inter-governmental setting and take account of the interests of the other member states, it also has to take account of the interest of Community institutions. At the end of 1982 the European Parliament was blocking the agreement of both the Council of Ministers and the Commission to Britain receiving a £500 million rebate on its 1982 Budget contributions. The EP had been blocking the repayment for two reasons: first, it wants to ensure that Britain spends the rebate money on specifically Community projects; second, it wants the Council to produce much more definitive plans for solving the Budget payment problems. In December 1982 Sir Geoffrey Howe, the Chancellor, underlined the urgency of the issue for Britain by suggesting, as in 1980, that if a solution was not found by the end of March 1983 Britain might halt its payment to the EC Budget.

At the time of writing, the dispute contains the following problems for a British government. (1) A British government might object to the EP gaining control of how repayments are used in Britain. This is not a new problem; Joel Barnett (1982, pp. 156–8) has recorded a similar instance of late 1978. At that time, he says, British officials persuaded Prime Minister Callaghan 'to give precedence to the other arm of our EEC policy, that is not to give greater powers to the European Parliament'. In other words, it was thought better to lose a little financial benefit from a bigger Regional Fund than to concede anything to the Parliament. (2) The most recent Commission proposals would relate national contributions to shares of the Gross Agricultural Production (GAP). This would reduce Britain and Germany's contributions but raise that of France, and thus would produce an inter-governmental dispute. The EC was unable to produce a complete settlement of the issue before the British general election in June 1983. Domestically, therefore, it seems that Britain's budgetary contributions will remain in the short-term, at least, a major irritant in the Conservative Party's desire to present EC membership as of positive benefit to Britain, and a major piece of ammunition to the Labour Party's attack on membership issues.[9]

THE NEGOTIATION OF THE COMMON FISHERIES POLICY (CFP)

With reference to the categories of governmental action developed in chapter 5, the British Government can be described as being a partner with the fishing industry in securing the best possible protection and promotion of British interests within the development of a Community policy. For British governments the CFP has been an issue similar to that of EC Budget reform; it has not divided the two main parties, both Labour and Conservative governments having sought the best deal possible for Britain. Because of the CFP's importance there are standing co-ordinating arrangements between the government departments involved.

The history of the efforts by the EC under the EEC Treaty to develop a Common Fisheries Policy (CFP), which started in 1970, shows evidence of conflict between the interests of member states and the Community's interests. The CFP, during its development, has had to take account not only of the interests of EC states in their traditional fishing areas, but also of the developments in the law of the sea at the UN Conference on the Law of the Sea (UNCLOS). Particularly relevant in the latter context, has been the gradual evolution of a customary right for coastal states to claim 200-mile Exclusive Economic Zones (EEZs) around their coasts.[10]

The principal aim of the CFP was to produce general principles to govern the management of fisheries in the EC area. In particular it was hoped that fishermen from an EC state could fish in the waters of *all* coastal states with the minimum of reserved fishing areas for nationals of coastal states. When Britain, Denmark and Eire joined in 1973 it was agreed to modify the CFP aims for ten years (i.e. until 1982) to reserve coastal fishing out to 12 miles for the sole use of the national or other fleets which had traditionally fished in those waters. Britain having vital national interests with regard to fishing as an industry, and the conservation of fish stocks, had a keen interest in the development of the CFP. Labour Foreign Secretary, David Owen (923 HC Deb. Col. 1070, 10 January 1977) told the Commons that the CFP was a very unique EC policy because: 'No other Community resource is subject to a regime of equal access in the way provided for fish. The Community does not require German coal or French farm land or our own North Sea oil and gas to be open territory for anyone in the Community.' However, he noted that the CFP was an EC obligation which we could not ignore, and therefore: 'It must be reformed in the spirit of achieving a Community solution.'

With regard to the EC's relationship to developments at UNCLOS, in September 1976 the Commission proposed a 200-mile EEZ for all EC coastal states. The Council of Ministers approved this step via a Resolution, which, not being binding, could only be implemented if the EC states passed the necessary domestic legislation. This was done in Britain by the passing of the 1976 Fishery Limits Act.

Parallel efforts were being made to produce an agreement on the details of the CFP. On behalf of Britain, in May 1976 Roy Hattersley, as Minister of State at the FCO, proposed that a variable belt up to 50 miles wide be reserved off the coasts of EC states for the nationals of each coastal state. The Commission's response in October 1976 only envisaged a retention of the old 12-mile limit. In addition arguments were also raised about reserving 'quotas' of the total possible EC area fish-catch in each year for particular states. In 1977 the Commission proposed that certain localized preferences might be granted so that countries could fish in traditional areas away from their coasts. In June 1977, John Silkin, Labour Minister of Agriculture, Fisheries and Food, told the Commons (933 HC Deb. col. 1785, 23 June 1977) that Britain would leave Roy Hattersley's proposals on the table in the EC but would discuss an exclusive zone for coastal states out to 12 miles, and a preferential area for coastal states from 12–50 miles, with fishing rights out to 200 miles being divided on a historic basis. He also said that the UK expected any quota allocation to give at least 45 per cent of the catch to Britain.

At the January 1978 Council meeting, which Mr John Silkin did not attend as the other EC states were not ready to concede the proposal quota to Britain, the other eight EC states accepted the main points of the Commission's proposals for internal Community CFP arrangements. However, the United Kingdom continued to refuse to accept the Commission's proposals and invoked the Luxembourg Accords to prevent their adoption by the other eight member states (Churchill, 1980, p. 26).

The British position at the end of the Labour Government's term of office was that 60 per cent of the fish caught in the EC's 200-mile 'pond' were caught off the coasts of the British Isles, and that any quota share for Britain should reflect that fact. Moreover, any concessions to the 'historic' fishing rights of other EC states off the British Isles had to be considered in the context of how much quota Britain was allocated. The Labour Government had reinforced its views on Britain's fishing claims and interest in conservation by being prepared to enact a number of fishery conservation orders in 1977–78 that ran counter to a strict interpretation of EC obligations. The legality of these orders were challenged (Churchill, 1980, pp. 32–3) in the Court of Justice by both France and the Commission.

In July 1982, the Conservative MAFF Minister, Peter Walker, made some concessions in proposing a 35 per cent quota for Britain, a 6-mile exclusive fishing zone, and a 6–12 mile preferential fishing zone in which only historic countries could continue fishing (France in the Channel, and Belgium, Netherlands and West Germany in the North Sea). However, hopes for an agreement in July 1982 were not fulfilled as this time Denmark blocked the process. The matter remained in dispute during the autumn of 1982, and Denmark did not finally agree to the CFP until 25 January 1983, in a catch quota deal worked out by the Commission which, in the end, gave Britain the largest quota share of 36.27 per cent. Britain's negotiating position on the CFP was strengthened by the fact that she has the largest Community fishing industry by weight of average annual catch, and some of the richest fishing grounds.

The three main parts of the CFP are:

(1) the quota shares of total allowable catch (TAC);
(2) 'access', or who has the right to fish where, inside EC waters (from 6–12 miles from member states' coasts and out to 200 miles);
(3) the reservation for Britain in the open EC waters (from 12–250 miles, two large areas around the Shetlands and the Orkeneys) of exclusive fishing rights for British boats and a limited number from other EC states.

BRITAIN AND THE EC HARMONIZATION PROPOSALS

Because the harmonization proposals cover so many diverse areas such as the rear registration plates of cars, non-automative weighing machines, textile names, detergents, cosmetics and food content law, all of which come under Article 100 (EEC),[11] and issues such as the incompatibility of state aids with the aims of the Common Market, Article 92 (EEC), it is evident that a British government will play more than one role in policy-making on these matters. In fact it can be seen in all the four roles identified in chapter 4, actor, partner, public sector guardian and agent. Generally the assessment[12] is that Britain's 'record for the adoption of "total" harmonization measures has been creditable . . . and even in the field of "optional" harmonization the performance of the UK has been at least as good as the average' (C. Twitchett (ed.), 1981, p. 23).

Dennis (1981) has examined the area of government aids to regions or sectors of the economy. Regional aids can be allowed providing they do not seriously affect other states' competitive abilities and the Commission has accepted the national importance of such government policies. Thus Britain was not challenged on the (approximately) £400 million worth of aid provided for in the 1972 Industry Act, although 'some of this finance would have provided aid which conflicted with Community policy' (Dennis, 1981, p. 26). Similarly, because of their political importance to Britain, there was no Commission interference in the granting of state aid to Chrysler (UK) and British Leyland. However, Butt Philip (1981) in his analysis of the ways in which the Community has approached a Community indus-trial policy, has provided examples of conflicts between Commission efforts and member states policies. For example, there were protests from other members about the Employ-ment Department's temporary employment subsidy (Butt Philip, 1981, p. 49). Most significantly, during the period of Labour government, 1974–79, government aid to the British Steel Corporation (BSC) was 'of constant concern to the Brussels authorities and other Member States . . . [especially] on the at times open-ended financing by the UK Govern-ment of BSC's operating losses' (Butt Philip, 1981, p. 56).

Carol Twitchett (1981, pp. 71–3) has looked at the impact of EEC Regulation 1463/70 requiring the installation and use of tachographs in commercial vehicles as from 1 January 1976. She remarks that the tachographs became, 'something of a *cause célèbre* in the domestic debate on United Kingdom membership of the European Community'. The (then) Transport Minister, William Rodgers, questioned the usefulness of this piece of harmonization, the Transport Workers' Union opposed the tachograph as the 'spy in the cab', and the transport firms raised concern over the cost of installation. The Commission started proceedings against Britain in October 1977, the Court of Justice ruled against Britain in February 1979, and British governments moved slowly towards implementation. This is a good example of the scope for national delay even where a clear Community obligation exists.

FOOD LAW HARMONIZATION[13]

Under treaty powers harmonization on food laws comes both under the CAP, with rules on composition and labelling, and under Article 100 (EEC) relating to descriptions of food and permitted additives in the context of improving Community trade. Britain has a long history of operating food laws at the local government level and at retail outlets. In particular Britain and Ireland differed from the other EC states in placing controls at the point of sale rather than, as in continental countries, at the point of manufacture.

In Britain, what may be described as the policy-making community for this issue comprises the food manufacturers, food traders, enforcement authorities and consumers' organizations. Government policy-makers seek wide consultations on food issues because they can arouse public interest very quickly if it appears that the traditional purchasing or eating habits are threatened; moreover, by law, under the Food and Drugs Act, ministers are obliged to consult with interested parties before making regulations.

In the proposal for a Directive on food labelling, first discussed in 1974, the Ministry of Agriculture consulted widely during the Commission working party stages, circulating the proposals to 200 interest groups and reporting back progress to about 50 of those groups. The House of Lords EC Committee produced a major report on the subject

(HL 393, Session 1975–76), and the matter was debated in the Commons in April 1977. It was, though, only a one-hour debate on a take-note notion relating to four EC legislative proposals and four reports of the Commons EC Scrutiny Committee. The implementation of EC labelling directives in Britain has proceeded quite smoothly under the auspices of the Trading Standards Officers which adds to local government work. However, in this instance the complexity of the EEC Treaty powers did produce a case before the Court of Justice (the Cassis de Dijon case 120/78 (ECR) 649) which opened up the whole question of the necessity for harmonization on this issue. The Court ruled that any product legally manufactured in one EC state must be admitted to the market of another.

Finally, not all harmonization provisions are the result of an over-enthusiastic Commission. There was much public outcry over the EC legislation on the brands of seeds gardeners could buy, and it was suggested that the EC was denying traditional seed brands to British gardeners. In fact the Commission had merely amalgamated nationally-produced lists.[14]

BRITAIN'S NON-PARTICIPATION IN THE EUROPEAN MONETARY SYSTEM (EMS)

The decision of the last Labour Government not to join the other EC states in the EMS, which was approved by the European Council in Brussels in December 1978, is an example of the Government as actor in its own policy sphere being able to sustain a national position apart from a Community policy. It is also an example of EC flexibility that a member state should be able to remain outside such a development.

In part, the proposals for an EMS go back to the 1974 Tindemans Report on European Union and also to national and Commission initiatives in 1976–77.[15] The basic aim was to produce a high degree of currency exchange rate stability for the members of such a union. At the Bremen European Council of August 1978, France and Germany produced a plan by which 'strong' EC currencies would be linked in a joint float and only allowed a narrow degree of exchange rate fluctuation (plus or minus 1 per cent), whilst weaker currencies like sterling would be allowed fluctuations of around (plus or minus) 2.25 per cent.

The British response was not totally unsympathetic to the EMS idea, but there were two important differences in the British attitude compared with the French and German approach. First, Britain had a more internationalist view of the currency reform problem, that is she favoured a broadly based Western economic recovery plan, involving America and promoting currency stability through the International Monetary Fund (IMF). Second, Britain, in the EC context, sought to link monetary union with EC budgetary reform. However, she did allow the pound to be included in the Euro-currency Unit which gave an informal relationship with the EMS and the option of joining later. Also Britain's non-participation was not unique, as France did not support the start of the EMS in January 1979. Statler (1979, p. 225) suggested that:

> The logic of development in the international system points in favour of working from within a strong regional grouping, even if this particular attempt at an EMS proves no more than a trial run. But a clear national consensus on Britain's place within either inside or outside is lacking; so is the will within either of the major parties to build such a consensus.

On the other hand, as the Chancellor of the Exchequer, Denis Healey, readily agreed in the Commons in January 1976 (960 HC Deb. Col. 1927), the fact that the EMS did not start to operate in January 1979 reflected French as well as British objections. Therefore, Britain was not alone in taking a non *communautaire* policy line over the proposed EMS.

On a purely political level, the British Government was acting in a way not dissimilar from other EC states faced at other times with domestic political problems. A general election was pending, the Labour Government naturally wished to maintain party unity, and monetary union raised the spectre of economic federalism. However, the way the EMS issue was handled by the Government did attract critical comment by the Commons Expenditure Committee (HC 60 Sess. 1978–9, p. xiii) which felt that the Treasury had not produced adequate evidence to allow for a broader debate on the EMS in Britain. The Treasury, and other economic experts, forecast lower expectation of British growth, output and employment if the country joined the EMS. The Expenditure Committee also criticized the Government for concentrating on the technical issues of the EMS and not recognizing its wider EC political significance as a stage in the Community's development. This perspective was later verified by the Committee on a visit to Brussels. In the Commons the ELC reported twice on the EMS (HC 29–xxxviii, Session 1977–78 and HC 10–iii, Session 1978–79).

In the Commons the EMS was debated at some length: for three hours, on 13 December 1978, in relation to specific EC documents on take-note notions; and for nine and a half hours, on 29 November 1978, in an Adjournment debate. The House, in the debate on 13 December agreed an amendment to the take-note notion (Ayes 111, Noes 33) welcoming the Prime Minister's refusal to join the EMS and his views on maintaining parliamentary and governmental control of national financial and economic affairs.

It was clear in the publicity over the EMS, as Butt wrote in *The Times* (26 October 1978), that: 'Discussion of most problems that concern the European Community is usually bedevilled in Britain by fixed not to say obsessive ideas about the original question of membership.' Chancellor Denis Healey was reported (*The Times* 29 November 1978) as reminding Labour Party critics of the EC that the EMS was not a bankers' plot as the Chairmen of both the Midland Bank and the Deutsche Budesbank were opposed to it. Also it was not a monetarists' plot as monetarist economists were against the EMS.

However, Britain's absence from the EMS should not be over stressed as being an important setback to EC development as a Community. Paul Taylor (1982, p. 741) has argued that during the 1970s 'there has been a significant reinforcement of pressures opposed to integration since the middle of

the decade.' Indeed Taylor (1982, p. 757) feels that by 1981
Prime Minister Thatcher 'could assert with little fear of
contradiction, "there is no such thing as a separate Community interest; the Community interest is compounded of
national interests of the ten member states."' Therefore
policy-making is carried out in a predominately inter-
governmental forum. An important point for Britain in this
context is to be sensitive to the interests and aspirations of
other member states and, as the overriding of our veto in
May 1982 reveals, to understand fully what forms of linkage
of issues may yield positive results and what will only
produce negative effects such as Britain trying to dominate
the agenda of Community meetings with the Budget
problem.

NOTES AND REFERENCES

1. An already published study on this topic is A. Newman,
   'Pressure Groups and Harmonization' in C. C. Twitchett
   (ed.) (1981) *Harmonization in the EEC*, London, Macmillan,
   pp. 102–13.
2. Comments made by Lord Carrington in an interview in
   London on 15 October 1982.
3. Information provided by the European Secretariat of the
   Cabinet Office at an interview, 14 Jan. 1983.
4. See the report of his speech in *The Economist*, 18 Nov. 1978,
   p. 62.
5. Reported in *Bulletin of the European Communities*, No. 11,
   1979; see also Commission *Background Reports*, B46/79.
6. For a useful discussion of Britain and *juste retour*, see
   G. Denton (1978) 'Reflections on Fiscal Federation in the
   EEC', *Journal of Common Market Studies*, 16, pp. 283–301 and
   also G. Denton (1982) 'The economics of EEC membership',
   Policy Studies, 3 (2), pp. 88–103.
7. See *The Economist*, 22-29 March 1980, p. 49.
8. Details of the settlement are contained in European Communities (1980), *Background Report*, B30/80.
9. See on the early 1983 situation: Cmnd 8789 (1983); *The
   Government Expenditure Plans 1983–1984 to 1985–86*, London,
   HMSO; and reports in *The Times* of 17 and 18 Dec. 1982, 27
   Jan. and 3 Feb. 1983.

10. For useful background information on Britain and the CFP see: R. Churchill (1980) 'Revision of the EEC's Common Fisheries Policy – Pt I', *European Law Review*, 5, pp. 3–37.

11. A useful list of Article 100 draft and adopted directives is contained as an Appendix in C. C. Twitchett (ed.), *op. cit.*

12. In this section I have drawn considerably on the analysis in C. Twitchett, *op. cit.*

13. This section is based, principally, upon a forthcoming Civil Service College publication and the authors are grateful to Dr Helen Wallace for providing an advance copy.

14. See J. Waterman (1981) 'Seeds of the gardeners' discontent', *Europe*, Nos 8/9, pp. 17–18.

15. For a useful discussion of European monetary integration efforts see D. C. Kruse (1980) *Monetary Integration in Western Europe: EMU, EMS and Beyond*, London, Butterworth.

CHAPTER SEVEN

Conclusions

After the General Election of 9 June 1983 and the Conservative landslide, Britain is clearly in the EC for at least the next five years. It is true that the Labour Party at its recent annual Party Conferences voted to withdraw from the EC (by 71 per cent in 1980 and 85 per cent in 1981) and included the commitment to leave the EC within the life of a single parliament in its 1983 Election manifesto. However, this does not seem to have been a vote winner. One may therefore hypothesize that a future Labour election manifesto could well be much more vague on the issue of EC membership.

Britain has just completed her first ten years of EC membership and, not surprisingly, a wide range of comments have been made concerning this period. In *Europe*, 82 (No. 12, December 1982) the Commission published a general survey of all the facets of Britain's membership of the EC covering such activities as trade, agriculture and women's rights. The report, whilst recognizing legitimate British grievances over budgetary contributions, does suggest some positive ways of viewing EC membership as well as calling for 'identification with the Community'. The report points out, for example, that almost 40 per cent of Britain's trade is with other EC states, and that since 1973 home food production has actually expanded allowing Britain's self-sufficiency in all foods to rise from 49 per cent in 1970/1 to 60.5 per cent in 1981. Moreover, looking at common grievances the Commission Report points out that Britain's budgetary contributions should be set against other items of government expenditure. In 1981 Britain's net EC budgetary contribution was £379 million, whilst in 1981–82 the British Government's spending on health and social security, etc. was £41,261 million. Moreover, the Commission argues that although food prices have increased by 293 per cent between 1971 and 1981, only 8–10 per cent can be attributed to the CAP.

At the start of this study it was argued that Britain had an essentially negative view of EC membership, and this point has been made by Patricia Clough in the *The Times* series 'Ten Years in the EEC'. She wrote in *The Times* (2 January 1983) that Britain 'still lacks a clear vision of how it would like the community to develop and tends merely to react to events as they happen'. This fact was recognized by Foreign Secretary, Francis Pym when he replied in *The Times* (10 January 1983) series. Mr Pym said 'I am emphatically with Helmut Schmidt when he says it is time we forget the "British problem". For years we have indulged ourselves and tried the patience of our friends. The job now is to build on the Community we have, and to make it work in all our interests. That is not to say we must be uncritical. But we must be constructive.' The Foreign Secretary described Britain's current EC policy as comprising increased efforts to solve the existing budgetary problems, special new efforts to regenerate European industry to try to reduce unemployment, and the strengthening of the EC's external role. By contrast, the Labour Party's chief economic spokesman, Peter Shore, was equally positive that Britain's future prosperity would be better secured by withdrawal from the EC.

It is not the purpose of this study to try and offer an answer to the very familiar question of whether Britain should or should not remain a member of the EC. Rather it has been the purpose of this study to examine the effects of EC membership upon the British system of government. Therefore the conclusions must relate to this, but it is also legitimate that they should reflect upon how the machinery of government could cope with a withdrawal from the EC.

In order to arrive at conclusions it is necessary to consider the machinery of government in its legislative, executive and administrative aspects. Before EC entry the declining powers of Parliament were well documented. EC entry has done nothing to halt that decline. The Commons have merely ceded yet more power to the executive without any comprehensive increase in its ability to hold the executive accountable. In the recent report of the Commons Liaison Committee (HC 92, pp. 75–6, 1982), the Chairman of the European Legislation Committee, Mr Julius Silverman MP, said that 'The Committee are broadly satisfied with their terms of reference.' However, he went on to stress that:

> No provision is made to govern ministerial actions in Brussels on documents which have not yet been examined by the Committee. The Resolution of the House only covers documents which have been recommened for debate by the Committee. If a document does not reach the Committee in time for it to be considered and reported on before agreement is reached in the Council of Ministers, the Committee have no possibility of recommending debate before agreement, and thus of activating the control over Ministerial actions, under the Resolution of 30 October 1980.

Mr Silverman also made the point that:

> the Committee recently have been much concerned by the controversy surrounding the overriding of the 'Luxembourg Compromise' at the time of the decisions on agricultural process on May 19. It is essential to our work that British Ministers should be able to protect the United Kingdom when they go to Brussels. If, because their power to insist on the protection of British interest is overruled, they are not able to respond to the views of the House reflected in the debates that take place, then the whole nature of the Community will have altered.

This comment relating to the expressing of views in the House is in turn related to another issue, namely the difficulty hard-presssed MPs have in attempting to monitor the consequences of EC membership. As one MP put it: 'the EEC is never less than two subjects, the technical specialist element, whatever the topic is, and the wider constitutional implications . . . Whenever an EEC related topic comes up, most members feel inhibited on one element or another.'[1]

For government ministers, the executive, the effects of membership are largely dependent upon their portfolio in terms of additional responsibilities. The Prime Minister has necessarily been heavily involved during the first ten years of membership because of the politically important disputes over the budgetary contributions. The current range of EC obligations and major issues most heavily involve the Foreign Secretary, the Treasury Minister and the Ministers responsible for Agriculture, Trade, Energy and the Environment. If there were to be, for example, a common industrial policy along the lines of the CAP, then of course the workload of the Industry Secretary would rise dramatically. Ministers need to be good at bargaining in order to maximize British interests and this may involve a considerable personal effort. Peter Shore has said that when he was Trade Secretary he would try and give himself a day in Brussels to prepare for a major Council meeting.[2] Ministers also need to adapt to the much slower Community pace of decision-making compared with the pace that may be attained nationally. The then Chancellor, Sir Geoffrey Howe, was quoted as saying (*The Times*, 7 January 1983), after the vote in the European Parliament in December 1982 to reject Britain's budget rebate, that 'Patience is one of the commodities which the Community generates in quite large quantities.'

The most significant increase in workload and in delegated power has gone to civil servants, large numbers of whom travel every year to Brussels to take part in working groups and other meetings in which the form of EC proposals is negotiated. As part of the preparation for these they work closely with British interest groups many of which will be involved in the implementation of EC instruments. To some degree, then, this is a policy-making model with which civil servants, ministers, Parliament and interest groups are familiar, one in which they form a policy community in which solutions are negotiated. The difference is, of course, that the negotiations take place not just at the national level but also at the Community level where Community institutions and European-wide interest groups are making inputs as well as the other member states. In such a model it is very hard to see how negotiations can be tied down to precise instructions. Civil servants can interrupt the agenda to refer back to their superiors but British ministers have no such excuse and from time to time have found themselves agreeing to settlements which were not acceptable to Cabinet or to Parliament.

It is not the scope of this study to attempt an explanation of why the Labour Party was so determined to leave the EC, or indeed to express the counter arguments put forward by Labour pro-marketeers, although this subject has been widely commented upon.[3] What can be considered, however, is the mechanics of a possible withdrawal. These have been succinctly analysed by Palmer (1982), who has pointed out in particular that 'it is an essential part of Labour's case that a future Labour government should negotiate for the United Kingdom on amicable withdrawal and an acceptable alternative relationship with its ex-partners.' Thus the Labour Party does not seek to govern Britain as though the EC simply did not exist. Therefore, although withdrawal involves the search for a new form of association with the EC it does implicitly recognize that an interdependent relationship between Britain and the EC is a political and economic fact which cannot be ignored.

Obviously, for withdrawal to occur, a Labour government must be first elected to office. However, given the controversies that a withdrawal policy would arouse, a mere electoral win would not be sufficient for such a policy to be carried through. Labour will need an adequate and loyal majority in the Commons. Assuming these conditions are met, Labour has proposed, first, to amend the 1972 EC Act to end the supremacy of future EC law in Britain, and to introduce provisions to repeal any sections of EC law which are unacceptable. They would also seek parliamentary approval of the timetable for withdrawal, as published in a White Paper. Given the necessary parliamentary majority, none of these proposals is impossible to achieve. Assuming a new form of relationship was agreed between Britain and the EC a Labour government would completely repeal the 1972

EC Act, again a step fully within the competence of a duly elected majority government. Thus, these withdrawal steps are completely consistent with normal British parliamentary practice and only differ in the degree of political significance from other examples such as the nationalization and de-nationalization of industries, and the enactment and repeal of Industrial Relations Acts.

However, when withdrawal is a step linked to a new relationship with the EC then it has to be acknowledged that all the components are not within the competence of a British government alone, unless that government simply decided, unilaterally, to break its treaty obligations. If it did this, then there would be no reason to assume that the other EC states would be under an obligation to assist Britain in any way. Labour, at present, envisages a period of about 12 months, from entry into office, to the repeal of the 1972 EC Act but recognizes that, for example, trading arrangements could take some time to negotiate and may go well beyond a 12-month period.

Palmer, (1982, p. 642) has pointed out that, even if one assumed the full and enthusiastic co-operation of other EC members: 'it is not generally appreciated in Britain that a new agreement between Britain outside the the European Community and its former EEC partners would be based on Article 236 of the Treaty of Rome, and would, therefore, be subject to ratification by the national parliaments of all other member states.' The negotiation of such a treaty could well take *more* than the life of one Parliament. If so, a change of the party in government could halt the process, and a new majority party could re-introduce an EC Act and seek to continue membership as before.

There could be other domestic difficulties in a withdrawal process. For instance:

the issue of the legality of a British government amending the 1972 European Communities Act before and not after the successful conclusion of negotiations with the Commission and the Council of Ministers. According to senior Commission experts Britain would remain fully subject to EEC law until withdrawal had been agreed. An amendment of the act before with-drawal would at least leave open the British govern-ment to being challenged not only in the . . . Court of Justice . . . but also in British courts . . . It is a matter of speculation how British courts would respond . . .' (Palmer, 1982, p. 641).

Moreover, comments by civil servants in the BBC pro-gramme 'No Minister' (No. 5, 'Brussels: a Mandarins' Paradise?') suggest that at the very least the loyalty of sec-tions of the Civil Service would be severely tested if called upon to undo the years of arduous work to integrate Britain into the EC.

As this book goes to press after the massive Conservative win in the June 1983 General Election, Britain's EC member-ship has taken on an air of much greater permanence. How-ever, the dilemmas for government remain, the new Conser-vative Foreign Secretary, Sir Geoffrey Howe, has to take on a major battle in the Community to change the system of financing the EC in order to produce a long-term solution to the level of Britain's budget contributions. The Labour Party, as an alternative government party, will have to re-examine its attitudes and policies towards the EC. As a consequence of Labour's electoral defeat it does seem that the controversy over Britain's EC membership is now somewhat muted. Nonetheless, it is not unreasonable to predict that contro-versies over the consequences of membership will continue.

NOTES AND REFERENCES

1. Letter to the authors from Mr Peter Lloyd MP, 13 Jan. 1983.
2. Comment to the authors in an interview at the House of Commons on 10 December 1982.
3. D. S. Bell (1980) 'Labour and the European Community' in D. S. Bell (ed.) *Labour into the Eighies*, London, Croom Helm, pp. 150–62; J. E. Turner (1981) 'The Labour Party – Riding the two horses', *International Studies Quarterly*, 25, pp. 385–437 and K. Featherstone (1981) 'Socialists and European Integration: the Attitudes of British Labour Members of Parliament', *European Journal of Political Research*, 9, pp. 407–19.

Abstracts from the Treaty Establishing the European Economic Community, Rome, 25 March 1957.*

PART ONE   PRINCIPLES

Article 1
By this Treaty, the High Contracting Parties establish among themselves a European Economic Community.

Article 2
The Community shall have as its task, by establishing a common market and progressively approximating the economic policies of Member States, to promote throughout the Community a harmonious development of economic activities, a continuous and balanced expansion, an increase in stability, an accelerated raising of the standard of living and closer relations between the States belonging to it.

Article 3
For the purpose set out in Article 2, the activities of the Community shall include, as provided in this Treaty and in accordance with the timetable set out therein:
(a)   the elimination, as between Member States, of customs duties and of quantitative restrictions on the import and export of goods, and of all other measures having equivalent effect;

*As amended by subsequent treaties. A useful source for the full text of the documents covered by Appendices 1 and 2 is Sweet & Maxwell's Legal Editorial Staff (1980) *Sweet & Maxwell's European Community Treaties* (4th edn), London, Sweet & Maxwell.

(b)   the establishment of a common customs tariff and of a common commercial policy towards third countries;

(c)   the abolition, as between Member States, of obstacles to freedom of movement for persons, services and capital;

(d)   the adoption of a common policy in the sphere of agriculture;

(e)   the adoption of a common policy in the sphere of transport;

(f)   the institution of a system ensuring that competition in the common market is not distorted;

(g)   the application of procedures by which the economic policies of Member States can be co-ordinated and disequilibria in their balances of payments remedied;

(h)   the approximation of the laws of Member States to the extent required for the proper functioning of the common market;

(i)   the creation of a European Social Fund in order to improve the raising of their standard of living;

(j)   the establishment of a European Investment Bank to facilitate the economic expansion of the Community by opening the fresh resources;

(k)   the association of the overseas countries and territories in order to increase trade and to promote jointly economic and social development.

Article 4

1   The task entrusted to the Community shall be carried out by the following institutions:
    – an Assembly
    – a Council
    – a Commission
    – a Court of Justice.
    Each institution shall act within the limits of the powers conferred upon it by this Treaty.

2   The Council and the Commission shall be assisted by an Economic and Social Committee acting in an advisory capacity.

3   The audit shall be carried out by a Court of Auditors acting within the limits of the powers conferred upon it by this Treaty.

Article 5
Member States shall take all appropriate measures, whether
general or particular, to ensure fulfilment of the obligations
arising out of this Treaty or resulting from action taken by
the institutions of the Community. They shall facilitate the
achievement of the Community's tasks.

They shall abstain from any measure which could jeopar-
dize the attainment of the objectives of this Treaty.

Article 6
1 Member States shall, in close co-operation with the
institutions of the Community, co-ordinate their respective economic policies to the extent necessary to attain the
objectives of this Treaty.
2 The institution of the Community shall take care not to
prejudice the internal and external financial stability of the
Member States.

Article 7
Within the scope of application of this Treaty, and without
prejudice to any special provisions contained therein; any
discrimination on grounds of nationality shall be prohibited.

PART TWO   Foundations of the Community

TITLE I   FREE MOVEMENT OF GOODS

Article 9
1 The Community shall be based upon a customs union
which shall cover all trade in goods and which shall
involve the prohibition between Member States of customs duties on imports and exports and of all charges
having equivalent effect, and the adoption of a common
customs tariff in their relations with third countries.

CHAPTER 2   *Elimination of quantitative restrictions between
Member States*

Article 30
Quantitative restrictions on imports and all measures having
equivalent effect shall, without prejudice to the following
provisions, be prohibited between Member States.

Article 31
Member States shall refrain from introducing between themselves any new quantitative restrictions or measures having equivalent effect. This obligation shall, however, relate only to the degree of liberalization attained in pursuance of the decisions of the Council of the Organization for European Economic Co-operation of 14 January 1955. Member States shall supply the Commission, not later than six months after the entry into the force of this Treaty with lists of the products liberalized by them in pursuance of these decisions. These lists shall be consolidate between Member States.

Article 34
1 Quantitative restrictions on exports, and all measures having equivalent effects shall be prohibited between Member States.

Article 36
The provisions of Articles 30 to 34 shall not preclude prohibitions or restrictions on imports, exports or goods in transit justified on grounds of public morality, public policy or public security; the protection of health and life of humans, animals or plants; the protection of national treasures possessing artistic, historic or archaeological value; or the protection of industrial and commercial property. Such prohibitions or restrictions shall not, however, constitute a means of arbitrary discriminations or a disguised restriction on trade between Member States.

Article 37
1 Member States shall progressively adjust any State monopolies of a commercial character so as to ensure that when the transitional period has ended no discrimination regardng the conditions under which goods are procured and marketed exists between nationals of Member States.

The provisions of this Article shall apply to any body through which a Member State, in law or in fact, either directly or indirectly supervised, determines or appreciably influences imports and exports between Member States. These provisions shall likewise apply to monopolies delegated by the State to others.

TITLE II   AGRICULTURE

1   The common market shall extend to agriculture and trade
in agricultural products. 'Agriculture products' means the
products of the soil, of stock-farming and of fisheries and
products or first-stage processing directly related to these
products.
2   Save as otherwise provided in Articles 39 or 46, the rules
laid down for the establishment of the common market
shall apply to agricultural products.
3   The operation and development of the common market
for agricultural products must be accompanied by the
establishment of a common agricultural policy among the
Member States.

Article 39
1   The objectives of the common agricultural policy shall
be:
(a)   to increase productivity by promoting technical
progress and by ensuring the rational development
of agricultural production and the optimum utiliza-
tion of the factors of production, in particular
labour;
(b)   thus to ensure a fair standard of living for the
agricultural community, in particular by increasing
the individual earnings of persons engaged in agriculture;
(c)   to stabilize markets;
(d)   to assure the availability of supplies;
(e)   to ensure that supplies reach consumers at reasonable
prices.
2   In working out the common agricultural policy and the
special methods for its application, account shall be taken
of:
(a)   the particular nature of agricultural activity, which
results from the social structure of agriculture and
from structural and natural disparities between the
various agricultural regions;
(b)   the need to effect the appropriate adjustments by
degrees;

(c) the fact that in the Member States agriculture constitutes a sector closely linked with the economy as a whole.

Article 40

1 Member States shall develop the common agricultural policy by degrees during the transitional period and shall bring it into force by the end of that period at the latest.

2 In order to attain the objectives set out in Article 39 a common organization of agricultural markets shall be established.

This organization shall take one of the following forms, depending on the product concerned;

(a) common rules on competition;
(b) compulsory co-ordination of the various national market organizations;
(c) a European organization.

3 The common organization established in accordance with paragraph 2 may include all measures required to attain the objectives set out in Article 39, in particular regulation of prices, aids for the production and marketing of the various products, storage and carryover arrangements and common machinery for stabilizing imports or exports.

The common organization shall be limited to pursuit of the objectives set out in Article 39 and shall exclude any discrimination between producers or consumers within the Community. Any common price policy shall be based on common criteria and uniform methods of calculation.

4 In order to enable the common organization referred to in paragraph 2 to attain its objectives, one or more agricultral guidance and guarantee funds may be set up.

TITLE III   FREE MOVEMENT OF PERSONS, SERVICES AND CAPITAL

CHAPTER I   *Workers*

Article 48

1 Freedom of movement for workers shall be secured

within the Community by the end of the transitional
period at the latest.

2   Such freedom of movement shall entail the abolition of
any discrimination based on nationality between workers
of the Member States as regards employment, remuneration and other conditions of work and employment.

3   It shall entail the right, subject to limitations justified on
grounds of public policy, public security or public health:
  (a)   to accept offers of employment actually made;
  (b)   to move freely within the territory of Member States
        for this purpose;
  (c)   to stay in a Member State for the purpose of
        employment in accordance with the provisions
        governing the employment of nationals of that State
        laid down by law, regulation or administrative
        action;
  (d)   to remain in the territory of a Member State after
        having been employed in that State, subject to
        conditions which shall be embodied in
        implementing regulations to be drawn up by the
        Commission.

4   The provisions of this Article shall not apply to employment in the public service.

Article 51

The Council shall, acting unanimously on a proposal from
the Commission, adopt such measures in the field of social
security as are necessary to provide freedom of movement
for workers; to this end, it shall make arrangements to secure
for migrant workers and their dependants:

(a)   aggregation, for the purpose of acquiring and retaining
      the right to benefit and of calculating the amount of
      benefit, of all periods taken into account under the laws
      of the several countries;

(b)   payment of benefits to persons resident in the territories
      of Member States.

CHAPTER 2   *Right of Establishment*

Article 52

Within the framework of the provisions set out below,
restrictions on the freedom of establishment of nationals of a

Member State in the territory of another Member State shall be abolished by progressive stages in the course of the transitional period. Such progresive abolition shall also apply to restrictions on the setting up of agencies, branches, or subsidiaries by nationals of any Member State established in the territory of any Member State.

Freedom of establishment shall include the right to take up and pursue activities as self-employed persons and to set up and manage undertakings in particular companies or firms within the meaning of the second paragraph of Article 58, under the conditions laid down for its own national by the law of the country where such establishment is effected, subject to the provisions of the chapter relating to capital.

Article 56

1   The provisions of this Chapter and measures taken in pursuance thereof shall not prejudice the applicability of provisions laid down by law, regulation or administrative action providing for special treatment for foreign nationals on grounds of public policy, public security or public health.

Article 57

1   In order to make it easier for persons to take up and pursue activities as self-employed persons, the Council shall, on a proposal from the Commission and after consulting the Assembly, acting unanimously during the first stage and by a qualified majority thereafter, issue directives for the mutual recognition of diplomas, certificates and other evidence of formal qualifications.

2   For the same purpose, the Council shall, before the end of the transitional period, acting on a proposal from the Commission and after consulting the Assembly, issue directives for the co-ordination of the provisions laid down by law, regulation or administrative action in Member States concerning the taking up and pursuit of activities as self-employed persons. Unanimity shall be required on matters which are the subject of legislation in at least one Member State and measures concerned with the protection of savings, in particular the granting of credit and the exercise of the banking profession, and

with the conditions governing the exercise of the medical and allied, and pharmaceutical professions in the various Member States. In other cases, the Council shall act unanimously during the first stage and by a qualified majority thereafter.

3 In the case of the medical and allied and pharmaceutical professions, the progressive abolition of restrictions shall be dependent upon co-ordination of conditions for their exercise in the various Member States.

CHAPTER 3 *Services*

Article 59
Within the framework of the provisions set out below restrictions on freedom to provide services within the Community shall be progressively abolished during the transitional period in respect of nationals of Member States who are established in a State of the Community other than that of the person for whom the services are intended.

The Council may, acting unanimously on a proposal from the Commission, extend the provisions of this Chapter to nationals of a third country who provide services and who are established within the Community.

Article 60
Services shall be considered to be 'services' within the meaning of this Treaty where they are normally provided for remuneration, in so far as they are not governed by the provisions relating to freedom of movement for goods, capital and persons,
'Services' shall in particular include:
(a)   activities of an industrial character;
(b)   activities of a commercial character;
(c)   activities of craftsmen;
(d)   activities of the professions.
Without prejudice to the provisions of the Chapter relating to the right of establishment, the person providing a service may, in order to do so, temporarily pursue his activity in the State where the service is provided, under the same conditions as are imposed by that State on its own nationals.

CHAPTER 4   *Capital*

Article 67

During the transitional period and to the extent necessary to ensure the proper functioning of the common market Member States shall progressively abolish between themselves all restrictions on the movement of capital belonging to persons resident in Member States and any discrimination based on the nationality or on the place of residence of the parties or on the place where such capital is invested.

2   Current payments connected with the movement of capital between Member States shall be freed from all restrictions by the end of the first stage at the latest.

Article 73

1   If movements of capital lead to disturbances in the functioning of the capital market in any Member State, the Commission shall, after consulting the Monetary Committee, authorize that State to take protective measures in the field of capital movements, the conditions and details of which the Commission shall determine. The Council may, acting by a qualified majority, revoke this authorization or amend the conditions or details thereof.

2   A Member State which is in difficulties may, however, on grounds of secrecy or urgency, take the measures mentioned above, where this proves necessary, on its own initiative. The Commission and the other Member States shall be informed of such measures by the date of their entry into force at the latest. In this event the Commission may, after consulting the Monetary Committee, decide that the State concerned shall amend or abolish the measures.

TITLE IV   TRANSPORT

Article 74

The objectives of this Treaty shall, in matters governed by this Title, be pursued by Member States within the framework of a common transport policy.

Article 75
1 For the purpose of implementing Article 74, and taking into account the distinctive features of transport, the Council shall, acting unanimously until the end of the second stage and by a qualified majority thereafter, lay down on a proposal from the Commission and after consulting the Economic and Social Committees and the Assembly:
(a) common rules applicable to international transport to or from the territory of a Member State or passing across the territory of one or more Member States;
(b) the conditions under which non-resident carriers may operate transport services within a Member State;
(c) any other appropriate provisions.

Article 84
1 The provisions of this Title shall apply to transport by rail, road and inland waterways.
2 The Council may, acting unanimously, decide whether, to what extent and by what procedure appropriate provisions may be laid down for sea and air transport.

PART THREE   Policy of the Community

TITLE I   COMMON RULES

CHAPTER I   *Rules on competition*

Section 1   Rules applying to undertakings

Article 85
1 The following shall be prohibited as incompatible with the common market: all agreements between undertakings, decisions by associations of undertakings and concerted practices which may affect trade between Member States and which have as their object or effect the prevention restriction or distortion of competition within the common market, and in particular those which:
(a) directly or indirectly fix purchase or selling prices or any other trading conditions;

(b) limit or control production, markets, technical development, or investment;

(c) share markets or sources of supply;

(d) apply dissimilar conditions to equivalent transactions with other trading parties, thereby placing them at a competitive disadvantage;

(e) make the conclusion of contracts subject to acceptance by the other parties of supplementary obligations which, by their nature or according to commercial usage, have no connection with the subject of such contracts.

2 Any agreements or decisions prohibited pursuant to this Article shall be automatically void.

3 The provisions of paragraph 1 may, however, be declared inapplicable in the case of:

- any agreement or category of agreements between undertakings;
- any decision or category of decisions by associations of undertakings;
- any concerted practice or category of concerted practices;

which contributes to improving the production or distribution of or to promoting technical or economic progress, while allowing consumers a fair share of the resulting benefit, and which does not:

(a) impose on the undertakings concerned restrictions which are not indispensible to the attainment of these objectives;

(b) afford such undertakings the possibility of eliminating competition in respect of a substantial part of the products in question.

Article 86

Any abuse by one or more undertakings of a dominant position within the common market or in a substantial part of it shall be prohibited as incompatible with the common market in so far as it may affect trade between Member States. Such abuse may, in particular consist of:

(a) directly or indirectly imposing unfair purchase or selling prices or unfair trading conditions;

(b) limiting production, markets or technical development to the prejudice of consumers;

(c) applying dissimilar conditions to equivalent transactions with other trading parties, thereby placing them at a competitive disadvantage;

(d) making the conclusion of contracts subject to acceptance by the other parties of supplementary obligations which, by their nature or according to commercial usage, have no connection with the subject of such contracts.

Section 3   Aids granted by states

Article 92

1 Save as otherwise provided in this Treaty, any aid granted by a Member State or through State resources in any form whatsoever which distorts or threatens to distort competition by favouring certain undertakings or the production of certain goods shall, in so far as it affects trade between Member States, be incompatible with the common market.

2 The following shall be compatible with the common market:

(a) aid having a social character, granted to individual consumers, provided that such aid is granted without discrimination related to the origin of the products concerned;

(b) aid to make good the damage caused by natural disasters or other exceptional occurrences;

(c) aid granted to the economy of certain areas of the Federal Republic of Germany affected by the division of Germany, in so far as such aid is required in order to compensate for the economic disadvantages caused by that division.

3 The following may be considered to be compatible with the common market:

(a) aid to promote the economic development of areas where the standard of living is abnormally low or where there is serious underemployment;

(b) aid to promote the execution of an important project of common European interest or to remedy a serious disturbance in the economy of a Member State;

(c)   aid to facilitate the development of certain economic activities or of certain economic areas, where such aid does not adversely affect trading conditions to an extent contrary to the common interest. However, the aids granted to shipbuilding as of 1 January 1957, shall in so far as they serve only to compensate for the absence of customs protection, be progressively reduced under the same conditions as apply to the elimination of customs duties subject to the provisions of this Treaty concerning common commercial policy towards third countries;

(d)   such other categories of aid as may be specified by decision of the Council acting by a qualified majority on a proposal from the Commission.

Article 93

1   The Commission shall, in co-operation with Member States, keep under constant review all systems of aid existing in those States. It shall purpose to the latter any appropriate measures required by the progressive development or by the functioning of the common market.

2   If, after giving notice to the parties concerned to submit their comments the Commission finds that aid granted by a State or through State resources is not compatible with the common market having regard to Article 92, or that such aid is being misused, it shall decide that the State concerned shall abolish or alter such aid within a period of time to be determined by the Commission.

3   If the State concerned does not comply with this decision within the prescribed time, the Commission or any other interested State may, in derogation from the provisions of Articles 169 and 170, refer the matter to the Court of Justice direct.

CHAPTER 3   *Tax Provisions*

Article 95

No Member State shall impose, directly or indirectly, on the products of other Member States any internal taxation of any kind in excess of that imposed directly or indirectly on similar domestic products.

Furthermore, no Member State shall impose on the products of other Member States any internal taxation of such a nature as to afford indirect protection to other products.

Member States shall, no later than at the beginning of the second stage, repeal or amend any provisions existing when this Treaty enters into force which conflict with the preceding rules.

CHAPTER 3   *Approximation of Laws*

Article 100
The Council shall, acting unanimously on a proposal from the Commission, issue directives for the approximation of such provisions laid down by law, regulation or administrative action in Member States as directly affect the establishment of functioning of the common market.

The Assembly and the Economic and Social Committee shall be consulted in the case of directives whose implementation would, in one or more Member States, involve the amendment of legislation.

Article 101
Where the Commission finds that a divergence between the provisions laid down by law, regulation or administrative action in Member States is distorting the conditions of competition in the common market and that the resultant distortion needs to be eliminated, it shall consult the Member States concerned.

If such consultation does not result in an agreement eliminating the distortion in question, the Council shall, on a proposal from the Commission, acting unanimously during the first stage and by a qualified majority thereafter, issue the necessary directives. The Commission and the Council may take any other appropriate measures provided for in this Treaty.

Article 102
1   Where there is reason to fear that the adoption or amendment of a provision laid down by law, regulation

or administrative action may cause distortion within the meaning of Article 101, a Member State desiring to proceed therewith shall consult the Commission. After consulting the Member States, the Commission shall recommend to the States concerned such measures as may be appropriate to avoid the distortion in question.

2 If a State desiring to introduce or amend its own provisions does not comply with the recommendation addressed to it by the Commission; other Member States shall not be required, in pursuance of Article 101, to amend their own provisions in order to eliminate such distortion. If the Member State which has ignored the recommendation of the Commission causes distortion detrimental only to itself, the provisions of Article 101 shall not apply.

TITLE II   ECONOMIC POLICY

CHAPTER I   *Conjunctural Policy*

Article 103
1 Member States shall regard their conjunctural policies as a matter of common concern. They shall consult each other and the Commission on the measures to be taken in the light of the prevailing circumstances.

Article 104
Each Member States shall pursue the economic policy needed to ensure the equilibrium of its overall balance of payments and to maintain confidence in its currency, while taking care to ensure a high level of employment and a stable level of prices.

Article 105
1 In order to facilitate attainment of the objectives set out in Article 104, Member States shall co-ordinate their economic policies. They shall for this purpose provide for co-operation between their appropriate administrative departments and between their central banks.

The Commission shall submit to the Council recommendations on how to achieve such co-operation.

CHAPTER 3 *Commercial Policy*

Article 110

By establishing a customs union between themselves Member States aim to contribute, in the common interest, to the harmonious development of world trade, the progressive abolition of restrictions on international trade and the lowering of customs barriers.

The common commercial policy shall take into account the favourable effect which the abolition of customs duties between Member States may have on the increase in the competitive strength of undertakings in those States.

Article 113

1 After the transitional period has ended, the common commercial policy shall be based on uniform principles, particularly in regard to changes in tariff rates, the conclusion of tariff and trade agreements, the achievement of uniformity in measures of liberalization, export policy and measures to protect trade such as those to be taken in case of dumping or subsidies.

2 The Commission shall submit proposals to the Council for implementing the common commercial policy.

3 Where agreements with third countries need to be negotiated, the Commission shall make recommendations to the Council, which shall authorize the Commission to open the necessary negotiations.

The Commission shall conduct these negotiations in consultation with a special committee appointed by the Council to assist the Commission in this task and within the framework of such directives as the Council may issue to it.

4 In exercising the powers conferred upon it by this Article, the Council shall act by a qualified majority.

TITLE III   SOCIAL POLICY

CHAPTER I   *Social Provisions*

Article 117

Member States agree upon the need to promote improved working conditions and an improved standard of living for workers, so as to make possible their harmonization while the improvement is being maintained.

They believe that such a development will ensue not only from the functioning of the common market, which will favour the harmonization of social systems, but also from the procedures provided for in this Treaty and from the approximation of provisions laid down by law, regulation or administrative action.

Article 118
Without prejudice to the other provisions of this Treaty and in conformity with its general objectives, the Commission shall have the task of promoting close co-operation between Member States in the social field, particularly in matters relating to:
– employment;
– labour law and working conditions;
– basic and advanced vocational training;
– social security;
– prevention of occupational accidents and diseases;
– occupational hygiene;
– the right of association, and collective bargaining between
  employers and workers.
To this end, the Commission shall act in close contact with Member States by making studies, delivering opinions and arranging consultations both on problems arising at national level and on those of concern to international organizations.

Before delivering the opinions provided for in this Article, the Commission shall consult the Economic and Social Committee.

Article 119
Each Member State shall during the first stage ensure and subsequently maintain the application of the principle that men and women should receive equal pay for equal work.

For the purpose of this Article, 'pay' means the ordinary basic or minimum wage or salary and any other consideration, whether in cash or in kind, which the worker receives, directly or indirectly, in respect of his employment from his employer.

Equal pay without discrimination based on sex means:

(a) that pay for the same work at piece rates shall be calculated on the basis of the same unit of measurement;

(b) that pay for work at time rates shall be the same for the same job.

CHAPTER 2 *The European Social Fund*

Article 123

In order to improve employment opportunities for workers in the common market and to contribute thereby to raising the standard of living, a European Social Fund is hereby established in accordance with the provisions set out below; it shall have the task of rendering the employment of workers easier and of increasing their geographical and occupational mobility within the Community.

Article 124

The Fund shall be administered by the Commission.

The Commission shall be assisted in this task by a Committee presided over by a member of the Commission and composed of representatives of Governments, trade unions and employers' organizations.

Article 125

1 On application by a Member State the Fund shall within the framework of the rules provided for in Article 127, meet 50 per cent of the expenditure incurred after the entry into force of this Treaty by that State or by a body governed by public law for the purposes of:

(a) ensuring productive re-employment of workers by means of: vocational retraining; resettlement allowances;

(b) granting aid for the benefit of workers whose employment is reduced or temporarily suspended, in whole or in part, as a result of the conversation of an undertaking of other production, in order that they may retain the same wage level pending their full re-employment.

2 Assistance granted by the Fund towards the cost of vocational retraining shall be granted only if the unemployed workers could not be found employment except

in a new occupation and only if they have been in productive employment for at least six months in the occupation for which they have been retrained.

Assistance towards resettlement allowances shall be granted only if the unemployed workers have been caused to change their home within the Community and have been in productive employment for at least six months in their new place of residence.

Assistance for workers in the case of the conversion of an undertaking shall be granted only if:

(a)   the workers concerned have again been fully employed in that undertaking for at least six months.

(b)   the Government concerned has submitted a plan beforehand, drawn up by the undertaking in question, for that particular conversion and for financing it;

(c)   the Commission has given its prior approval to the conversion plan.

TITLE IV   THE EUROPEAN INVESTMENT BANK

Article 129
A European Investment Bank is hereby established; it shall have legal personality.

The members of the European Investment Bank shall be the Member States.

The Statute of the European Investment Bank is laid down in a Protocol annexed to this Treaty.

Article 130
The task of the European Investment Bank shall be to contribute, by having recourse to the capital market and utilizing its own resources, to the balanced and steady development of the common market in the interest of the Community. For this purpose the Bank shall, operating on a non-profit-making basis, grant loans and give guarantees which facilitate the financing of the following projects in all sectors of the economy:

(a)   projects for developing less developed regions;

(b)   projects for modernizing or converting undertakings or

for developing fresh activities called for by the progressive establishment of the common market, where these
projects are of such a size or nature that they cannot be
entirely financed by the various means available in the
individual Member States;
(c) projects of common interest to several Member States
which are of such size or nature that they cannot be
entirely financed by various means available in the
individual Member State.

PART FOUR Association of the Overseas Countries and Territories

Article 131
The Member States agree to associate with the Community
the non-European countries and territories which have
special relations with Belgium, France, Italy, the Netherlands
and the United Kingdom.

The purpose of association shall be to promote the
economic and social development of the countries and
territories and to establish close economic relations between
them and the Community as a whole.

In accordance with the principles set out in the Preamble to
this Treaty association shall serve primarily to further the
interests and prosperity of the inhabitants of these countries,
and territories in order to lead them to the economic, social
and cultural development to which they aspire.

PART SIX General and Fiscal Provisions

Article 210
The Community shall have legal personality.

Article 223
1 The provisions of this Treaty shall not preclude the
application of the following rules:
(a) No Member State shall be obliged to supply
information the disclosure of which it considers
contrary to the essential interest of its security;

(b)   Any Member State may take measures as it considers necessary for the protection of the essential interests of its security which are connected with the production of or trade in arms, munitions and war materials; such measures shall not, however, adversely affect the conditions of competition in the common market regarding products which are not intended for specifically military purposes.

Article 224

Member States shall consult each other with a view to taking together the steps needed to prevent the functioning of the common market being affected by measures which a Member State may be called upon to take in the event of serious internal disturbances affecting the maintenance of law and order, in the event of war or serious international tension constituting a threat of war, or in order to carry out obligations it has accepted for the purpose of maintaining peace and international security.

Article 228

1   Where this Treaty provides for the conclusions of agreements between the Community and one or more States or an international organization, such agreements shall be negotiated by the Commission. Subject to the powers vested in the Commission in this field, such agreement shall be concluded by the Council, after consulting the Assembly where required by this Treaty.
    The Council, the Commission or a Member State may obtain beforehand the opinion of the Court of Justice as to whether an agreement envisaged is compatible with the provisions of this Treaty. Where the opinion of the Court of Justice is adverse, the agreement may enter into force only in accordance with Article 236.
2   Agreements concluded under these conditions shall be binding on the institutions of the Community and on Member States.

Article 229

It shall be for the Commission to ensure the maintenance of all appropriate relations with the organs of the United

Nations, of its specialized agencies and of the General Agreement on Tariffs and Trade.

The Commission shall also maintain such relations as are appropriate with all international organizations.

Article 235
If action by the Community should prove necessary to attain, in the course of the operation of the common market, one of the objectives of the Community and this Treaty has not provided the necessary powers, the Council shall acting unanimously on a proposal from the Commission and after consulting the Assembly take the appropriate measures.

Article 236
The Government of any Member State or the Commission may submit to the Council proposals for the amendment of this Treaty.

If the Council, after consulting the Assembly and, where appropriate the Commission, delivers an opinion in favour of calling a conference of representatives of the Governments of the Member States, the conference shall be convened by the President of the Council for the purpose of determining by common accord the amendments to be made to this Treaty.

The amendments shall enter into force after being ratified by all the Member States in accordance with their respective constitutional requirements.

Article 237
Any European State may apply to become a member of the Community. It shall address its application to the Council, which shall act unanimously after obtaining the opinion of the Commission.

The conditions of admission and the adjustments to this Treaty necessitated thereby shall be the subject of an agreement between Member States and the applicant State. This agreement shall be submitted for ratification by all the contracting States in accordance with their respective requirements.

Article 238
The Community may conclude with a third State, a union of States or an international organization agreements

establishing an association involving reciprocal rights and obligations, common action and special procedures.

These agreements shall be concluded by the Council, acting unanimously after consulting the Assembly.

Where such agreements call for amendments to this Treaty, these amendments shall first be adopted in accordance with the procedure laid down in Article 236.

Abstracts from the European Communities Act 1972 (1972, c. 68)

An Act to make provisions in connection with the enlarge-
ment of the European Communities to include the United
Kingdom, together with (for certain purposes) the Channel
Islands, the Isle of Man and Gibraltar (17 October 1972).

PART I   General Provisions

Short title and interpretation

2   In this Act –
'the Communities' means the European Economic Community, the European Coal and Steel Community and the
European Atomic Energy Community;
'the Treaties' or 'the Community Treaties' means, subject to
subsection (3) below, the pre-accession treaties, that is to say,
those described in Part I of Schedule 1 to this Act, taken with

(a)   the Treaty relating to the accession of the United
      Kingdom to the European Economic Community and
      to the European Atomic Energy Community, signed at
      Brussels on the 22 January 1972; and

(b)   the decision, of the same date, of the Council of the
      European Communities relating to the accession of the
      United Kingdom to the European Coal and Steel
      Community;

3   If Her Majesty by Order in Council declares that a treaty
specified in the Order is to be regarded as one of the
Community Treaties as herein defined, the Order shall be
conclusive that it is to be so regarded; but a treaty entered
into by the United Kingdom after the 22 January 1972, other

than a pre-accession treaty to which the United Kingdom accedes on terms settled on or before that date, shall not be so regarded unless it is so specified, nor be so specified unless a draft of the Order in Council has been approved by resolution of each House of Parliament.

4   For purposes of subsection (2) and (3) above, 'treaty' includes any international agreement, and any protocol to annex to a treaty or international agreement.

General Implementation of Treaties

2 – (1) All such rights, powers, liabilities, obligations and restrictions from time to time created or arising by or under the Treaties, and all such remedies and procedures from time to time provided for by or under the Treaties, as in accordance with the Treaties are without further enactment to be given legal effect or used in the United Kingdom shall be recognized and available in law, and be enforced, allowed and followed accordingly; and the expression 'enforceable Community right' and similar expressions shall be read as referring to one to which subsection applies.

(2) Subject to Schedule 2 to this Act, at any time after its passing Her Majesty may by Order in Council, and any designated Minister or department may by regulations, make provision –

(a)   for the purpose of implementing any Community obligation of the United Kingdom, or enabling any such obligation to be implemented, or of enabling any rights enjoyed or to be enjoyed by the United Kingdom under or by virtue of the Treaties to be exercised; or

(b)   for the purpose of dealing with matters arising out of or related to any such obligation or rights or the coming into force, or the operation from time to time, of subsection (1) above;

and in the exercise of any statutory power or duty, including any power to give directions or to legislate by means of orders, rules, regulations or other subordinate instrument, the person entrusted with the power or duty may have regard to the objects of the Communities and to any such obligation or rights as aforesaid.

In this subsection 'designated Minister or department' means such Minister of the Crown or government department as may from time to time be designated by Order in Council in relation to any matter or for any purpose, but subject to such restrictions or conditions (if any) as may be specified by the Order in Council.

(3) There shall be charged on and issued out of the Consolidated Fund or, if so determined by the Treasury, the National Loans Fund the amounts required to meet any Community obligation to make payments to any of the Communities or member States, or any Community obligation in respect of contributions to the capital or reserves of the European Investment Bank or in respect of loans to the Bank, or to redeem any notes or obligations issued or created in respect of any such Community obligation; and, except as otherwise provided by or under any enactment –

(a) any other expenses incurred under or by virtue of the Treaties or this Act by any Minister of the Crown or government department may be paid out of the moneys provided by Parliament; and

(b) any sums received under or by virtue of the Treaties of this Act by any Minister of the Crown or government department, save for such sums as may be required for disbursements premitted by any other enactment, shall be paid into the Consolidated Fund or, if so determined by the Treasury, the National Loans Fund.

Decisions on, and proof of, treaties and Community instruments, etc.

3 – (1) For the purposes of all legal proceedings any question as to the meaning or effect of any of the Treaties, or as to the validity, meaning or effect of any Community instrument, shall be treated as a question of law (and, if not referred to the European Court, be for determination as such in accordance with the principles laid down by and any relevant decision of the European Court).

(2) Judicial notice shall be taken of the Treaties, of the Official Journal of the Communities and of any decision of, or expression of opinion by, the European Court on any such

question as aforesaid; and the Official Journal shall be admissable as evidence of any instrument or other act thereby communicated of any of the Communities or of any Community institution.

PART II Amendment of Law

General provision for repeal and amendment

4 – (1) The enactments mentioned in Schedule 3 to this Act (being enactments that are superseded or to be superseded by reason of Community obligations and of the provision made by this Act in relation thereto or are not compatible with Community obligations) are hereby repealed, to the extent specified in column 3 of the Schedule, with effect from the entry date or other date mentioned in the Scheule; and in the enactments mentioned in Schedule 4 to this Act there shall, subject to any transitional provision there included, be made the amendments provided for by that Schedule.

(2) Where in any Part of Schedule 3 to this Act is provided that repeals made by that Part are to take effect from a date appointed by order, the orders shall be made by statutory instrument and an order may appoint different dates for the repeal of different provisions to take effect, or for the repeal of the same provision to take effect for different purposes and an order appointing a date for a repeal to take effect may include transitional and other supplementary provisions arising out of that repeal, including provisions adapting the operation of other enactments included for repeal but not yet repealed by that Schedule, and may amend or revoke any such provisions included in a previous order.

Customs duties

5 – (1) Subject to subsection (2) below, on and after the relevant date there shall be charged, levied, collected and paid on goods imported into the United Kingdom such Community customs duty, if any, as is for the time being applicable in accordance with the Treaties or, if the goods are not within the common customs tariff of the Economic

Community and the duties chargeable are not otherwise fixed by any directly applicable Community provision such duty of customs, if any, as the Treasury, on the recommendation of the Secretary of State, may by order specify.

For this purpose 'the relevant date' in relation to any goods, is the date on and after which the duties of customs that may be charged thereon are no longer affected under the Treaties by any temporary provision made on or with reference to the accession of the United Kingdom to the Communities.

(2) Where as regards goods imported into the United Kingdom provision may, in accordance with the Treaties, be made in derogation of the common customs tariff or of the exclusion of customs duties as between member States, the Treasury may by order make such provision as to the customs duties chargeable on the goods, or as to exempting the goods from any customs duty, as the Treasury may on the recommendation of the Secretary of State determine.

The common agricultural policy

6 – (1) There shall be a Board in charge of a government department, which shall be appointed by and responsible to the Ministers, and shall be by the name of the Intervention Board for Agricultural Produce a body corporate (but not subject as a statutory corporation to restriction on its corporate capacity); and the Board (in addition to any other functions that may be entrusted to it) shall be charged, subject to the direction and control of the Ministers, with such functions as they may from time to time determine in connection with the carrying out of the obligations of the United Kingdom under the common agricultural policy of the Economic Community.

(2) Her Majesty may by Order in Council make further provision as to the constitution and membership of the Board, and the remuneration (including pensions) of members of the Board or any committee thereof, and for regulating or facilitating the discharge of the Board's functions, including provisions for the Board to arrange for its functions to be performed by other bodies on its behalf

and any such provision as was made by Schedule 1 to the Ministers of the Crown Act 1964 in relation to a Minister to whom that Schedule applied; and the Ministers:

(a) may, after consultation with any body created by a statutory provision and concerned with agriculture or agricultural produce, by regulations modify or add to the constitution or powers of the body so as to enable it to act for the Board, or by written directions given to the body require it to discontinue or modify any activity appearing to the Ministers to be prejudicial to the proper discharge of the Board's functions; and

(b) may by regulations provide for the charging of fees in connection with the discharge of any functions of the Board.

(3) Sections 5 and 7 of the Agriculture Act 1957 (which make provision for the support of arrangements under section 1 of that Act for providing guaranteed process or assured markets) shall apply in relation to any Community arrangements for or related to the regulation of the market for any agricultural produce as if references, in whatever terms, to payments made by virtue of section 1 were references to payments made by virtue of the Community arrangements by or on behalf of the Board and as if in section 5(1)(d) the reference to the Minister included the Board.

(4) Agricultural levies of the Economic Community, so far as they are charged on goods exported from the United Kingdom or shipped as stores, shall be paid to and recoverable by the Board; and the power of the Ministers to make orders under section 5 of the Agriculture Act 1957, as extended by this section, shall include power to make such provision supplementary to any directly applicable Community provision as the Ministers consider necessary for securing the payment of any agricultural levies so charged, including provision for the making of declarations or the giving of other information in respect of goods exported, shipped as store, warehoused or otherwise dealt with.

(5) Except as otherwise provided by or under any enactment, agricultural levies of the Economic Community, so far as they are charged on goods imported into the United Kingdom, shall be levied, collected and paid, and the

proceeds shall be dealt with, as if they were Community customs duties . . .

(7) Where it appears to the Ministers, having regard to any such Community arrangements as aforesaid (and any obligations of the United Kingdom in relation thereto), that section 1 of the Agriculture Act 1957 should cease to apply to produce of any description mentioned in Schedule I to that Act, they may by order make by statutory instrument, which shall be subject to annulment in pursuance of a resolution of either House of Parliament, provide that as from such date as any be prescribed by the order (but subject to such savings and transitional provisions as may be so prescribed) the Act shall have effect as if produce of that description were omitted from Schedule I.

(8) Expressions used in this section shall be construed as if contained in Part I of the Agriculture Act 1957; and in this section 'agricultural levy' shall include any tax not being a customs duty, but of equivalent effect, that may be chargeable in accordance with any such Community arrangements as aforesaid and 'statutory provision' includes any provision having effect by virtue of any enactment and in subsection (2), any enactment of the Parliament of Northern Ireland or provision having effect by virtue of such an enactment.

Furnishing of information to Communities

12 – Estimates, returns and information that may under section 9 of the Statistics of Trade Act 1947 or section 80 of the Agriculture Act 1947 be disclosed to a government department or Minister in charge of a government department may, in like manner, be disclosed in pursuance of a Community obligation to a Community institution.

SCHEDULES

SECTION 2.   *Schedule 2*

Provisions as to subordinate legislation
1 – (i) The powers conferred by section 2(2) of this Act to make provision for the purposes mentioned in section 2(2)(a) and (b) shall not include power:

(a) to make any provision imposing or increasing taxation; or

(b) to make any provision taking effect from a date earlier than that of the making of the instrument containing the provision; or

(c) to confer any power to legislate by means of orders, rules, regulations or other subordinate instrument, other than rules of procedure for any court or tribunal;

(ii) Sub paragraph (1)(c) above shall not be taken to preclude the modification of a power to legislate conferred otherwise than under section 2(2), or the extension of any such power to purposes of the like nature as those for which it was conferred; and a power to give directions as to matters of administration is not be be regarded as a power to legislate within the meaning of sub-paragraph (i)(c).

2 – (i) Subject to paragraph 3 [relating to Northern Ireland], where a provision contained in any section of this Act confers power to make regulations (otherwise than by modification or extension of an existing power), the power shall be exercisable by statutory instrument.

(ii) Any statutory instrument containing an Order in Council or regulations made in the exercise of a power so conferred, if made without a draft having been approved by a resolution of each House of Parliament, shall be subject to annulment in pursuance of a resolution of either House.

APPENDIX 3

List of Interviews Conducted

Former Ministers

The Rt Hon. Lord Carrington
The Rt Hon. Lord Peart
The Rt Hon. Peter Shore, MP

Members of Parliament

Mr Peter Lloyd, MP (Fareham)
Mr Nigel Spearing, MP (Newham South)

Officers of the House of Commons

Mr R. W. G. Wilson, Clerk to the European Legislation
    Committee and the Clerk/Advisers to the Committee
Sir Charles Davis, CB, Counsel to the Speaker, European
    Legislation, etc.

Members of HM Civil Service

Mr G. Stapleton, European Secretariat, Cabinet Office
Mr N. Spreckley, European Community Division, FCO
Miss J. Court, HM Treasury
Mr J. Ingram, Department of Industry
Mr R. Wells, Department of Trade
Mr M. Smart, Department of Employment
Mr A. C. Morrison, Department of Environment
Mr J. Halliwell, Department of Health and Social Security
Mr K. Reere, Department of Health and Social Security

Other experts

Dr Helen Wallace, Civil Service College
Mr Tom Jenkins, TUC
Ms Daphne Grose, Consumers Association
Ms Penny Duckham, Consumers Association
Ms Susan Leather, Consumers in the EC Group
Mr Roy Manley, National Council of Voluntary Organizations
Mr Bill Scary, National Council of Voluntary Organizations
Mr Paul Bongers, British Section, International Union of Local Authorities/Council of European Municipalities
Mr Bird, Association of Metropolitan Authorities
Mr Roberts, Associaiton of County Councils
Mrs Virginia Crowe, Royal Institute of Public Administration

Bibliography

BOOKS AND ARTICLES

Akehurst, M. (1982) *A Modern Introduction to International Law* (4th edn), London, George Allen & Unwin.

Allen, D. (1978) 'Foreign policy at European level: beyond the nation state?' in W. Wallace, and W. E. Patterson (eds) *Foreign Policy Making in Western Europe*, Farnborough, Saxon House.

Arbuthnot, H. and Edwards, G. (eds) (1979) *A Common Man's Guide to the Common Market*, London, Macmillan.

Barnett, J. (1982) *Inside the Treasury*, London, Deutsch.

Bates, T. St J. N. (1976) 'The scrutiny of European secondary legislation', *European Law Review*, 1.

Bell, S. (1981) 'How to abolish the Lords', London, Fabian Tract 476.

Bell, D. S. (1980) 'Labour and the European Community' in D. S. Bell (ed.) *Labour into the Eighties*, London, Croom Helm, pp. 150–62.

Boardman, R. and Groom, A. J. R. (eds), (1973) *The Management of Britain's External Relations*, London, Macmillan.

Bogdanor, V. (1979) *Devolution*, Oxford, Oxford University Press.

Bowett, D. W. (1963) *The Law of International Institutions*, London, Methuen.

Brew, D. (1979) 'National parliamentary scrutiny of European Community legislation: the case of the United Kingdom Parliament', in V. Herman and R. van Schendelen (eds) *The European Parliament and National Parliaments*, Farnborough, Saxon House.

Bridge, J. W. (1976) 'Community Law and English Courts and Tribunals: general principles and actionary rulings', *European Law Review*, 1, pp. 13–21.

Bridge, J. W. (1981) 'National legal tradition and Community Law: legislative drafting and judicial interpretation in England and the European Community', *Journal of Common Market Studies*, XIX (4) pp. 351–76.

British Bankers' Association (1982) *EEC Checklist*, London.

Bromhead, P. (1958) *The House of Lords and Contemporary Politics 1911–1952*. London, Routledge and Kegan Paul.

Brown, G. (1971) *In My Way*, London, Gollancz.

Butler, D. and Marquand, D. (1981) *European Elections and British Politics*, London and New York, Longman.

Butler, D. and Kitzinger, U. (1976) *The 1975 Referendum*, London, Macmillan.

Butt Philip, A. (1981) 'The harmonisation of industrial policy and practices' in C. C. Twitchett (ed.) *Harmonisation in the EEC*, London, Macmillan, pp. 47–62.

Camps, M. (1965) *Britain and the European Community*, Oxford, Oxford University Press.

Camps, M. (1967) *European Unification in the Sixties, London, Oxford University Press, and RIIA*.

Castle, B. (1980) *The Castle Diaries, 1974–76*, London, Weidenfeld & Nicolson.

Charlton, M. (1982) 'How Britain at last made up its mind', *Europe 82*, No. 4, pp. 16–18.

Churchill, R. (1980) 'Revision of the EEC's Common Fisheries Policy – Pt I' *European Law Review*, 5, pp. 3–37.

Civil Service College, 'Annual Report by the Principal to the Civil Service College Advisory Council 1970–71, (and subsequent reports) London, HMSO.

Civil Service Department, *Civil Service Year Book*, 1973 (and subsequent edn) London, HMSO.

Cook, C. and Francis, M. (1979) *The First European Elections*, London, Macmillan.

Coombes, D. (1981) 'Parliament and the European Community', in S. A. Walker and D. Ryle (eds) *The Commons Today*, London, Fontana, pp. 237–59.

Crossman, R. (1977) *The Diaries of a Cabinet Minister, Vol. 3 Secretary of State for Social Services 1968–70*, London,

Hamish Hamilton and Jonathan Cape.

Dicey, A. V. (1965) *Law of the Constitution* (10th edn), with introduction by E. C. S. Wade, London, Macmillan.

Dike, C. (1974) 'The case against parliamentary sovereignty' *Public Law*, pp. 283–97.

Dennis, G. (1981) 'The harmonisation of non-tariff barriers', in C. C. Twitchett, (ed.) *Harmonisation in the EEC*, London, Macmillan, pp. 18–32.

Denton, G. (1978) 'Reflections on fiscal federation in the EEC' *Journal of Common Market Studies*, 16, pp. 283–301.

Denton, G. (1981) 'How to prevent the EC Budget reinforcing divergence: a British view', in M. Hodges and W. Wallace (eds) *Economic Divergence in the EC*, London, RIIA, Allen & Unwin.

Denton, G. (1982) 'The economics of EEC membership' *Policy Studies*, 3 (2), pp. 88–103.

Department of Trade (1983) 'Harmonisation of Company and Related Law in Europe – timetable and progress of Draft Directives and other proposals', London, Companies Legislation Division.

Department of Transport (1982) *Information on Progress of EC Legislation*, London, International Transport Division.

Dorwick, F. E. (1982) 'Overlapping international and European laws', *International and Comparative Law Quarterly*, 31 (1), pp. 59–98.

Douglas, R. (1980) *The History of the Liberal Party 1895–1970*, London, Sidgwick and Jackson, p. 274.

Drew, J. (1979) *Doing Business in the European Community*, London, Butterworth.

Edwards, G. and Wallace, H. (1977) *The Council of Ministers of the European Community and the President-in-Office*, London, Federal Trust for Education and Research.

Englefield, D. D. (1981) *Parliament and Information*, London, Library Association.

Erridge, A. (1980) *Decision-making in the European Community: An Exercise*, Civil Service College.

Featherstone, K. (1979) 'Labour in Europe: the work of a national party delegation to the European Parliament', in V. Herman and R. van Schendelen (eds) *The European*

Parliament and National Parliaments, Farnborough, Saxon House, pp. 81–110.

Featherstone, K. (1981) 'Socialists and European integration: the attitudes of British Labour Members of Parliament', *European Journal of Political Research*, 9, pp. 407–19.

Feld, W. J. (1979) *International Relations: a Transnational Approach*, California, Alfred.

Fitzmaurice, J. (1978a) *The European Parliament*, Farnborough, Saxon House.

Fitzmaurice, J. (1978b) 'Direct elections and the future of the European Parliament', *West European Politics*, XI (2).

Fitzmaurice, J. (1980) 'Reflections on the European elections', *West European Politics*, 3, pp. 233–41.

Gibbs, J. (1977) 'The French and British National Administrations and the European Economic Community', unpublished MSc thesis, Bristol University.

Godley, W. (1980) 'The UK and the Community Budget', in W. Wallace (ed.) *Britain in Europe*, London, Heinemann.

Goodwin, G. (1977) 'The external relations of the European Community – shadow and substance', *British Journal of International Studies*, 3, pp. 39–54.

Haas, E. B. (1958) *The Uniting of Europe*, London, Stevens.

Hansard Society (1977) *The British People: their Voice in Europe*, Farnborough, Saxon House.

Hartley, T. C. and Griffith, J. A. G. (1975) *Government and Law*, London, Weidenfeld & Nicolson.

Henig, S. (1980) *Power and Decision in Europe*, London, Europotentials Press.

Herman, V. and Lodge, J. (1978) *The European Parliament and the European Community*, New York, St Martin's Press.

Herman, V. and Hagger, M. (1980) *The Legislation of Direct Elections to the European Parliament*, Farnborough, Gower.

Holland, M. (1981) 'The selection of Parliamentary candidates: contemporary developments and the impact of the European Elections', *Parliamentary Affairs*, XXXIV, 1981, pp. 28–46.

Hood Phillips, O. and Jackson, P. (1978) *O. Hood Phillips' Constitutional and Administrational Law*, (6th edn) London, Sweet and Maxwell.

Howe, G. (1973) 'The European Communities Act 1972'

International Affairs, 49 (1), pp. 1–13.

Hull, C. and Rhodes, R. A. W. (1977) *Intergovernmental relations in the European Community*, Farnborough, Saxon House.

Hurd, D. (1979) *An End to Promises – Sketch of a Government 1970–74*, London, Collins.

Johnstone, D. (1975) *A Tax Shall Be Charged*, Civil Service Studies, 1, London, HMSO.

Judge, D. (1981) *Backbench Specialization in the House of Commons*, London, Heinemann Educational.

Kerr, A. J. C. (1977) *The Common Market and how it Works*, Oxford, Pergamon Press.

King, A. (1977) *Britain Says Yes*, Washington DC, American Enterprise Institute for Public Policy Research.

Kitzinger, U. (1968) *The Second Try: Labour and the EEC*, Oxford, Pergamon.

Kitzinger, U. (1973) *Diplomacy and Persuasion*, London, Thames & Hudson.

Kolinsky, M. (1975) 'Parliamentary scrutiny of European legislation', *Government and Opposition*, 10, pp. 46–69.

Kruse, D. C. (1980) *Monetary Integration in Western Europe: EMU, EMS and Beyond*, London, Butterworth.

Laing, M. (1972) *Edward Heath – Prime Minister*, London, Sidgwick and Jackson.

Lasok, D. and Bridge, J. W. (1982) *Law and Institutions of the European Communities* (3rd edn), London, Butterworth.

Leiber, R. J. (1970) *British Politics and European Unity*, London and Los Angeles, University of California Press.

Lindberg, L. N. and Scheingold, S. A. (eds) (1971) *Regional Integration: Theory and Research*, Cambridge, Harvard University Press.

Lodge, J. and Herman, V. (1982) *Direct Elections to the European Parliament*, London, Macmillan.

Mackintosh, J. P. (1982) *The Government and Politics of Britain* (5th edn), London, Hutchinson.

Macmillan, H. (1972) *Pointing the Way 1959–61*, London, Macmillan.

Marquand, D. (1979) *Parliament for Europe*, London, Jonathan Cape.

Marquand, D. (1981) 'Parliamentary accountability and the

European Community', *Journal of Common Market Studies*, XIX (3), pp. 221–36.

Mathijsen, P. S. R. F. (1972) *A Guide to European Community Law*, London, Sweet and Maxwell.

Meyer, P. (1974) 'Divided loyalties – civil servants at home and in Europe', *Public Administration Bulletin*, No. 17, pp. 44–52.

Michelmann, H. J. (1978) *Organisational Effectiveness in a Multi-national Bureaucracy*, Farnborough, Saxon House.

Miller, H. N. (1977) 'The influence of British Parliamentary Committees on European Community legislation', *Legislative Studies Quarterly*, II (1), pp. 45–75.

Mitchell, J. D. B. (1979) 'The sovereignty of Parliament and Community Law: the stumbling block that isn't there', *International Affairs*, 55 (1), pp. 33–46.

Moore, C. (1979) 'The Role of the House of Lords in the Scrutiny of European Economic Communities Legislation', unpublished BA dissertation, Department of Politics, University of Hull.

Morgan, A. (1976) *From Summit to Council Evolution in the EEC*, London, Chatham House and PEP.

Morgan, J. P. (1975) *The House of Lords and the Labour Government 1964–70*, Oxford, Clarendon Press.

Morgan, R. (1980) 'Britain's role in the European Community', *Policy Studies*, I.

Nau, H. R. (1974) *National Politics and International Technology – Nuclear Reactor Development in Western Europe*, London and Baltimore, Johns Hopkins University Press.

Neville-Rolfe, E. (1982) 'The Community Agricultural Policy: aspects for reform', *Policy Studies* 2, pp. 116–30.

Newman, A. (1981) 'Pressure Groups and Harmonisation', in C. C. Twitchett (ed.) *Harmonisatoin in the EEC*, London, Macmillan, pp. 102–13.

Norton, P. (1978) *Conservative Dissidents*, London, Temple Smith.

Norton, P. (1980), 'The changing face of the British House of Commons in the 1970s', *Legislative Studies Quarterly*, V (3), pp. 333–57.

Norton, P. (1980b) *Dissension in the House of Commons 1974–79*, Oxford, Clarendon Press.

Norton, P. (1981) *The Commons in Perspective*, Oxford, Martin Robertson.

Norton, P. (1983) 'Party committees in the House of Commons' *Parliamentary Affairs*, 36, pp. 7–27.

Open University (1974) *The European Economic Community, National and International Impact*, Milton Keynes, Open University.

Palmer, J. (1982) 'Britain and the EEC: the withdrawal option', *International Affairs*, 58, pp. 638–47.

Palmer, M. (1981) *The European Parliament*, Oxford, Pergamon Press.

Pearce, J. (1981) 'The CAP: a guide to the Commission's new proposals', *The World Today*, 37, pp. 339–47.

Pfaltzgraff, R. L. Jr (1969) *Britain Faces Europe*, Philadelphia, University of Pennsylvania Press.

Plaskitt, J. (1981) 'The House of Lords and legislative harmonisation in the European Community', *Public Administration*, 59, pp. 203–14.

Pridham, G. and P. (1979) 'The new European Party federations and direct elections', *The World Today*, 35, pp. 62–70.

Pridham, G. and P. (1981) *Transnational Party Co-operation and European Integration*, London, Allen & Unwin.

Pryce, R. (1973) *The Politics of the European Community*, London, Butterworth.

Richards, P. G. (1967) *Parliament and Foreign Affairs*, London, George Allen and Unwin.

Richardson, J. J. and Jordan, A. G. (1979) *Governing under Pressure*, Oxford, Martin Robertson.

Robins, L. J. (1977) *The Reluctant Party: Labour and the EEC*, Ormskirk, G. W. & A. Hesketh.

Robinson, A. (1983) 'MPs and MEPs – Channels of Communication', *Policy Studies*, 3 (4), pp. 288–304.

Rudden, B. and Wyatt, D. (1980) *Basic Community Laws*, Oxford, Clarendon Press.

Ryan, M. and Isaacson, P. (1974–75) 'Parliament and the European Communities', *Parliamentary Affairs*, 28 (2), pp. 199–215.

Schermers, H.G. (1972) *International Institutional Law*, vols I & II, Leiden, Sijthoff.

Schwarzenberger, G. (1967) *A Manual of International Law*, London, Stevens.

Sedgemore, Brian (1980) *The Secret Constitution*, London, Hodder and Stoughton.

Soames, Sir Christopher (1972) 'Whitehall into Europe', *Public Administration*, vol. 50, pp. 271–9.

Stack, F. (1983) 'The House of Commons and European Community Policy: inevitable executive dominance?', unpublished Political Studies Association conference paper.

Statler, J. (1979) 'The European monetary system: from conception to birth', *International Affairs*, 55 (2), pp. 206–25.

Stevens, A. (1976–77) 'Problems of parliamentary control of European Community policy', *Millenium, Journal of International Studies*, 5 (3).

Street, H. and Brazier, R. (eds) (1981) *Constitutional and Administrative Law*, de Smith, (4th edn), London, Penguin.

Taylor, J. (1975) 'British membership of the European Communities: the question of parliamentary sovereignty', *Government and Opposition*, X, pp. 278–93.

Taylor, P. (1981) 'The European Communities and the obligations of membership: claims and counter-claims', *International Affairs*, 57 (2), pp. 236–53.

Taylor, P. (1982) 'Intergovernmentalism in the European Communities in the 1970s: patterns and perspectives', *International Organisation*, 36, pp. 741–66.

The Encyclopedia of European Community Law (1983), Vols A, B and C, London, Sweet and Maxwell.

Trindade, F. A. (1972) 'Parliamentary sovereignty and the primacy of European Community Law', *Modern Law Review*, 35, pp. 325–402.

Twitchett, C. C. (ed.) (1981) *Harmonisation in the EEC*, London, Macmillan.

Twitchett, C. C. (1982) 'The Falklands – Community diplomacy at work', *Europe 82*, July 1982, pp. 10–11.

Twitchett, C. C. and K. (1981) *Building Europe: Britain's Partners in Europe*, London, Europa Press.

Twitchett, K. J. (1979) 'Britain and Community Europe 1973–79', *International Relations*, vi, pp. 698–714.

Usher, J. (1981) *European Community Law and National Law, The Irreversible Transfer?* London, Allen & Unwin.

Wall, E. M. (1973) *European Communities Act 1972*, London, Butterworth.

Wallace, H. (1971) 'The impact of the European Communities on national policy-making', *Government and Opposition*, pp. 520–38.

Wallace, H. and W. (1972–73) 'The impact of Community membership on the British machinery of government', *Journal of Common Market Studies*, pp. 243–62.

Wallace, H. (1973) *National Governments and the European Community*, London, Chatham House/PEP.

Wallace, H. (1974a) 'Administrative change as a consequence of British membership of the EC', *Public Administration Bulletin*, 16, pp. 18–21.

Wallace, H. (1974b) 'The European Community and the organization of British government' in the Open University, *The European Economic Community*, Milton Keynes, Open University, p. 933.

Wallace, H. and W. (eds) and Webb, C. (1977) *Policy-making in the European Communities*, London, Wiley.

Wallace, H. (1979) 'Direct elections and the political dynamics of the European Communities', *Journal of Common Market Studies*, XVII (4), pp. 281–96.

Wallace, W. (1977) *The Foreign Policy Process in Britain*, London, RIIA, Allen & Unwin.

Wallace, W. (ed.) (1980) *Britain in Europe*, London, Heinemann for NIESR, PSI, RIIA.

Waltz, K. N. (1967) *Foreign Policy and democratic politics: the American and British experiences*, Boston, Little, Brown and Company.

Willis, V. (1983) *Britons in Brussels*, London, Policy Studies Institute.

Wilson, H. (1979) *Final Term*, London, Weidenfeld & Nicolson, and Michael Joseph.

Winterton, G. (1976) 'The British Grundnorm: parliamentary supremacy re-examined', *Law Quarterly Review*, 92, pp. 591–617.

Wood, D. M. (1982) 'Comparing Parliamentary Voting on European Issues in France and Britain' *Legislative Studies*

Quarterly, VII (1), pp. 101–17.

Yardley, D. C. M. (1974) *Introduction to British Constitutional Law* (4th edn) London, Butterworth.

Young, H. and Sloman, A. (1982) *No Minister*, London, BBC.

PARLIAMENTARY PAPERS — EC COMMITTEES OF THE COMMONS AND LORDS

Report from the Joint Committee on Delegated Legislation, HL 184, HC 475, Session 1971–72.

HOUSE OF COMMONS

Session 1972–73

First Report from the Select Committee on European Community Secondary Legislation, HC 143.
Second Report from the Select Committee on European Secondary Legislation, HC 463 I and II.
Minutes of Evidence to the above Select Committee, HC 121 ii–xiii, and HC 121–xv.

Session 1974–75

Twelfth Report Select Committee on European Secondary Legislation, HC 45–XII.
Second Special Report from the Select Committee on European Secondary Legislation, HC 234.
Third Special Report from the Select Committee on European Secondary Legislation, HC 613.
Minutes of Evidence to above Select Committee, HC 87–I, HC 87–III, HC 87–IV and HC 87–VI.

Session 1976–77

Thirteenth Report, Select Committee on European Secondary Legislation, 'European Regional Development Fund', HC 41–xiii and HC 76–i–iii.
Minutes of Evidence to above Select Committee, HC 43–ii, HC 43–iii and HC 43–vi.

Session 1977–78

Special Report from the Select Committee on European Legislation, HC 642.

Session 1981–82

Fourth, Thirteenth, Eighteenth, Nineteenth, Twenty-third, Twenty-ninth Reports of the Select Committee on European Legislation, HC 21–iv, –xviii, –xix, –xxiii and –xxix.

Session 1982–83

First Report of the Select Committee on European Legislation, HC 34–i.

HOUSE OF LORDS

Session 1972–73

First Report by the Select Committee on Procedures for Scrutiny of Proposals for European Instruments, HL 67.
Second Report by the Select Committee on Procedures for Scrutiny of Proposals for European Instruments, HL 194.
Minutes of Evidence to the above Select Committees, HL 115–i to 115–ii.

Session 1974–75

Thirteenth Report from the Select Committee of the House of Lords on the European Communities, HL 115.

Session 1975–76

Twenty-second Report from the Select Committee of the House of Lords on the European Communities, 'Direct Elections to the European Assembly'.
Minutes of Evidence to the above Select Committee, HL 119 and HL 119–i.

Session 1976–77

Eleventh Report from the Select Committee of the House of Lords on the European Communities, 'European social policy', HL 60.

Session 1977–78

Forty-fourth Report from the Select Committee of the House of Lords on the European Communities, 'Relations between the United Kingdom Parliament and the European Parliament after Direct Elections', HL 256–I and 256–II.

REPORTS BY OTHER HOUSE OF COMMONS COMMITTEES

Session 1974–75

First Report from the Select Committee on Procedure, HC 249.

Session 1977–78

Report of the Select Committee on Procedure, HC 588–I and II.

Session 1978–79

First Report from the Expenditure Committee, 'The European Monetary System', HC 60.

Session 1979–80

First Report from the Agriculture Committee, 'Economic, social and health implications for the UK of the Common Agricultural Policy on milk and dairy products', HC 687.
   First Special Report, Government Reply to First Report, HC 826.
First Report from the Transport Committee, 'The European Commission's green paper on transport infrastructure', HC 466–v and Minutes of Evidence, HC 466 i–iv.
Second Report from the Select Committee on House of Commons (Services), HC 461.

Session 1981–82

Fifth Report from the Industry and Trade Committee, 'European air fares', HC 431.

Session 1982–83

First Report from the Liaison Committee, 'The Select Committee system', HC 92.
Report from the Select Committee on Standing Orders (Revision), HC 244.

COMMAND PAPERS

Cmnd 9346, 'Agreement concerning relations between the UK and the ECSC', Dec. 1954.
Cmnd 3269, 'Membership of the European Communities', May 1967.
Cmnd 3274, 'The Common Agricultural Policy of the European Economic Community', May 1967.
Cmnd 3301, 'The legal and constitutional implications of membership of the European Communities', May 1967.
Cmnd 4289, 'Britain and the European Communities – an economic assessment', Feb. 1970.
Cmnd 4715, 'The United Kingdom and the European Communities', July 1979.
Cmnd 5179–I and II, 'Treaty concerning the accession, etc.', Jan. 1973.
Cmnd 5460–I, 'Royal Commission on the Constitution: Memorandum of Dissent', October 1973.
Cmnd 5699, 'Intervention Board for Agricultural Produce, Report for the calendar year 1973', July 1974.
Cmnd 5925, 'Referendum on United Kingdom membership of the European Community', Mar. 1975.
Cmnd 5999, 'Membership of the European Community: statement on behalf of Her Majesty's Government made by the Prime Minister to the House of Commons on Tuesday, March 18 1975', Mar. 1975.
Cmnd 6003, 'Membership of the European Community: report on renegotiation', Mar. 1975.

Cmnd 6394, 'Direct Elections to the European Assembly', Feb. 1976.

Cmnd 6768, 'Direct Elections to the European Assembly', Apr. 1977.

Cmnd 7348, 'Report, European Assembly Constituencies. Boundary commission for England', Dec. 1978.

Cmnd 8525, 'Developments in the European Communities', 1977 (These reports on developments in the EC are published twice a year).

Cmnd 8789, 'The Government Expenditure Plans 1983–1984 to 1985–86', 1983.

PUBLICATIONS OF THE EUROPEAN COMMUNITY

European Parliament (1975) 'The effects on the United Kingdom of membership of the European Communities', Brussels, Directorate General for Research and Documentation. Doc. PE 37.460–37.464/III/rev.

European Parliament (1978) 'Powers of the European Parliament', London, Information Office of the European Parliament.

European Parliament (1979) 'Purse strings of Europe – the European Parliament and the Community Budget', London, Information Office of the European Parliament.

European Communities (1980) *Register of Current Community Legal Instruments*, Vol. I, 'Analytical register', and Vol. III 'Chronological Index', Brussels and Luxembourg.

Office for Official Publications of the EC (1981), 'The Court of Justice of the European Communities' (2nd edn), Luxembourg, Periodical 1/1981, Cat. No. CB–NC–81–001–EN–C.

Office for Official Publications of the EC (1982) 'The Economy of the European Community', Luxembourg. Periodical 1–2/1982 Cat. No. CB–NC–82–002–EN–C.

European Commission (yearly) *Annual General Report on the Activities of the European Communities presented to the European Parliament by the Commission.*

EUROPEAN COMMUNITIES COMMISSION:
BACKGROUND REPORTS

ISEC/B40/78 'Supremacy of European Community Law, the Simmenthal Case', 1978.
ISEC/B42/79 'Reforming the Commission', 1979.
ISEC/B46/79 'Budgetary questions: divergence and con-vergence', 1979.
ISEC/B13/80 'The European Institutions – past and future', 1980.
ISEC/B37/80 'Community Budget: British repayments', 1980.
ISEC/B64/80 'Landmark in liberalizing trade – The Cassis de Dijon Case', 1980.
ISEC/B24/82 'Community voting procedures', 1982.

Index